The Great Race

The Great Race

*The Race Between the English and
the French to Complete the Map of Australia*

DAVID HILL

Little, Brown

LITTLE BROWN

First published in Australia in 2012 by William Heinemann
First published in Great Britain in 2014 by Little, Brown

Maps on pp.viii-xvi © Ice Cold Publishing
Cover: map detail © South Australian Museum.
Chart of Duff's Track in the Pacific Ocean, 1797 –
'A Missionary Voyage to the Southern Pacific Ocean
performed in the years 1796, 1797 and 1798
in the Ship *Duff*, London, 1799.
Ships from the painting *HMS Investigator and L'Geographe* by Ian Hansen
from the collection of the Australian National Maritime Museum
and reproduced with kind permission of Ian Hansen.
Cover design by Christabella Designs

A CIP catalogue record for this book
is available from the British Library.

ISBN 978-1-4087-0642-8

Typeset in Sabon by Midland Typesetters, Australia
Printed and bound in Great Britain by
Clays Ltd, St Ives plc

Papers used by Little, Brown are from well-managed forests
and other responsible sources.

MIX
Paper from
responsible sources
FSC
www.fsc.org   FSC® C104740

Little, Brown
An imprint of
Little, Brown Book
100 Victoria Embankment
London EC4Y 0

An Hachette UK Company
www.hachette.co.uk

www.littlebrown.co.uk

CONTENTS

To Stergitsa

AUTHOR'S NOTE

Wherever possible I have avoided the word 'discover' in relation to European forays around and into Australia and other parts of the New World, but in some instances it was unwieldy to avoid the verb. Where I have used 'discovered' in relation to European exploration, I do so meaning the first *European* discovery. I hope readers are comfortable with this – it does not indicate that I believe Australia or any other lands were undiscovered before Europeans landed on or settled them.

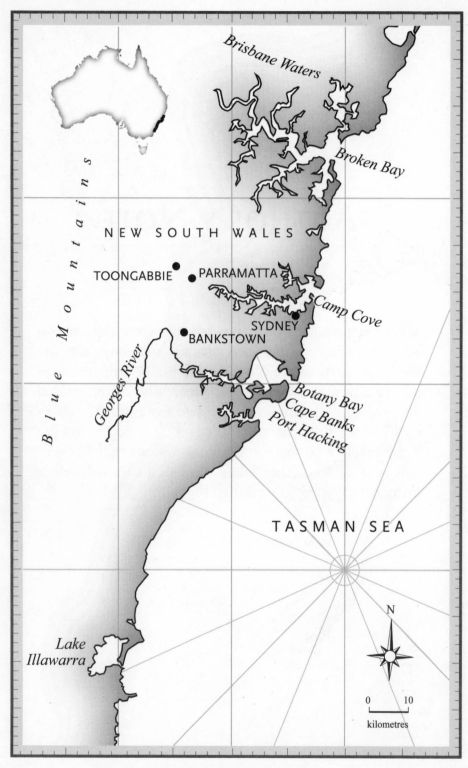

Sydney and its environs

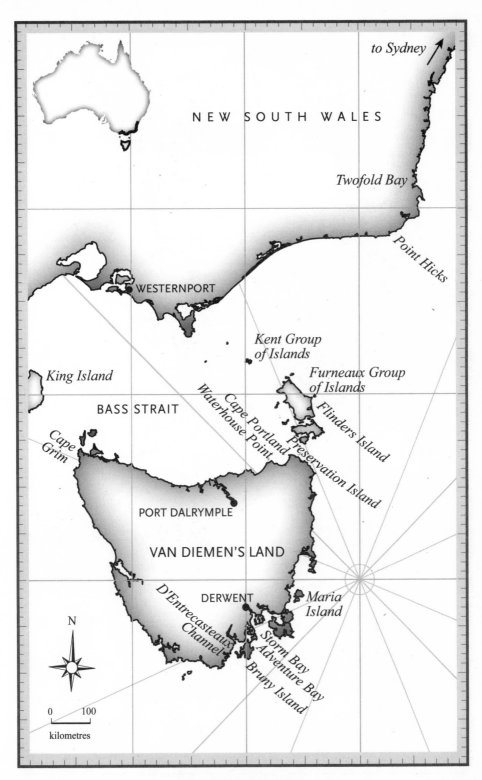

Van Diemen's Land

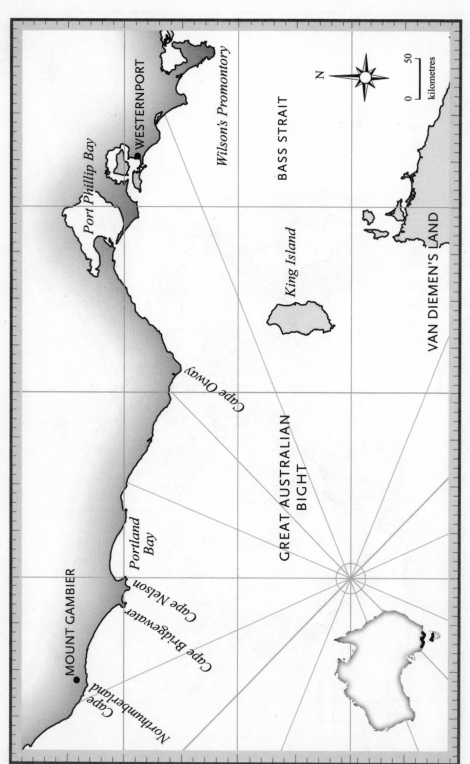

South-eastern coast

South Australian gulfs

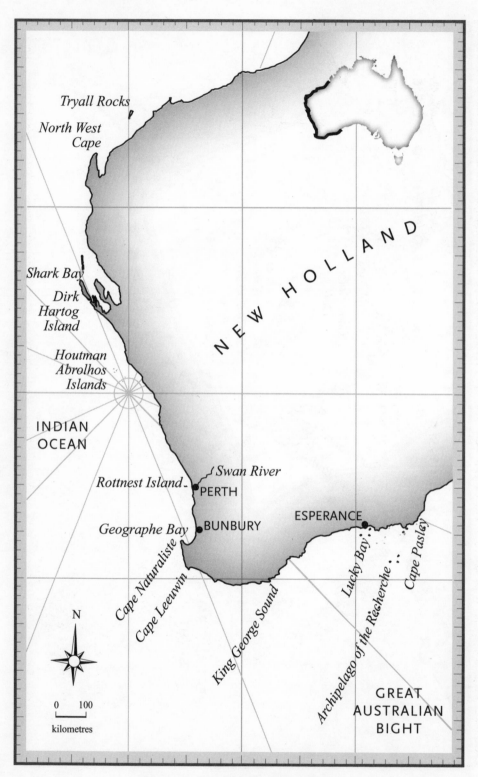

Tryall Rocks

North West
Cape

Shark Bay

Dirk
Hartog
Island

Houtman
Abrolhos
Islands

INDIAN
OCEAN

NEW HOLLAND

Rottnest Island

Swan River
PERTH

Geographe Bay

BUNBURY

ESPERANCE

Cape Naturaliste

Cape Leeuwin

King George Sound

Lucky Bay

Archipelago of the Recherche

Cape Pasley

N

0   100

kilometres

GREAT
AUSTRALIAN
BIGHT

West coast to North West Cape

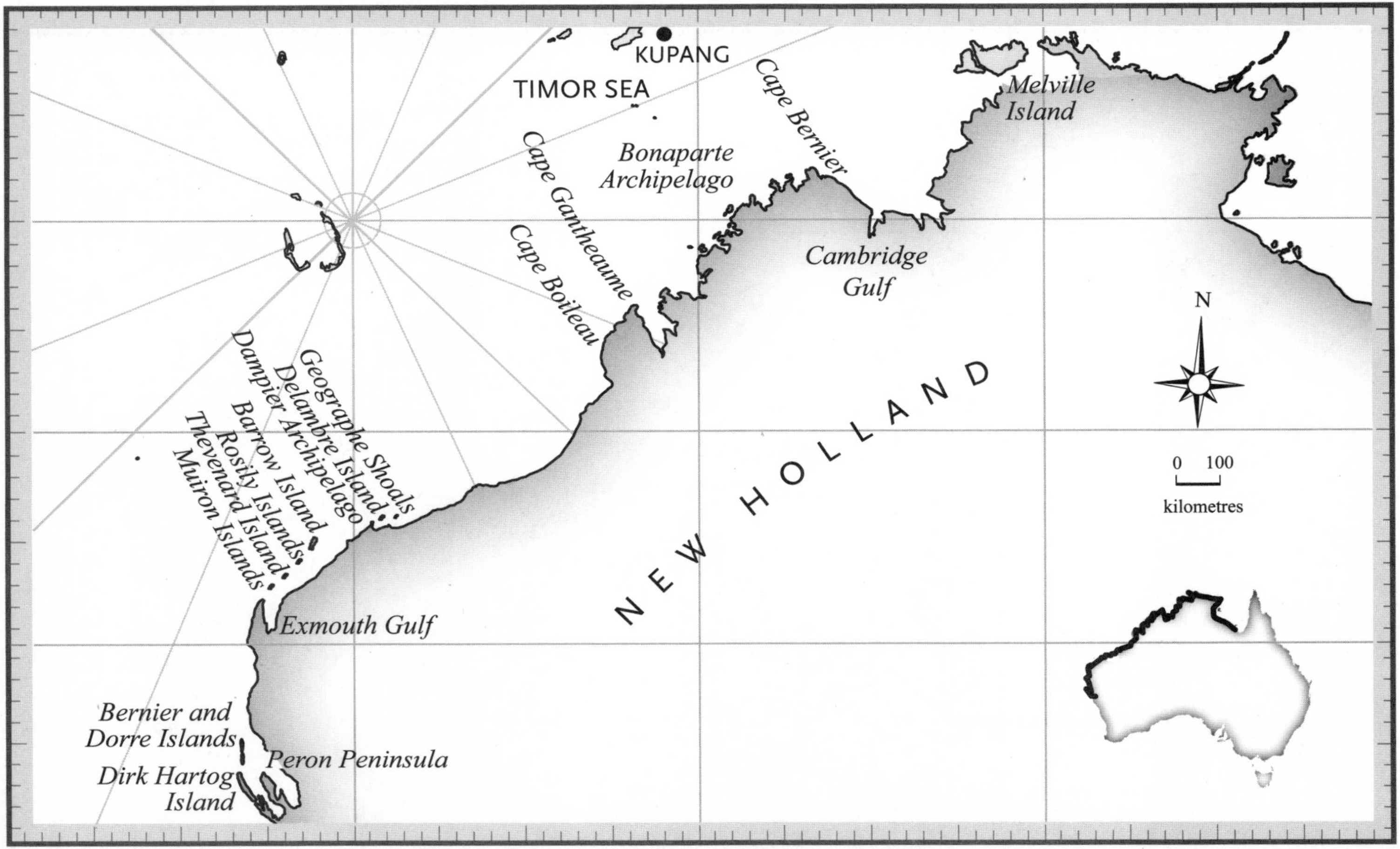

TIMOR SEA

KUPANG

Melville
Island

Cape Bernier

Cambridge
Gulf

NEW HOLLAND

Bonaparte
Archipelago

Cape Gantheaume

Cape Boileau

Geographe Shoals
Delambre Island
Dampier Archipelago
Barrow Island
Rosily Islands
Thevenard Island
Muiron Islands

Exmouth Gulf

Peron Peninsula

Bernier and
Dorre Islands
Dirk Hartog
Island

North West Cape

N

0   100
kilometres

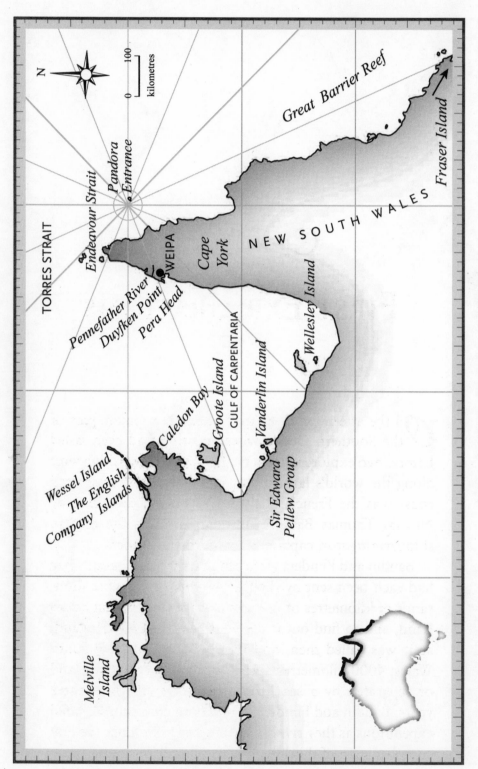

Gulf of Carpentaria to Fraser Island

CHAPTER 1

FIRST EXPLORATIONS

On the afternoon of 8 April 1802, in a remote part of the Southern Ocean where no ship had ever sailed before, two explorers had a chance encounter. Sailing west along the world's largest remaining stretch of uncharted coast was the French ship *Le Géographe*, captained by Nicolas Thomas Baudin; heading east was the English ship *Investigator*, captained by Matthew Flinders.

Baudin and Flinders were both on the same quest. They had each been sent by their government to explore thousands of kilometres of unknown coast of the Great South Land, and to find out if the west coast of New Holland, as it was called then, and the east coast of New South Wales, 4000 kilometres away, were part of the same land or separated by a sea, or a strait. Over the next three years, Baudin and Flinders would both command ill-fated expeditions as they rivalled each other to produce the first complete map of this largely unexplored continent.

*

The French and the British were both relative latecomers to the Great South Land. For more than 200 years, other European navigators and explorers had visited, and some had charted, various parts of its coast.

The first documented European visits to Australia were both in 1606: one by a Spanish explorer, Luis Váez de Torres; and one by a Dutchman, Willem Janszoon. But there is some pretty compelling evidence suggesting that other Europeans had arrived much earlier, including surviving maps indicating Portuguese seafarers may have sailed along large sections of the Australian coast in the early 1500s.

The Portuguese were the first Europeans to sail into the Indian Ocean, when Bartholomeu Diaz navigated the Cape of Good Hope in 1486 and, a little more than a decade later, in 1497, Vasco da Gama sailed two ships to India and then back to Lisbon. Over the next century, the Portuguese developed a network of trading routes in the southern hemisphere, connecting South America, southern Africa, India and the Pacific as far as Timor. A major impetus for the trade was to collect spices and herbs that were not then available in Europe, including ginger, cloves, nutmeg, cinnamon, lemongrass, curry, vanilla and fennel.

The theory that the Portuguese may also have reached as far as Australia is largely based on old maps that contain a number of coastal features strikingly similar to the Australian shoreline. The beautifully made French Dieppe maps are believed to be reproductions of Portuguese originals, and they show a land mass named Java la Grande between Indonesia and Antarctica. They were made by the Dieppe Cartography Department for wealthy and royal patrons and included the Dauphin map of 1547, which was ordered by King Francis I of France as a gift to his son the Dauphin, who later became King Henry II. The map, which is now in the British Library, depicts a coastline that appears similar to the features of the Australian coast from Cape York to the current-day southern Victoria.

Other surviving charts from this period include a book of maps dated 1542 that was presented to England's King Henry VIII by Frenchman Jean Rotz, an artist-cartographer who was a member of the Dieppe School. The Jean Rotz maps depict a coastline similar to some of Australia's north and east coasts. Then in 1566 Nicolas Desliens created a world map whose depiction of Australia had similar features to one of the far north-east coast of the continent made 200 years later by Captain James Cook. Also supporting the theory of an earlier Portuguese discovery of Australia was the claim in 1836 by two whalers that they had found the remains of a sixteenth-century Portuguese ship on a deserted stretch of beach on the southern Australian coast near Warrnambool. There were other reported sightings over the next few decades, but no more evidence has been found since the 1880s, despite the offer of a $250,000 reward by the Victorian state government in the late 1970s.

Historians are divided as to whether the maps are proof that the Portuguese had, albeit unwittingly and presumably unknowingly, discovered Australia in the early sixteenth century. Some argue the coastal features on the maps are too accurate for their likeness to the Australian coast to be a coincidence. The explorer Matthew Flinders was among those who thought the Portuguese had been to the Great South Land many years before him; he said of the surviving maps that 'the direction given to some parts of the coast, approaches too near the truth, for the whole to have been marked by conjecture alone'.[1]

Others, however, argue the maps are merely theoretical constructs and not the result of actual discovery.[2] They point out that the theory of earlier Portuguese discoveries rests almost entirely on the Dieppe maps. There are no surviving Portuguese charts from the sixteenth century that show any traces of a large landmass, and there are no records of any European sailing along the coast of Australia before 1606.[3] It has also been argued that the features of Java la Grande on the Dieppe maps could resemble the coast of Indonesia and Indochina as much as they do Australia.

It is known that, by the end of the eighteenth century, men from Malaya had a well-established trade fishing for turtles and trepang, or sea cucumbers, on the north and west coasts of Australia. The men arrived in October and November in fleets of small wooden boats that fanned out across the Top End to fish throughout the summer. Each boat weighed about twenty tons and had a crew of about twenty men who lived on deck in bamboo cabins. The trepang were taken ashore and boiled, sun-dried and then smoked, before being sold in China, where they were regarded as a great delicacy. In 1803 Flinders met some of these seamen and speculated they had fished large parts of the coast for many years, as he had seen traces of them 'so abundantly along the coast of the Gulf'.[4] The French explorer Nicolas Baudin also recorded seeing the fishermen on a different part of the north coast of Australia on his expedition in the same year.

It has been claimed that the Chinese reached the east coast of Australia as early as the time of the Han Dynasty (202 BC–AD 220) and perhaps even further back, in the undocumented past.[5] In recent decades a number of books have argued that ancient maps suggest Chinese navigators charted parts of the east coast of Australia up to a century before the Portuguese.[6]

However, the first documented European visits to Australia were by the Dutchman Willem Janszoon and, separately, the Spaniard Luis Váez de Torres in 1606 – one coming from the west and the other from the east, and, in an amazing coincidence, both reaching the same parts of the north Australian coast within months of each other.

Willem Janszoon was thirty-five years old when he was sent by his employer, the Dutch East India Company, to search 'the vast land of Nova Guinea and other east and south lands'.[7] Janszoon was not sent on a voyage of scientific exploration but to look for gold and new trading opportunities for the Dutch, who by now had taken over most of the former Portuguese trade routes and become the dominant economic power in the East Indies. Unlike the French and the British, who more than a century later would send well-equipped ships on expeditions of scientific inquiry, the Dutch, like the Portuguese and the Spanish, were only interested in discovery for commercial gain.

The Dutch East India Company, or VOC (Vereenigde Oostindische Compagnie), was created in 1602 by the Dutch government, amalgamating competing Dutch merchants and granting them a monopoly in the spice trade in Asia. Janszoon had joined the Dutch East India Company as a sixteen-year-old cadet in 1586 and was on his third trip to the East Indies, having first sailed there as a mate on the *Hollandia* in 1598. The company and those who were part of it were given wide-ranging powers by the Dutch government, including the authority to establish colonies, negotiate treaties, coin money and wage war. They were at liberty to exploit any resources or riches they found, and they ruthlessly crushed all local resistance. In the East Indies, the VOC was effectively a government in its own right and answerable to no one.

The first Dutch trading settlement was established in Bantam, in West Java, in 1602. By the beginning of the seventeenth century, the Dutch had become the most prominent European traders in the East Indies, having taken over many of the ports from the Portuguese and the Spanish, as both empires were in decline. In 1619, the governor-general of the VOC, Jan Pieterszoon Coen, invaded Batavia (current-day Jakarta) with a fleet of nineteen warships, routed the local resistance and established the Dutch provincial capital of Batavia. Over the next half-century, with Batavia as its provincial capital, the Dutch expanded their ports across South-East Asia, including Kupang (in Timor), Makassar, Manado, Sulawesi and Malacca.

Willem Janszoon arrived in Java as part of a convoy in 1605, commanding the *Duyfken* (Little Dove), before he was sent by the Dutch East India Company to search for possible trading opportunities to the south-east. The *Duyfken* was a tiny ship – only nineteen metres long – but, being smaller than other ships of that time, it was more manoeuvrable and suitable for exploring closer to shore. Included in the crew of roughly ninety men was a senior company representative, Lodewijksz van Rosingeyn.[8] The ship probably carried about ten guns. Eight would have been small bronze or iron cannons and the remaining two the old-style stonepieces, so called for the stone balls they shot from a swivel, across a wide angle.[9]

Unfortunately no log or journal survives of this expedition, but later copies of the charts of the voyage show that Janszoon first saw land near the mouth of the Pennefather River, about 150 kilometres south of the top of Cape York Peninsula. Seeing nothing of commercial value, he continued south for about 300 kilometres along the eastern side of the coast, which was still thought to be an extension of New Guinea, until he reached what is today known as Weipa, on the Gulf of Carpentaria side of the Cape York Peninsula.

It was on the Janszoon voyage that the first violent clashes between Europeans and Aboriginal people are claimed to have occurred. They are said to have taken place at a spot marked on Janszoon's map as Cabo Keerweer (Cape Turn-about), not far from Weipa. While no firsthand account survives, a number of later Dutch records say that the local Aboriginal people attacked and killed nine of the *Duyfken*'s crew who had gone ashore. Nearly forty years later, when the navigator Abel Tasman was to embark on his second great voyage in this same area, he was warned of 'places inhabited by wild, cruel, black savages, by whom some of the [*Duyfken*] crew were murdered'.[10]

However, in the oral history of the local Wik people that was passed down and recorded in the late twentieth century, it was alleged that the killings were in retaliation for the murder of local Aboriginals and the abduction of some Aboriginal women. In one account, it was claimed that 'the Dutch shot many Aboriginal people along the river and in the bush land. Also the warriors speared and killed some Dutchmen and made the Dutch go back to their ship.'[11]

Janszoon and his Dutch masters were at the time unaware of the significance of his discovery. They thought the *Duyfken* had been charting a southern extension of the New Guinea coast and were unaware they had been the first Europeans known to have set foot on Australia.

Janszoon's voyage offered very little in the way of possible trading opportunities, so it was of scant use to the Dutch. If, however, his voyage had shown prospects for profitable trade, Australia might well have gone on to become a Dutch possession.

After returning to Batavia, over the following two decades Janszoon served in a number of senior posts, including as an admiral and governor of the Dutch East

Indian settlement of Banda, near current-day Ambon. He returned to the Netherlands in 1629 and is believed to have died the following year, aged about sixty.

In a remarkable coincidence, only months after Janszoon was in the Gulf of Carpentaria, Spaniard Luis Váez de Torres sailed from the east through the islands that separated New Guinea from Australia.

While the Portuguese had been developing trade routes from Lisbon, via the Cape of Good Hope, to the east since the early 1500s, the Spanish had been coming around Cape Horn at the southernmost tip of South America. Ferdinand Magellan was the first to open up the East Indies to Spanish traders from the east when he sailed from the Atlantic, through the narrow strait at the bottom of South America that bears his name, and into the Pacific Ocean – the quiet sea. In addition to controlling large parts of the Caribbean, and Central and South America, the Spanish established a network of trading centres in the Pacific, including the Philippines, Guam and parts of Formosa (Taiwan).

Torres was commander of the *San Pedro*, one of three Spanish ships of an expedition led by Pedro Fernández de Quirós that left Callao, in Peru, in December 1605 to search for the much-discussed but never-found Great South Land that had appeared on the earlier Dieppe maps.

Little is known about Torres, and most of the information about his voyage comes from a letter he wrote to King Philip III of Spain in 1607 and from a later account written by one of his fellow officers, Don Diego de Prado y Tovar.

After sailing for six months and discovering the New Hebrides (Vanuatu), the *San Pederico* and the third ship, *Los Tres Reyes Margos*, became separated from de Quirós's flagship, the *San Pedro*. Following contingency instructions, Torres continued to search for the Great South

Land and, with great care, eventually managed to navigate the dangerous reef that separates the north of Australia from New Guinea. Torres then explored part of the New Guinea coast, which he claimed on behalf of King Philip III of Spain, before heading north and reaching Manila in May 1607, after which his name disappears from history.

Torres did not know that, as he passed through the strait, he had sailed past the Great South Land; he recorded seeing only some 'very large islands' to the south.[12]

The Spanish did not divulge Torres's discoveries to their European rivals, and it was not until the British came into possession of the charts more than 150 years later that the passage became more widely known and named Torres Strait, after its discoverer.

After the visits by Torres and Janszoon, a number of other Dutch East India Company ships were sent to explore the north coast of this land, but over the next fifty years many more landed by accident or were wrecked on the west coast of what later became known as New Holland.

In December 1610, Dutchman Henrik Brouwer discovered a route that reduced to about six months the journey time from Europe to the Dutch East Indies, which had been well over a year. Up until Brouwer's discovery, ships bound for the East Indies travelled on much the same route as the Portuguese had sailed a hundred years before: around the Cape of Good Hope, then north through the Mozambique Channel, which separates the eastern African coast from Madagascar, sometimes calling at India, then east across the Indian Ocean.

Brouwer discovered that by sailing south after the Cape of Good Hope to a latitude of around forty degrees or more, a ship would be driven much more quickly by the strong westerly winds, which became known as the roaring forties. Once across the south of the Indian Ocean, the ship could then turn north for the Dutch East Indian ports. Even though the distance was greater, the voyage was completed more quickly. The 'Brouwer route' soon became the standard route for all European ships bound for the east.

However, by going too far east before turning north, many ships unwittingly reached the west coast of New Holland and were wrecked on the shore. Travelling the Brouwer route was more hazardous for early navigators because of the difficulty of calculating their longitude, or the distance they had travelled from west to east.

Estimating longitude did not become a science until the invention of reliable mechanical clocks. It was then possible to keep the clock on board ship on the same time as that at the port of departure. By sighting the sun at its highest point during the day, seamen could tell the time difference between local noon and noon at the ship's original location, and from that they could calculate how far east or west they had travelled. But it was not until the second half of the seventeenth century that the first marine chronometers were introduced, and it would be almost another century before dependable and reliable clocks were invented.

Calculating latitude, or distance travelled north or south, was easier. Since ancient Greek times, navigators had known how to measure the distance from the equator by making a geometric calculation based on the angle of the sun in relation to the horizon at noon.

In the meantime, to measure the distance they had travelled east or west, navigators continued to rely on crude systems, which were far from reliable. One way was dead reckoning, which involved calculating the time travelled between fixed points on land, but this was obviously difficult for a ship out of sight of land. Another method involved calculating a ship's speed by throwing a heavy piece of wood tied to a rope over the side and timing how long it took to reach the end of the rope. Using such methods, shipwrecks were almost inevitable.

For a while, the British adopted the Brouwer route, but they abandoned it following the wrecking of the *Tryal* in 1622. The *Tryal* became the first British ship known to have reached Australian waters when it crashed onto rocks near Montebello and Barrow islands off the north-west coast of the mainland (near current-day Exmouth). The ship was owned by the English East India Company, which had been formed in 1600. In addition to trading in spices and herbs and other fine goods, as the VOC did, the English East India Company became a dominant trader in tea and opium, particularly with China.

When the *Tryal* left England under the command of Captain John Brooke with a cargo of silver, neither the captain nor any of his crew had any experience sailing the southerly route in the roaring forties. When it was about ten degrees longitude – or more than 600 kilometres – further east than it should have been, the *Tryal* was wrecked on what became known as Tryal Rocks.

Brooke said that following the wind, 'veering to the south east', the ship hit the rocks at around eleven at night on 25 May 1622. He immediately gave orders to steer in a westerly direction, but 'the rock being sharp the ship was presently full of water' and within three hours they began to abandon it. Brooke claimed everything was done to save the crew but the ship broke up too quickly and most were drowned: '[I] made all the means I could to save . . . as many . . . as I could . . . The [long]boat put off at 4 in the morning and half an hour after . . . part of the ship fell in pieces!'[13]

According to Thomas Bright, who also survived, '128 souls [were] left to God's mercy and only 36 were saved'.[14] After searching for water on nearby islands, Brooke and the surviving crew headed in the *Tryal*'s longboat for Batavia, where they arrived, according to Brooke, with the boat '1/3 full of water' and rations nearly exhausted on 25 June.

In a letter sent from Batavia to his masters in the English East India Company, Brooke denied responsibility for the wreck. He said that he had been following the charts of another English captain, Humphrey Fitzherbert, who on the *Royal Exchange* had sailed that way two years before, in 1620.[15] Brooke claimed that at the time of the wreck they had seen land 'formerly seen by the [Dutch]'. However, it is unlikely that the *Tryal* was the first English ship to sight the Australian mainland, because Tryal Rocks is about one hundred kilometres off the north-west Australian coast.[16]

The exact site of the *Tryal* wreck remained a mystery for more than 300 years – despite many searches in the nineteenth and twentieth centuries – until it was found by a team of divers from Western Australia in 1969.

The first Dutchman known to have followed the Brouwer route and unintentionally sailed too far, thus reaching the west coast of Australia, was Dirk Hartog, in 1616. Thirty-six-year-old Hartog was an experienced local sailor when he was appointed commander of the cargo ship the *Eendtracht* (Concord), which was on its maiden voyage to the Dutch East Indies and weighed 700 tons, making it a large ship for its time. Leaving the Dutch port of Texel in an icy cold January, with ten chests containing 80,000 reals (pieces of eight), the ship reached the Cape of Good Hope on 27 August, after a very slow journey. Following the Brouwer route, the expedition reached an island on the edge of the western Australian coast, which became known as Dirk Hartog Island, at the entrance to the current-day Shark Bay. A week later, and before leaving to sail north, they left an inscription on a flattened pewter plate – the first record of a European landing left in Australia:

> 1616. 25 October is here arrived the ship the *Eendracht* of Amsterdam, the upper merchant Gillis Miebais of Liege, skipper Dirk Hatchs of Amsterdam; the 27th ditto set sail again for Bantam, the under merchant Jan Stins, the upper steersman Peter van Bill, Anno 1616.

(More than eighty years later, another Dutch explorer, Willem de Vlamingh, took the plaque and replaced it with a new one, which included a copy of the original text and a record of his own visit. Vlamingh took the original plaque to Batavia, from where it was later taken back to Holland, and it is now in the Rijksmuseum in Amsterdam.)

Hartog's discovery was to have a major impact. What had been a mythical continent known as Terra Australis Incognita (the unknown southern land) began to appear on European maps, bearing the name of Hartog's ship: Land van de Eendracht (Land of *Eendracht*).

A decade after Hartog's historic landing, a fellow Dutchman, twenty-eight-year-old Pieter Nuyts, became the first to sail along a large part of the unmapped south coast of the continent.

Nuyts was born in Leiden in 1598, the son of a textile merchant. After attending university, he worked in his father's business before joining the Dutch East India Company. By 1626 he was a senior official with the VOC. Subsequently he left his pregnant wife in Amsterdam to take up a company posting in Batavia. Taking his older son, Laurens, with him, Nuyts boarded the *Guilden Seepart* (Golden Seahorse), captained by François Thijssen, and left the Netherlands in May 1626 with 158 crew and passengers. Included in the passengers were six women, who were either accompanying or joining husbands who had been posted to Dutch trading settlements in the East Indies.

Seven months later, on 26 January 1627, the *Guilden Seepart* reached Cape Leeuwin, on the south-west tip of the continent. One hundred and sixty-one years later to the day, Captain Arthur Phillip would claim the site of Sydney on the east coast for the British, on what would become known as Australia Day.

Then, instead of heading north along the western Australian coast to its destination of Batavia, the *Guilden Seepart* continued east along the uncharted south coast. As scant information about the voyage survives, other than some copies of Nuyts's charts, it is not clear whether he was instructed to explore the unknown coast or search for an alternative route to the Dutch East Indies, or was simply blown too far east. After sailing more than 1600 kilometres, he found a group of islands off the southern Australian coast opposite current-day Ceduna, which he charted. He named the two largest St Francis and St Peter, after François Thijssen and Pieter Nuyts. The islands are the oldest named parts of South Australia.

After reaching St Peter and St Francis islands, the *Guilden Seepart* turned around and sailed back the way it had come, to Cape Leeuwin then north along the west coast to Batavia, where it arrived on 10 April 1627.

In Batavia, Pieter Nuyts was promoted to become the Dutch East Indian ambassador to Japan, but after encountering difficulties with the Japanese, he settled on Formosa. Nuyts's time as a diplomat was controversial. In Formosa he married a local – his first wife, Cornelia, had died – but is said to have conducted a number of affairs. Eventually recalled to Batavia, he returned to the Netherlands in 1636, where he again married in 1640.

But his new wife, Anna van Driel, died during childbirth later that year. Nuyts subsequently became a landowner in Holland and the mayor of both Hulster Ambacht and Hulst, and he married again in 1649, to Agnes Granier. When he died, in 1655, aged fifty-seven, it was found that many of the taxes he collected on behalf of the local government were unaccounted for, and eventually they had to be paid by his surviving son.

After the voyage of the *Guilden Seepart*, Dutch charts would name the southern shoreline 'Landt van P. Nuyts'. The two islands of St Peter and St Francis are believed to have later been the inspiration for Jonathan Swift's Lilliput and Blefuscu in *Gulliver's Travels*, first published almost a century later, in 1726.

Two years after Nuyts's epic journey, another Dutch ship was not so lucky when it became one of the most celebrated shipwrecks in history by foundering on the rocks off the coast of Western Australia.

The *Batavia*, the pride of the Dutch East India Company fleet, was on its maiden voyage. Built in 1628, the ship was fifty-seven metres long and weighed 650 tons, almost twice the size of a typical ship of that time. It left the Dutch port of Telex in October 1628 with a large sum of money and 314 crew and passengers, including women and children on their way to settle with their husbands and fathers in the Dutch provincial towns and cities of the East Indies. Captained by Ariaen Jacobsz and leading a convoy of eight other ships, the *Batavia* also carried the fleet commander, Francisco Pelsaert.

Making good time and taking the Brouwer route, the *Batavia* sailed too far and reached the west coast of Australia, where, before daylight on 5 June 1629, the ship was wrecked on the rocks of the Houtman Abrolhos islands, about fifty kilometres off the coast of current-day Geraldton.

During the day, using the *Batavia*'s small boats, the crew managed to ferry almost 240 people across to two nearby islands, but many others were drowned or stranded on the stricken ship. The survivors had only a small amount of food, and, while they were able to fish and hunt some sea lions, they could not find any significant quantity of drinking water.

Commander Francisco Pelsaert decided to take the *Batavia*'s nine-metre-long boat to the mainland to fetch some water for the castaways, then send for help to the Dutch provincial capital on Java, some 1500 kilometres to the north:

> Since on all the islands or reefs round about our foundered ship Batavia, there is no water to be found, in order to feed and keep the saved people alive, therefore the Commander has earnestly besought us and proposed that we should sail to the mainland in order to see if God will grant that we find water there, to assist the people with as many trips from there until we can be certain that they will be able to remain alive for some considerable time, and meanwhile command someone to bring our sad happenings to the Hon. Lord General, to which we the undersigned have consented now that the need has been placed before us of how greatly important it is to be responsible before God and the high authorities. Have agreed and resolved to do our utmost duty in order to help our poor companions in their distress.[17]

However, according to Pelsaert, who wrote a journal of events after the wrecking of the *Batavia*, at first they could not even land on any of the nearby islands or on the mainland:

The coast here stretches mostly N by W and S by E. It is bad rocky land without trees, [the cliffs] about as high as Dover in England . . . We saw a small inlet . . . where we intended to land, but approaching, noticed that there was a big surf and many breakers near the shore; very suddenly the swell became heavy.[18]

A week later, they managed to land, only to find few waterholes and not much water:

The 16 [June] in the morning continued to see whether there were more such holes . . . But our search was in vain, it appeared that it had not rained there for a long time, nor was there any sign of running water.[19]

The following day, they decided to head north for Batavia, which they reached a fortnight later, with almost no drinking water left. Remarkably, all forty-eight people who had crowded on the little boat had survived the month since the sinking of the *Batavia*.

After arriving in port, on Monday, 10 July, Pelsaert had to confront Lord Governor Coen. Coen had been eagerly awaiting the *Batavia*, with its much-needed money and desperately needed reinforcements for the fortress at Batavia. The town was badly under-defended from attacks by local Bantam forces, who had never entirely ceased their onslaught since the Dutch invasion ten years before.

Commander Pelsaert was immediately ordered by Coen to take the *Sardam* to rescue the *Batavia*'s survivors, who had now been stranded with insufficient water for more than a month. The *Sardam* had only recently arrived in Batavia, but it was quickly readied for sail and left the following Saturday, 15 July.

Batavia's Captain Jacobsz was not as fortunate: he and his boatswain, Jan Evertszoon, were both thrown in jail to answer charges about the sinking of the *Batavia* and a number of incidents on her voyage out from Holland, including the abuse of a woman passenger on her way to Batavia to meet up with her husband.

Pelsaert made good time and reached the Houtman Albrolhos islands on 10 August, but spent another month searching among the various islands before he found the wreck of the *Batavia* on 16 September, and the ghastly story emerged of what had happened to the survivors in the three months since the shipwreck.

A senior member of the *Batavia's* crew – the *onderkoopman*, or under-merchant, Jeronimus Cornelisz, who had been left in charge of the survivors – had embarked on a reign of terror and murder. In order to control the limited water and food, and crush any possible dissent, his followers began a killing spree, drowning, strangling, stabbing and bludgeoning to death more than 120 men, women and children.

When Pelsaert returned and forcibly took control of the scene, he immediately tried and executed the ringleaders, including Cornelisz, with the more serious offenders having both hands cut off before being hanged.

Two of the youngest offenders, Walter Loos and a young cabin boy, who were considered to have committed only lesser crimes, were abandoned on the mainland. Many years later, British settlers noticed unusually light-skinned Aboriginal people, which fuelled speculation that the two Dutchmen may have survived and become part of a local community. However, it is also possible that if there were Dutchmen living on the mainland, they could have come from other Dutch shipwrecks on the same part of the coast, including that of the *Zuytdorp*, which was wrecked in a similar area in 1712.

By 5 December, seven months after the wreck, only sixty-three of the original 341 people who sailed on the *Batavia* had survived to reach Batavia.

The dreadful *Batavia* story has become etched in Australia's history and remains the country's biggest ever mass murder. More than 300 years later, in 1963, divers discovered the remains of the wreck, and on nearby islands they have found burial sites and remnants of the survivors' camps. In 1972 the wreck of the ship was retrieved from the sea, and it is now exhibited in the Western Australian maritime museum, in Fremantle.

*

One of the greatest navigation achievements by the Dutch during this period – and, indeed, all of history – was by Abel Tasman, who, in two separate expeditions in 1643 and 1644, discovered large parts of the Australian coast.

Tasman was born in Lutjegast, in today's province of Groningen, in 1603. Nothing is known of his parents or other relatives, but his later journals suggest he was reasonably well educated. It is believed that he began working with the Dutch East India Company as a *vaerentgesel*, or common seaman, in 1632 and gradually worked his way through the ranks.[20] By twenty-nine years of age, he was widowed. After remarrying, he sailed to Batavia with the company in 1633. After a visit back to Holland, he returned to the East Indies in 1636 and captained trading missions to Formosa, Japan and Sumatra. By all accounts, Tasman gave the impression of being a man unfazed by pressure, who consulted his colleagues and was prepared to take their advice.

In 1642 he embarked on the first of his two great voyages of discovery when he was sent by the company to explore the Great South Land. Unlike many of the Dutch sailors who had reached the coast by accident in preceding years, Tasman was sent specifically to explore new trading opportunities for the Dutch East India Company by sailing thousands of kilometres deep into the Great Southern Ocean, where no one had ever ventured before.

In its instructions to Tasman, the Dutch East India Company made it clear that as great wealth had been found by explorers of the New World in the northern hemisphere, the same should reasonably be expected in the southern hemisphere:

> Seeing that in many countries north of the line Equinoctial (in from 15 to 40 degrees Latitude), there are found many rich mines of precious and other metals, and other treasures, there must be similar fertile and rich regions situated south of the Equator . . . so that it may be confidently expected that the expense and trouble that must be bestowed in the eventual discovery of so large a portion of the world, will be rewarded with certain fruits of material profit and immortal fame.[21]

For the expedition, Tasman was assigned two small ships, the 120-ton *Heemskerck* and the 200-ton *Zeehaen*; and with a total crew of 110 men, they left Batavia on 14 August 1642.[22] There was twelve to eighteen months' worth of provisions on board, and Tasman carried samples of minerals and spices so they could show any local people they might encounter the sorts of goods the Dutch were interested in taking.

Tasman was also looking for the possibility of new sailing routes east to South America. His comprehensive written instructions from the Dutch East India Company called for the most thorough exploration and description of the lands and the people they came to:

All the lands, islands, points, turnings, inlets, bays, rivers, shoals, banks, sands, cliffs, rocks, etc., which you shall meet with and pass, you will duly map out and describe, and also have proper drawings made of their appearance and shape . . . to gather information concerning the situation of the country, the fruits and cattle it produces, their method of building houses, appearance and shape of the inhabitants, their dress, arms, manners, diet, means of livelihood, religion, mode of government, wars and the like notable things, especially whether they are kindly or cruelly disposed.[23]

In accordance with his instructions, Tasman sailed in a wide arc – first almost 6000 kilometres west of Batavia – and reached the small island of Mauritius in the Indian Ocean in October 1642. Mauritius had first been used by the Portuguese on voyages to the East Indies at the beginning of the fifteenth century, but by the time Tasman arrived it had been a Dutch-controlled settlement for almost four decades.

Tasman stayed a month on the island, where his ships were repaired for the daunting journey ahead. Here they loaded firewood and fresh food, including more than twenty live goats and ten pigs. Tasman said that while they were in port he agreed to cut his crew's grog ration at the request of the local governor:

The worshipful Van de Ste informed us that he got positive orders . . . not to serve out more than one pympetien of arrack to each of their men, and this only to such as are cold, wet and dirty. In order to maintain peace among the men and prevent discontent, ill will and envy . . . we have deemed it best to serve out only half a small glass of arrack to our men while we were lying in this roadstead.[24]

Before leaving Mauritius to sail into the Southern Ocean, Tasman described a meeting of the senior officers of both ships with the Dutch East India Company to discuss contingency plans if things went wrong:

> After due deliberation we summoned on board all our skippers, first and second mates, and informed them that we desired all persons present to give their advice in writing what place were best to fix upon for a rendezvous, in case we should get separated from each other by rough weather, storms or other accidents (which we hope will be spared us and God in his mercy advert).[25]

Sailing vast distances in tiny leaking wooden ships – all of them leaked – on voyages that could last for several years was extremely dangerous, and death rates of more than fifty per cent of the crew were far from uncommon. The hazards included accidents, often involving falling from the rigging onto the deck or into the sea; shipwrecks; fire on board; fighting enemies at sea or being killed by hostile locals on land; starvation; and disease. However, for hundreds of years, until into the nineteenth century, the largest single killer of sailors was scurvy, which was responsible for about half of all deaths at sea. It would take the Europeans almost 250 years from the first voyages of discovery in the early fifteenth century to find the simple remedy to this terrible disease, which caused livid spots to appear all over the body, bleeding from every orifice, the loss of teeth, debilitating fatigue, depression and death. Eventually, in the mid-eighteenth century, it was learned that scurvy could be largely avoided with a regular intake of fresh food, particularly fruit and vegetables, which are a source of vitamin C. By the time of his great expeditions in the 1760s and 1770s, Captain James Cook had successfully controlled the disease, but it was still wide-spread on long voyages when fresh food was not available.

After leaving Mauritius, Tasman and his men headed south, reaching the latitude of 47 degrees, where, despite it being the southern hemisphere summer, it was freezing cold and wet, making the small ships not only cramped but also damp. In the high seas and strong winds, Tasman recorded in his journal that the 'gale was attended with hail and rain to such a degree that we feared the ship would not live through it'.[26]

Weeks later Tasman complained of 'hail and snow' and very high seas and the crew suffering 'from the severe cold'.[27]

Finally, on 24 November they came across land they realised had never been sighted by any Europeans before them. Tasman recorded in his journal:

> This land being the first land we have met with in the South Seas and not known to any European nation we have conferred on it the name of Anthony van Diemen's land in honour of the Honourable Governor General, our illustrious master, who sent us to make this discovery.[28]

When charting the location of his new discovery, Tasman calculated its longitude with an error of only 2.05 degrees from Greenwich – or 140 kilometres – which, after a journey of two months and sixteen days and covering nearly 10,000 kilometres from Mauritius, was a remarkable piece of navigation.

If Tasman believed that he had found the southernmost tip of the continent that had been touched on by many of his countrymen over the previous forty years, he made no mention of it. On 2 December, almost five months since leaving Batavia, a number of the Dutch were sent ashore to look for firewood and fresh water. They found that in contrast to the barren north, west and south coast of New Holland, Van Diemen's Land had an abundance of good timber, drinking water and some edible vegetable matter:

> About three hours before nightfall the boats came back, bringing various samples of vegetables which they had seen growing there in great abundance, some of them in appearance not unlike a certain plant growing at the Cape of Good Hope and fit to be used as pot-herbs.[29]

They did not meet any local Aboriginal people but regularly saw smoke from fires, which Tasman said meant 'there can be no doubt there must be men here of extraordinary nature'. Tasman said his men also found traces of wildlife, including evidence of what later became known as the Tasmanian tiger:

> On the ground they had observed certain footprints of animals, not unlike those of tiger's claws; they brought on board certain specimens of animal excrement voided by quadrupeds, so far as they could surmise and observe, together with a small quantity of gum . . . which had exuded from the trees.[30]

Later, the Dutch on shore saw more smoke and fireplaces and suspected that they were being closely watched by men hiding nearby. Tasman said they made no attempt to search for the local people as they were in a hurry to look for trade potential for the Dutch East India Company:

> We had ordered them to return speedily, partly in order to be made acquainted with what they had seen, and partly that we might be able to send

them to other points if they should find no profit there, to the end that no precious time might be wasted.[31]

On 3 December, only a day before leaving the newly discovered land, Tasman became the first European to claim legal ownership of Australian territory on behalf of his country:

> In the afternoon we went to the south-east side of the bay in the boats . . . we carried with us a pole with the company's mark carved into it, and the Prince flag [of Holland] to be set up there, that those who shall come after us may become aware that we have been here, and we have taken possession of the said land as our lawful property.[32]

Tasman left Van Diemen's Land, continued east and made a similar territorial claim nine days later, when he became the first European to reach what later became known as the South Island of New Zealand. He then headed north, via the Friendly Islands (Tonga), and around the top of New Guinea, and arrived back in Batavia on 15 June after a voyage of ten months.

Although Tasman had found little of intrinsic trading value on his voyage of discovery, he and the crew were paid a bonus by the Dutch East India Company:

> although in fact no treasures or profitable commodities have been found . . . we have unanimously resolved . . . to award a recompense . . . to the Commander, skippers, supercargoes and sub-cargoes, steersmen, inclusive of the book-keeper, two months' pay each, and to the common sailors one month's pay each.[33]

Almost immediately after reaching Batavia and with the support of the governor, Anthony van Diemen, Tasman was sent off on another exploration in 1644, with instructions to:

> obtain a thorough knowledge of the extensive countries, the discovery whereof has begun . . . [It] now only remains for the future to discover whether New Guinea is one continent with the great south land, or separated by channels and islands lying between them, and also whether the new Van Diemen's Land is the same continent.

Again the aim of the company was the discovery of new wealth, and after Tasman's expedition they intended to send more ships to search for riches:

> By September next, when the projected discovery of the north coast of the south land is likely to have been successfully effected, we also intend to dispatch two or three yachts for the further exploration of the newly discovered South-lands, with express orders to ascertain what advantages for the Company may be obtained there. They will especially have to inquire whether in these vast regions there are any silver-, gold-, or copper-mines, which we deem very likely, seeing they are situated under a climate especially adapted for such mines, and resembling that of the silver- and gold-bearing regions of Peru, Chile, China and Japan.[34]

In the event that Tasman found gold or silver, he was instructed to cheat the locals by not indicating how valuable it was:

> Find out what commodities their country yields, likewise inquiring after gold and silver . . . making

them believe that you are by no means eager for precious metals, so as to leave them ignorant of the value of the same; and if they should offer you gold or silver in exchange for your articles, you will pretend to hold the same in slight regard, showing them copper, pewter or lead and giving them an impression as if the minerals last mentioned were by us set greater value on.[35]

For the expedition, the Dutchman was given three small ships – the *Limmer*, the *Zeemeeuw* and the *Bracq* – with a total crew of ninety-four sailors and seventeen soldiers. We know nothing about how Tasman felt about his next great assignment, because no log or journal of his second epic voyage survives. However, the charts of his journey tell us where he sailed. After leaving Batavia in February 1644, he sailed east in the direction of Torres Strait, reaching the western side of Cape York Peninsula at nearly the site where fellow Dutchman Janszoon had first begun his journey in the gulf nearly forty years before. Tasman then sailed south and west around the Gulf of Carpentaria, passing a large island that had been seen by another Dutch sailor, Willem van Coolsteerdt, twenty years before but had remained nameless. Tasman gave it its European name, Groote Eylandt.

He then sailed west around the top of what is now the Northern Territory and south along the west coast to what is today North West Cape, in a voyage of six months and around 5000 kilometres, which was by far the longest exploration of Australia's coastline yet.

It is believed that Tasman's beautifully reproduced map of 1695 was a copy of one that was first made immediately after he finished his second voyage, in 1644. An inscription on the map, which is described as 'The Secret Atlas of the East India Company' states:

> These lands were discovered by the [Dutch East India] Company's explorers except for the northern part of New Guinea and the west end of Java. This work is put together from different writings as well as from personal observations by Abel Tasman, AD 1644, by order of his excellency the Governor-General Antonio van Diemen.

It was from Tasman's maps of his second voyage that the south land gained the new name of New Holland, which it would keep for more than 150 years, until the publication of Matthew Flinders's maps in 1814.

Tasman's was a remarkable navigational achievement. He was the first European to travel so far south across the world's most southern oceans; to discover Van Diemen's Land and New Zealand; and to sight the Fiji islands. And, as a result of his two great voyages, the Dutch were able to use his charts and those of earlier explorers to complete the map of large parts of Australia's northern, western and southern coasts.

However, the Dutch East India Company was not overly excited by his achievement, as – again – he had brought back no treasure or promise of profitable trade. The land he discovered was relatively unproductive, with no apparent new sources of minerals, spices or tradeable food, and nor had he found any new passage to South America, which might have been of value to the Dutch.

Nonetheless, when he returned to Batavia, Tasman was granted a promotion and a pay rise and was appointed to the Council of Justice. In 1647, he commanded an expedition to Siam (Thailand), taking gifts to its king. The following year he commanded a fleet of eight ships sent against rival Spanish ships. He retired in comfortable circumstances as a merchant and landowner in 1653 and died in 1659, aged fifty-six.

After Tasman, Holland showed little further interest in Australia, and nor did any other European country until more than half a century later, when an English pirate made an unplanned visit.

CHAPTER 2

THE FIRST ENGLISHMAN

The first Englishman known to have visited the Australian mainland was William Dampier, who arrived in 1688, forty years after Abel Tasman and more than seventy years before Captain James Cook.

Pirate, navigator, writer, natural historian, naval officer and adventurer, Dampier was the first person to circumnavigate the globe three times, visiting Australia twice. He was born in East Coker, Somerset, in 1651 but little is known about his childhood. As a boy he attended a local grammar school and was able to read and write well. His father, who made his living on a small rented farm, died when William was ten years old; his mother died six years later. As an orphaned teenager, he said he was pleased when he was apprenticed to the master of a merchant, because he wanted to see the world:

> My friends did not originally design me for the sea,
> but bred me at school till I came to years fit for

a trade. But on the death of father and mother . . .
and having removed me from Latin school to learn
writing and arithmetic, they soon placed me with a
master of a ship at Weymouth, complying with the
inclinations I had very early of seeing the world.[1]

Dampier first sailed to France and then on a longer journey
to Newfoundland but complained when he returned that
he found it too cold. He was about to abandon a career
at sea when the offer came for a voyage to the warmer
climate of the East Indies.

But so pinched with the rigour of a cold climate,
that upon my return I was absolutely against going
to these parts of the world . . . Yet going up a while
after London, the offer of a warm voyage, and a
long one, both of which I always desired, soon
carried me to sea again.[2]

At eighteen years old, he signed on to the *John and
Martha* and sailed to Bantam, on the island of Java, the
voyage lasting more than a year. Dampier said that the
earlier voyages had 'qualified' him but that on this voyage
he gained 'more experience in navigation'.[3]

In 1673, following the outbreak of war between England
and the Netherlands, twenty-two-year-old Dampier grew
weary of staying ashore and enlisted on the *Royal Prince*.
On the ship, he took part in two indecisive naval battles
at Schooneveld, on the Dutch coast, in which more than
eighty English and French ships fought sixty-four Dutch
ships. The British had intermittently been at war with its
trading rival the Netherlands for more than twenty years
when, in May and June 1673, Britain and its French allies
failed in both their attempts to crush the Dutch navy, which
would have opened the way for an invasion of Holland.

Dampier said that he 'fell very sick' and witnessed a third sea battle with the Dutch later in the year from a hospital ship. The following year, after 'languishing a great while' and recuperating at his brother's house, Dampier recovered his 'old inclination for the sea' and sailed to Jamaica, where he became the manager of a sugar plantation.

After only a short time, he admitted that he was unsuited to the planter's life, so he quit and went back to sailing.

> I was clearly out of my element there and therefore as soon as [my employer] Captain Heming came thither I disengaged myself from him and took my passage on board a sloop.[4]

Within months Dampier had changed jobs again, and for the next three years he was cutting and trading timber in the highly profitable logwood trade in the Gulf of Mexico.[5] At the time, logwood was prized in Europe as a source of quality timber and also for the rich dye from its sap, which was used in the making of ink and printing of textiles. However, in mid-1676 Dampier was struggling to make a living from logging, and when his settlement was devastated by a storm, he turned to pirating:

> For when the violent storm . . . took us, I was but just settling to work and not having a stock of wood to purchase such provision as was sent from Jamaica, . . . I with many more in my circumstances, was forced to range about to seek subsistence in company of some privateers then in the bay.[6]

There were at the time many English sailors pirating across the Spanish Main, the Carribean Sea, the Pacific side of Central America, and across the Pacific as far as the Philippine Islands. The Spanish Empire was largely one of plunder: the Spanish took gold, gems, spices, hides and much of the natural wealth from its domain; and in turn, pirates from England and other European countries raided Spanish ships and Spanish settlements.

Although Dampier described his business on the Spanish Main as privateering, it was in fact simple pirating. Privateers were 'legalised' by their own governments, in that they were licensed in wartime to raid enemy ships in return for a cut in the proceeds. The men Dampier joined were adventurers with no legal sanction from any government; they regarded any ship as fair game and shared their loot with no one.

Leaving Jamaica in April 1678, twenty-nine-year-old Dampier returned to England in August, and married. We know little about his wife, Judith, other than that she worked in the household of the Duke and Duchess of Grafton. Dampier made no mention of her in his extensive journals, and the only known record of her appears in an amended will of 1703, which was subsequently revoked.[7]

Six months after their marriage, in January 1679, Dampier returned, alone, to the Caribbean and resumed a life of piracy. He said it had been his original intention to return to Jamaica as a trader but his associates there had by now become pirates, so he decided to join them.

In 1680 Dampier, buccaneer Captain Bartholomew Sharp and a band of several hundred other pirates crossed the Darien isthmus (where the Panama Canal was later built) to plunder Spanish settlements on the Pacific coast.

Two years later, Dampier said, he and about twenty other pirates 'took one of the vessels and our share of the [stolen] goods and ended up in Virginia', which had been settled by Europeans earlier in the century and become a flourishing tobacco-growing region. He didn't say why he went there or anything about the 'trouble that befell' him while he was there, but a little more than a year later he joined another famous English pirate, John Cooke, and seventy other men sailing to Chile and Peru on what would become Dampier's first voyage around the world. Dampier emphasised that because of the length of their intended voyage, it was necessary during the preparation of the ship for the pirates to reach 'an agreement on particular rules, especially temperance and sobriety'.[8]

After leaving North America, the pirates sailed on the eighteen-gun *Revenge* for the Cape Verde Islands and south along the West African coast, then to the southwest, and in early 1684 they rounded Cape Horn, where they met up with another pirate ship. Together they began raiding Spanish and Indian settlements along the west coast of South and Central America, including Chile, the Galápagos Islands, Peru, Mexico, Panama and southern California. As the ships came in sight of Cape Blanco (in current-day Costa Rica), Dampier wrote that Captain John Cooke, who had been ill,

> then died all of a sudden; though he seemed in the morning likely to live . . . but it is usual with sick men coming from the sea, where they have nothing but sea air, to die off as soon as ever they come within view of the land.'[9]

Over the next two years, the pirates captured a number of ships and attacked several Spanish settlements along the Pacific coast, including Payta, in Peru, and Leon, in Nicaragua. The climax to the voyage might have been in May 1685, with the capture of a Spanish fleet in the Bay of Panama that was carrying treasure to Peru. A fleet of ten pirate ships with more than 900 men had assembled against the Spanish fleet of twenty-four smaller vessels, but the Spanish carried more guns and on the second day of the encounter, Dampier admitted, the pirates 'were glad to escape'.[10]

By early in 1686 he seemed to begin to feel jaded by the 'fatigues, hardships and losses' that his lifestyle entailed, and was tempted by the prospect of greater treasure to switch to another English ship, the *Cygnet*, commanded by Captain Charles Swan, who was planning a voyage westward across the Pacific to the East Indies.[11] Dampier said that some of the men still thought the world ended somewhere further to the west.

> Here Captain Swan proposed to go into the East Indies. Many were well pleased with the voyage; but some thought, such was their ignorance, that he would carry them out of the world; for about two-thirds of our men did not think there was any such way to be found; but at last he gained their consents.

So on 31 March 1686, seven years after leaving England, Dampier joined about 150 other pirates on the *Cygnet* and another captured ship and sailed from the Mexican coast for Guam, more than 8000 kilometres across the Pacific. They knew that a little more than a hundred years before, in 1579, the Englishman Francis Drake had sailed this route in fifty days and that Thomas Cavendish had done it in forty-eight days in 1588. However, Dampier said they embarked on the journey with too little food:

> We had not sixty days provisions at little more than ½ a pint of maize a day for each man and no other provision, except for 3 meals of salted Jew-fish, and we had a great many rats aboard, which we could not hinder from eating part of our daily maize.[12]

They reached the coast of Guam two months later, nearly starving. Dampier said they had only three days of provisions left and that the crew had been planning to eat him and the captain – but the captain first because he was meatier:

> It was well for Captain Swan that we got sight of [the coast] before our provisions were spent, of which we had but enough for three days more, for I was afterwards informed the men had contrived first to kill Captain Swan and eat him when the victuals was gone, and after him all of us who were accessory to the voyage. This made Captain Swan say to me after our arrival at Guam, 'Ah! Dampier, you would have made them but a poor meal', for I was lean and the Captain was lusty and fleshy.[13]

After landing in Guam, they found plenty of fresh food, including rice, watermelons, pineapples, oranges and limes. Dampier also provided the first English account of breadfruit, which was a significant source of local food. The English interest in cultivating breadfruit as a cheap source of food was the main reason for William Bligh's later expedition to the Pacific and, thus, led to the mutiny on the *Bounty*.

> The breadfruit (as we know it) grows on a large tree, as big and as high as our largest apple trees. It has a spreading head full of branches, and dark leaves. The fruit grows on boughs like apples: it is as big as a penny loaf, when wheat is at five shillings a bushel. It is of a round shape, and has a thick tough rind. When the fruit is ripe, it is yellow and soft; and the taste is sweet and pleasant. The natives of this island use it for bread: they gather it in when it

is full grown, while it is green and hard, then they
bake it in an oven, which scorcheth the rind and
makes it black: but they scrape off the outside black
crust, and the inside is soft, tender and white, like
the crumb of a penny loaf ... the fruit lasts in season
about eight months of the year; during which time
the natives eat no other sort of food of bread kind.[14]

After replenishing the ship, they headed further east for
more than 2000 kilometres to St John, on the east of
the Philippine island of Mindanao, which they had been
told by a local friar was 'exceedingly well stored with
provisions'.[15]

They were 'well provided' at Mindanao by the locals,
who feared the oppressive Spanish and, more recently, the
Dutch traders more than they feared the pirates. Captain
Swan was in no hurry to leave Mindanao, enjoying his
time ashore, since he had the money to do so. Dampier
explained in his log that about one-third of the crew lived
ashore 'with their comrades . . . and some with women
servants, who they hired . . . as concubines'.[16] However,
most of the crew had run out of money and were forced
to live on the ship. These men wanted to move on, since
'want of being busy ... made them so uneasy'.[17] To occupy
themselves, having learned from the locals that many
ships – mostly Chinese, Portuguese and Spanish – were
going to and from the harbour of Manila, over the next
months they waited for unescorted ships, chased them
down, took their cargo and abandoned their prisoners on
the nearest land.

When Swan could not be persuaded to leave Mindanao,
the crew took possession of the ship while he was ashore,
elected John Read as their new captain and finally left
on the *Cygnet* on 14 January 1687, after more than five
months.

For the next year they sailed about the China Sea, including Cambodia and Siam (Thailand), then returned to the Philippines, Celebes (Sulawesi) and Timor, pirating and taking 'what that country could afford us'.[18] Dampier said they were careful to avoid the shipping routes that Dutch and English warships might use, as the pirates would certainly have been hanged if caught.

From the middle of March till the middle of April 1687 they beached the *Cygnet* in a sheltered bay to make repairs, renew the sails and replace rotting timbers. All ships took carpenters and spare timber with them to allow for this necessity and they also cut down trees where they could.

By late June they were heading along the south China coast, off the province of Guangdong, where Dampier made many detailed observations on local customs, dress, fine silks, lacquer works, art, sugar and tea, rice growing, religious ceremonies, the widespread use of drugs and the popularity of gambling:

> The Chinese are very great gamesters and they will never be tired with it, playing night and day till they have lost all their estates; then it is usual with them to hang themselves. This was frequently done by the Chinese factors at Manila, as I was told by Spaniards that lived there. The Spaniards themselves are much addicted to gaming and are very expert at it; but the Chinese are too subtle for them, being in general a very cunning people.[19]

He also provided one of the early accounts of the foot binding of young Chinese girls:

> The women have very small feet, and consequently but little shoes, for from infancy their feet are kept swathed up with bands, as hard as they can possibly

endure them, and from the time they can go till the time they have done growing they bind them up every night. This they do to hinder them growing, esteeming little feet to be a great beauty. But by this unreasonable custom they do in a manner lose the use of their feet . . . They seldom stir abroad, and one would be apt to think, that, as some have conjectured, their keeping of their fondness for this fashion were a strategy of the men, to keep them from gadding and galloping about.[20]

For recreation, they regularly stopped to engage with the local women made available by the local men, who appeared willing to prostitute them. Dampier wrote, '[They] would bring them aboard, and offer them to us, and many of our men hired them for a small matter.'[21]

By now, the pirates were travelling aimlessly; they had some old maps but no knowledge of the region or what to expect. After leaving the mainland of China they headed to the Pescadores Islands between China and Formosa, where they encountered a terrible storm that threatened to sink the ship:

It blew exceedingly hard, and the rain poured down as through a sieve and the sea seemed all of a fire about us, for every sea that broke sparkled like lightning. The violent wind raised the sea presently to a great height . . . and began to break in on our deck . . . I was never in such a violent storm in all my life; so said all the company.[22]

Towards the end of the year, they sailed south to Celebes Island and on to Timor, which they reached on 29 December 1687. They were now at the end of the known world, so they decided to head for New Holland, with little design other than the knowledge that the prevailing winds would take them there:

> Being now clear of all the islands, we stood off south, intending to touch at New Holland, a part of Terra Australis Incognita, to see what that country would afford us. Indeed, as the winds were, we could not keep our intended course (which was first westerly, then northerly) without going to New Holland, unless we had gone back again among the islands: But this was not a good time of year to be among the islands to the south of the Equator, unless in a good harbour.[23]

In January 1688 – almost one hundred years before Captain Arthur Phillip founded the British colony in New South Wales – Captain Read, Dampier and the crew became the first Englishmen to reach the Australian mainland. They landed in a cove in the Kimberley region of north-west Australia at what became known as King Sound and the mouth of the Fitzroy River.[24] Dampier was convinced that this huge tract of land was a separate continent: 'It is not yet determinate whether it is an island or a main continent; but I am certain that it joins neither Asia, Africa, nor America.'[25]

His first impressions were that the country was not rich:

> The land is of a dry sandy soil, destitute of water, except you make wells, yet producing diverse sorts of trees; but the woods are not thick, nor the trees very big . . . There was pretty long grass growing under the trees; but it was very thin. We saw no trees that bore fruit or berries . . . We saw no sort of animal. Nor any track of beast, but once; and that seemed to be the tread of a beast as big as a great

mastiff dog. Here there are a few small land birds, but none bigger than a black bird; and but a few sea fowls. Neither is the sea very plentifully stored with fish, unless you reckon of the Manatee and Turtle as such. Of these creatures there is plenty; but they are extraordinary shy; though the inhabitants cannot trouble them much, having neither boats nor iron.[26]

Dampier also made an unflattering assessment of the local Aboriginal people.

The Inhabitants of this country are the miserablest people in the World . . . [They] have no houses and skin garments, sheep, poultry, and fruits of the earth, ostrich eggs etc.; as the Hodmadods have; And setting aside their human shape, they differ but little from brutes. They are tall, straight-bodied, and thin, with small long limbs. They have great heads, round foreheads, and great brows. Their eye-lids are always half closed, to keep the flies out of their eyes; they being so troublesome here, that no fanning will keep them from coming to one's face; and without the assistance of both hands to keep them off, they will creep into one's nostrils, and mouth too, if the lips are not shut very close, unless they hold up their heads as if they were looking at somewhere over them . . . They have great bottle noses, pretty full lips, and wide mouths.[27]

He noted that the Aboriginal men typically had had some front teeth removed, an observation made by later explorers in other parts of Australia.[28]

The two front-teeth of their upper jaw are wanting in all of them, men and women, old and young;

whether they were drawn out, I know not: Neither
have they any beards. They are long visaged, and
of a very unpleasing aspect, having no one graceful
feature in their faces. Their hair is black, short and
curly, like that of the negroes. The colour of their
skins, both of their faces and the rest of their body,
is coal black, like the negroes of New Guinea.[29]

Dampier and his crew were on shore for two months,
which was the longest known stay by any Europeans in
Australia up to that time. They replenished their water,
fished and hunted fresh food and careened the ship, which
meant running it up the beach at high tide, laying it on its
side as the tide went out and replacing rotten timbers.

After 'time enough to clean [the] ship's bottom . . .
mend the sails', collect water and enjoy some local fish
and turtles, they sailed from Australia on 12 March 1688,
ultimately landing on Great Nicobar Island in the Indian
Ocean, about 300 kilometres from the north-west tip
of Sumatra.[30]

On Great Nicobar Island some of the crew of the
Cygnet wanted to jump ship – indeed, Dampier himself
said he wanted to leave to start a local trading business
between Great Nicobar Island and Aceh, at the northern
end of Sumatra. He said he saw the 'prospect of advancing
a profitable trade for ambergrease [ambergris] . . . and of
gaining a considerable fortune' for himself.[31] Ambergris
is a waxy biliary excretion from sperm whales' intestines,
which was prized for use in perfume making and burned
as incense. It can be collected floating on the water or
washed up on the beach.

Arguments followed on board the *Cygnet*. Dampier
said that he and two other crew members were then
rowed ashore, and the pirate ship sailed off. The next day,
he and his colleagues bought a canoe with an outrigger

and a small sail from the natives, loaded it with coconuts, breadfruit and water, and, with four locals, headed south back to Sumatra. After five days and nights in a hurricane in the tiny boat, Dampier and his colleagues reached the coast of Sumatra and staggered up the beach, from where they were helped into a nearby village by friendly locals.

For more than a year Dampier worked in a number of odd jobs around Sumatra, including teaching navigation, instructing a French missionary in how to make gunpowder and working as a gunner at the fort of Bencoolen (now Bengkulu) on the south-west of the island. He never again mentioned his ambition to develop a business in ambergris.[32]

Eventually, in early 1691, Dampier admitted that he had begun to long for his native country, 'after so tedious a ramble from it'.[33] So on 25 January he deserted his post and managed to secure a working passage on the English ship *Defence*, which was returning to England with a cargo of pepper. After sailing via the Cape of Good Hope, Dampier reached England on 16 September 1692.

He had completed his first circumnavigation of the world, a voyage that had taken eight years on a number of different ships, boats and canoes. After being away for more than twelve years, he reached home empty-handed except for some journals and papers. He also brought with him a native of the Philippines named Jeoly, and Jeoly's mother. He had bought the 'curiously and most exquisitely painted' man in a slave market and intended to exhibit him in England. However, short of money, he sold the Filipino 'prince' shortly after arriving in London, and the new owners displayed the man until he died of smallpox in Oxford in 1692.

Little is known of the next few years of Dampier's life. He never mentioned his wife and whether at any stage they were reunited, or if he still owned the house he had previously bought in Dorset. However, five years later, in 1697, his book *A New Voyage around the World*, based on the journals and papers he had brought back from his travels, was released and became an instant, spectacular success, running to four editions over the next two years.

As well, Dampier became a celebrity and attracted the attention of the Royal Society and of the government, which was particularly interested in his report of the flora and fauna and indigenous people of New Holland.

The fact that Dampier had been a pirate for most of the previous decade did not seem to bother his admirers. Among the eminent men who met with him were the president of the Royal Society, Charles Montague (later the Earl of Halifax); the Earl of Orford, who was one of the Lord Commissioners of the Treasury; and the Lord High Admiral, the Earl of Pembroke. John Evelyn, a popular London diarist at the time, reflected on the fascination with William Dampier in England when he wrote of a dinner at which Dampier appeared:

> I dined with Mr Pepys, where was Captain Dampier, who had been a famous buccaneer, had brought hither the painted prince Job [Jeoly], and printed a relation of his very strange adventure . . . He was now going abroad again by the King's encouragement, who furnished a ship of 290 tons. He seemed a more modest man than one would imagine by relation of the crew he had associated with.[34]

The year after the success of his book, and possibly influenced by his new supporters, the British government appointed Dampier to lead an expedition back to Australia, even though in all his years of seafaring he had never commanded a ship before. He was commissioned to explore the land, and his instructions ordered him to assess its potential for settlement as part of the British Empire.

The expedition was to be the British navy's first dedicated to both exploration and scientific discovery. Dampier was instructed to survey 'all islands, shores, capes, bays, creeks and harbours, fit for shelter as well as defence'. He was to bring back specimens of the native flora and fauna, and was provided with an artist for the voyage to 'sketch birds, beasts, fishes and plants'. He was also told to bring back one of the natives 'provided they shall be willing to come along'.

So on 14 January 1699, William Dampier, now nearly fifty years old, left England with a crew of sixty-three on the navy ship the *Roebuck*, which weighed 299 tons and was twenty-nine metres long and just less than eight metres wide.

The voyage was soon in trouble: constant arguments between Dampier and his deputy, First Lieutenant George Fisher RN, divided the ship. The two men were apparently 'behaving equally as boors without a spark of dignity or self-respect . . . alternately drinking together, backbiting one another to their confidants, and breaking into personal abuse and even fisticuffs in presence of the crew'.[35] The *Roebuck* called first at the Canary Islands, which was a regular first stop for European ships sailing to the South Seas to stock up on fresh food, water, wine and brandy. They then sailed further south to the Cape Verde Islands, off the West African coast, before crossing the Atlantic to Brazil, which Dampier planned to make his last stop before sailing around the Cape of Good Hope for New Holland:

> For designing that my next step should be quite to New Holland and knowing that after so long a run nothing was to be expected there but fresh water,

if I could meet even with it there, I resolved at putting in first at some port in Brazil. Besides refreshing and furnishing my men, I aimed also at inuring them gradually and by intervals to the fatigues that were to be expected in the remainder of the voyage, which was to be to a part of the world they were altogether strangers to; none of them, except two young men, having ever crossed the line [the equator].[36]

Dampier stayed a month in Brazil. But before he left, he and Fisher's disagreements came to a head in a terrible fight, during which Dampier beat up Fisher, had him clapped in irons and left him in a Brazilian jail.

Now the *Roebuck* headed south-easterly towards the Cape of Good Hope. By early June it had sailed past it. With strong winds, less than two months later, on 25 July, the crew saw 'some weeds' float by them so that they did not doubt that they would quickly see land.[37]

A few days later they passed Dirk Hartog Island and entered a large inlet, which Dampier would name Shark Bay.

Dampier was very quick to learn what Dutch seafarers before him had discovered on this stretch of barren coastline: it contained little fresh water.

As soon as I came to anchor in this bay . . . I sent my boat ashore to seek fresh water, but in the evening the men returned, having found none. The next morning I went ashore myself carrying pick-axes and shovels with me, to dig for water and axes to cut wood. We tried in several places for water, but finding none after several trials, nor in several miles of compass, we left any further search for it and . . . we went aboard for the night.[38]

While they had difficulty finding water, they found plenty of oysters, mussels, fish, green turtles weighing as much as ninety kilograms and sharks, which the *Roebuck*'s master, Jacob Hughes, claimed were up to six metres long. Inside the stomach of one of the largest sharks, they found the bones and head of what Dampier claimed was a hippopotamus but was probably one of the dugongs, or sea cows, fairly common in the area.

The *Roebuck* spent two weeks exploring Shark Bay, the men making sketches and collecting flowers and plants, many of which Dampier kept pressed between the pages of his books. He then charted north along the coast for 1000 kilometres, at the end of which he found a group of islands now known as the Dampier Archipelago, near current-day Karratha.

The *Roebuck*'s master, Jacob Hughes, said the crew, as with so many European explorers landing on Australian shores, was overwhelmed and irritated by an 'abundance of small flies, tickling their faces and buzzing about their ears'.[39] And while on the shore and still attempting to find water, the English had their first close encounter with a group of Aboriginals; Dampier shot one of them when he thought one of his crew was in danger:

> Upon their seeing me, one of them threw a lance at me, that narrowly missed me. I discharged my gun to scare them but avoided shooting any of them; till finding the young [crew] man in great danger from them, and myself in some; and that though the gun had a little frightened them at first, yet they had soon learnt to despise it, tossing up their hands, and crying pooh, pooh, pooh; and coming on afresh with a great noise, I thought it high time to charge again, and shoot one of them, which I did. The rest, seeing him fall, made a stand again;

and my young man took the opportunity to disen-
gage himself, and come off to me; my other man
also was with me, who had done nothing all this
while, having come out unarmed; and I returned
back with my men, designing to attempt the natives
no farther, being very sorry for what had happened
already. They took up their wounded companion;
and my young man, who had been struck through
the cheek by one of their lances, was afraid it had
been poisoned: but I did not think that likely. His
wound was very painful to him, being made with a
blunt weapon: but he soon recovered of it.[40]

By now, Dampier's crew was developing scurvy. Faced
with the outbreak and declining stocks of water and
food, he reluctantly decided to quit the coast for Timor,
disappointed that he had discovered so little of value in
New Holland.

The *Roebuck* reached the Dutch East Indian port of
Kupang, in Timor, less than a week later, on 14 September.
The Dutch authorities on Timor were initially suspicious
of the English but eventually allowed the *Roebuck* to
anchor and, finally, to stock up on fresh water and food.

From Timor the ship headed east across the top of
New Guinea, where Dampier passed through the strait
he named Dampier's Passage (now Dampier Strait) and
discovered the island to the north-east of New Guinea,
which he named Nova Britannia (New Britain).[41]

By April 1700 he was only one hundred miles from
the northern tip of the east coast of Australia. Had the
Roebuck been in better condition for sailing and its
timbers not so rotten, he may have beaten James Cook to
his discovery of New South Wales by more than seventy
years. But the *Roebuck* was already in a nearly hopeless
condition, so Dampier struck a course for home.

He headed first to the Dutch port of Batavia, which was 4000 kilometres to the east. It took almost four months to get there, and after another four months of repairs, the *Roebuck* began its homeward journey.

By the end of 1700, the ship had reached the Cape of Good Hope and started the 10,000-kilometre voyage north to England. However, on 21 February the *Roebuck* could be sailed no more and limped to tiny Ascension Island in the middle of the Atlantic Ocean, 1600 kilometres off the African coast. 'The plank was so rotten it broke away like dirt, and now it is impossible to save the ship,' wrote Dampier.[42]

The ship sank at its moorings, and the crew had just enough time to collect their personal effects and food to sustain them until rescue arrived. Dampier managed to save some of his journal but many of his books and papers were lost. Six weeks later they were picked up by the *Canterbury*, an East Indiaman on its way back to England, and they arrived home in August 1701, having been away for thirty-one months.

Shortly after reaching England, Dampier's career as a captain in the Royal Navy came to an inglorious end, when he was court martialled, sacked and had all his wages withheld for beating up and jailing his deputy, George Fisher, in Rio de Janeiro almost two years before. Fisher had managed to get back to England before Dampier to press charges against his former captain. The court was of the opinion that Dampier was guilty of 'very hard and cruel usage towards Lieutenant Fisher in beating him' on board the ship and 'confining him in irons for a considerable time, and afterwards imprisoning him on shore in a strange country', when it did not appear that there had been 'any grounds for this ill usage of him'. It also stated:

the said Captain Dampier falls under [the] 33rd Article for these his irregular proceedings, and the Court does adjudge that he be fined all his pay . . . and it is further opinion of the Court that the said Capt. Dampier is not a fit person to be employed as commander of any of her Majesty's ships.[43]

Dampier was bitter about the conviction, but his dismissal from the navy did not stop him publishing *A Voyage to New Holland*, which was issued in two volumes in 1703 and 1709 and was, as his previous books had been, very popular.

Dampier returned to the sea and twice more circumnavigated the globe. In 1703, while England was at war with Spain and France, he was given command of the *St George*, a privateer licensed by the British government to plunder enemy shipping for a cut of the booty. The *St George* was 200 tons, with twenty-six guns and a crew of 120. It was accompanied by the small *Cinque Ports*, which had sixteen guns and sixty-three crew.

They left England on 30 April 1703 and sailed to the south Atlantic and around Cape Horn into the Pacific, where they attacked and sank some small Spanish ships off the South American coast but without winning any great treasure.

In October the following year, the *Cinque Ports* was leaking badly and its twenty-three-year-old quartermaster, Alexander Selkirk, contended that the ship was dangerously unseaworthy. At his insistence, he was dropped off on one of the small uninhabited Juan Fernández Islands, about 700 kilometres west of the South American coast. He was given food and water, a gun and ammunition, and tools and some books, including a Bible.

Selkirk was probably correct about the condition of the *Cinque Ports*, because it was later wrecked, with only eight survivors, who were captured and imprisoned by the Spanish and took years to get back to England.

Meanwhile, Dampier and the *St George* continued pirating along the South American coast with only limited success, before crossing the Pacific and reaching Batavia, then Cape Town, and finally returning to England at the end of 1707. Dampier's second circumnavigation of the globe had taken a little more than three years.

Less than a year later, Dampier was off again, privateering under captain Woodes Rogers on the 320-ton, thirty-gun *Duke*, accompanied by the 260-ton, twenty-six-gun *Duchess*. Leaving England on 2 August 1708, the ships sailed first to the south Atlantic and around Cape Horn, where they were more successful in plundering Spanish ships and towns along the South American coast.

In late January the following year, as they passed by what were believed to be the uninhabited Juan Fernández Islands, they saw a large fire on the shore. Sent to investigate, an armed landing party found a hairy Alexander Selkirk dressed in goatskins. The privateers were amazed at how he had survived. When his ammunition had run out, he had learned to outrun and kill the wild goats that lived on the island. He had built solid cabins of timber and used nails as needles to sew clothes from goatskins when those he had landed with became rags. Selkirk had harvested much of the local food, including fruit, vegetables and fish, and had even crafted knives from the iron rings of a barrel he had on the island.

Dampier readily took Selkirk aboard, and found that the Scotsman had temporarily lost the ability to speak, having spent the past four years and four months with only goats, rats and some cats for company. Before leaving the island, Selkirk was able to help many of his rescuers, who were suffering from scurvy, by cooking them stews of goat, seal and local cabbage and turnips. The Selkirk story was the inspiration for Daniel Defoe's *Robinson Crusoe*, published a little more than a decade later, in 1719.

Resuming their privateering, the *Duke* and the *Duchess* successfully attacked a number of Spanish ships and captured the Spanish town of Guayaquil in current-day Ecuador, where they were paid a ransom for the hostages they had taken.

A year later, in January 1710, they headed west across the Pacific to Guam and eventually to Batavia, which they reached the following June. After three months repairing their ship and replenishing supplies, they headed home via Cape Town and reached England in October 1711. They had been away for a little more than three years. Dampier had completed his third circumnavigation of the globe and was received enthusiastically in London for having successfully taken so much treasure from the Spanish.

Not much is known of the last years of Dampier's life, and he died in London in 1715, aged sixty-four. Over the next twenty years, seven editions of his books would be published and translated into Dutch and French.

In addition to having been involved in the events that inspired Defoe's *Robinson Crusoe*, Dampier also influenced Jonathan Swift's *Gulliver's Travels*, which was published in 1726, a decade after Dampier's death. Lemuel Gulliver refers affectionately to 'Cousin Dampier', and the ship that Gulliver sails from England to the South Seas has the same name, the *Antelope*, as one that for a time sailed with the *Roebuck*. Samuel Taylor Coleridge, who is believed to have been influenced by Dampier when he wrote the *Rime of the Ancient Mariner*, described Dampier as 'among men of genius'.[44] Later scientists and navigators also commended Dampier. Charles Darwin recommended his recording of Australia's natural history, and Captain James Cook and Matthew Flinders praised his discourses on winds, tides and navigation – as did the French explorer Nicolas Baudin, who a century later was the next European after Dampier to sail along Australia's North West Cape.

But for all Dampier's later influence, the British must have been disappointed that his expedition had yielded so little immediate potential for the British Empire. As Dampier himself admitted, he had found little along the coast of New Holland that was of much value to the British, and he certainly found no suitable sites for settlement.

After Dampier, there was limited British interest in exploring the Great South Land until 1768, when a navy lieutenant was sent on a solitary ship to the South Pacific to make astrological observations.

CHAPTER 3

THE BRITISH SETTLEMENT

*M*ore than half a century after William Dampier returned from his second voyage to Australia, Captain James Cook was sent by the Royal Society and the British government on what was to be the first of his three great voyages to the Pacific.

Cook was born in Yorkshire in 1728 into relatively humble circumstances. His father, a farmer, was Scottish, and his mother was from Yorkshire. He grew up on the farm on which his father worked as a labourer and attended a village school before going to work for a local shopkeeper. Eighteen months later, aged eighteen, he took an apprenticeship on a merchant ship that was to sail from Whitby to the Baltic Sea. In 1755 he joined the Royal Navy as a master's mate on the *Eagle* and two years later was promoted to master on the *Pembroke*, sailing with the Channel fleet. In 1758, at twenty-nine years of age, he served in the Seven Years War against the French and was part of the successful siege of Fort Louisburg, on the St Lawrence River in Canada, which opened the way for the British to take Quebec the following year and end French rule in North America.

By the time Cook arrived back in England in 1762, his navigation and mapping brilliance in Newfoundland, Nova Scotia and on the St Lawrence River were already recognised. In a letter to the Secretary to the Admiralty, Admiral Lord Colville recommended Cook for 'greater undertakings' and referred to his 'genius and capacity'.[1] On a number of voyages over the next few years, Cook mapped large sections of the North American Atlantic coast for the Royal Navy, and these maps were later praised by the Admiralty for their 'truly astonishing' accuracy.[2]

While he was back in England in 1762, the thirty-four-year-old Cook married Elizabeth Batts at Barking, Essex. Although married for seventeen years, they spent only four of those years together, because of Cook's extensive travelling. Nevertheless they had six children, though three died in infancy.

In 1768 Cook was sent to the South Seas, principally to observe the transit of the planet Venus, which is best seen in the southern hemisphere. The transit takes place when Venus moves across the face of the sun and is similar in principle to a solar eclipse by the moon. Observations of such transits helped scientists calculate the distance of the Earth from the sun and other planets, which in turn was helpful in navigation. Transits of Venus are predictable phenomena that come in pairs – eight years apart – and each pair of eclipses occurs about every one hundred years. A transit had occurred in 1761, and Cook was sent to observe the second of the pair.[3] He was instructed that after he had witnessed the transit of Venus, he should 'proceed southwards in order to make discovery of the continent'. If he found it, he was to diligently explore as great an extent of the coast as he could, carefully observing and making charts and records of bays, harbours, the nature of the soil, 'the beast and fowls', fish, mines, minerals and valuable stones. He was to bring home specimens of seeds, fruits and grains, and 'observe the games, temper, disposition and number of natives'.[4]

The Royal Society had proposed that the expedition to the Pacific be headed by Alexander Dalrymple, who in 1767 had published *An Account of the Discoveries Made in the South Pacific Ocean, Previous to 1764*, which included the charts of the Dutch and other earlier explorers. However, the Admiralty, which was providing and equipping the ship, insisted that James Cook, who was more qualified to command one of its vessels, lead the voyage.

Cook left England on 26 August 1768. He was provided with a thirty-two-metre coal-carrying ship, the *Earl of Pembroke*, which had been purchased by the navy, refitted with extra cabins for the scientists on the expedition and renamed the *Endeavour*. In addition to the crew of eighty-three sailors and marines, there were civilian scientists, including astronomer Charles Green, artists Sydney Parkinson and Alexander Buchan, and naturalist Joseph Banks. Not only did Banks have two assistants, Daniel Solander and Herman Spöring, he also took aboard a suite of staff – including two botanists, gardeners and two servants – and his two pet greyhounds.

The upper-class Banks was the only son of a wealthy landowner. Both his father and grandfather had been members of parliament, and one of Banks's roles was adviser to King George III. Already passionate about botany, Banks used his position to lobby the King to support the exploration of unknown lands. Before his journey on the *Endeavour*, Banks had already travelled as a botanist on a ship bound for Newfoundland and had been elected a member of the Royal Society. He was to prove a hugely valuable and influential member of this first expedition of Cook's.

With eighteen months' supply of food, the *Endeavour* made its first stop for fresh water and food at Madeira, where the master's mate, Robert Weir, was accidentally killed when he was caught in the anchor chain. He was replaced by a sailor the crew kidnapped from an American sloop anchored nearby. The kidnapping of other ships' crew members, or 'shanghaiing' as it later became known, was widely practised on ships from most countries when they would otherwise be unable to leave port because of a shortage of crew.

The *Endeavour* left Madeira, crossed the Atlantic to reach Rio de Janeiro and headed down the South American coast and around Cape Horn in January 1769. Though it was the height of the southern hemisphere summer, the ship had a difficult passage around the cape, enduring freezing temperatures and high seas. After stopping on the Pacific side of the coast at the Bay of Good Success, Banks and his team went ashore on a cold but sunny day to collect botany samples. They had planned to return to the ship by nightfall, but miscalculated and were caught in a snowstorm with no food, tent or blankets. As they tried to force their way through the snow, Banks's servants, Tom Richmond and George Dorlton, died. Eventually the rest of the party made it back to the ship.

Heading north-west into the Pacific, they reached Tahiti on 10 April, with plenty of time for astrologer Charles Green to observe the transit of Venus on 3 June. The *Endeavour* was the third European ship ever to have called in at Tahiti. Two years before Cook, thirty-nine-year-old English sea captain Samuel Wallis, on an expedition of circumnavigation of the globe on his ship the *Dolphin*, was the first European to land on Tahiti, which he named

King George III Island. The following year, French explorer Louis Antoine de Bougainville visited the island, and his account of the earthly paradise where men and women lived happily and innocently away from the corruption of modern society did much to shape Europeans' romantic images of the place.

Cook recorded the friendliness of the Tahitians, saying they were 'open, affable and courteous' and from all he could see, 'free from treachery'; but he also said they were 'thieves to a man' and would put to 'shame the most noted pickpocket in Europe'.[5] He also made observations on Tahitian customs, diet, religion, housing, social organisation, lifestyle and even the widespread practice of marking the skin with 'tattows' (tattoos), which many of the crew brought back to Europe on their bodies as souvenirs. And he critically noted the Tahitian's open attitude to sex:

> Sunday, 14th. This day closed with an odd scene at the gate of the fort, where a young Fellow above 6 feet high made love to a little girl about 10 or 12 years of age publicly before several of our people and a number of the natives. What makes me mention this is because it appeared to be done according to custom, for there were several women present . . . and these were so far from showing the least disapprobation that they instructed the girl how she should act her part, who, young as she was, did not seem to want it.[6]

The botanist Joseph Banks said that the local women freely offered sex to the English without any concern for privacy:

> We walked freely about several large houses attended by the ladies who showed us all kind of civilities . . .

indeed we had no reason to doubt any part of their politeness, as by their frequently pointing to the mats on the ground and sometimes by force seating themselves and us upon them they plainly showed that they were much less jealous of observation than we were.[7]

When the *Endeavour* had left Tahiti, Cook wrote in his diary that his crew had 'too free use of the women' and 'half of them had got the venereal disease'.[8]

After completing his primary mission of observing the transit of Venus, Cook sailed south-west looking for the great continent that some believed extended around the South Pole. Finding no land, he headed for New Zealand and became only the second European to arrive there since Dutch explorer Abel Tasman had more than a century before. Cook spent six months charting the coast and confirmed that the country consisted of two major islands, before he headed west to look for the east coast of New Holland.

At six in the morning of 20 April 1770, Lieutenant Zachary Hicks, who was on watch on the *Endeavour*, sighted the east coast of Australia at a point that Cook would name Point Hicks (on the eastern coast of present-day Victoria). There was no natural harbour near Point Hicks, so Cook decided to follow the coast northward until they got to its northernmost point – five months later, after a voyage of more than 3000 kilometres.

Ten days into the voyage, Cook entered a large bay, which he initially called Stingray Bay because of the quantity of huge stingrays caught by the crew. It was later named Botany Bay, after Joseph Banks and his team collected hundreds of plants and seeds from the area. The *Endeavour* arrived at Botany Bay on 29 April 1770 and left on 7 May. Banks went ashore with his colleague

Daniel Solander on five of the days they were there, and on the second day ashore Banks wrote that the 'soil, wherever we saw it, consisted either of swamps, or lightly sandy soil on which grew very few species of trees'.[9]

Four days later, on 4 May, he ventured further inland:

> We went a good way in to the country which in this place is very sandy and resembles something of the moors of England, as no trees grow upon it but everything is covered with a thin brush of plants about as high as the knees.[10]

Cook stayed only seven days in Botany Bay, which was long enough to collect fresh water and wood and for Banks to collect his specimens before heading off to the north. He could have had no inkling that eighteen years later the British would choose this spot to establish their largest ever convict colony.

Cook's next major stop was unplanned: the *Endeavour* was nearly wrecked on a reef almost 3000 kilometres further north. For more than seven weeks the ship was beached on the banks of what became known as the Endeavour River – the later site of Cooktown.

After the ship had been repaired, Cook successfully navigated his way through the Torres Strait – by the time of his voyage, the British had copies of Torres's early charts. When he was finally through the strait, the crew went ashore on what Cook would call Possession Island, and on 22 August 1770 he claimed the entire east coast of Australia for Britain. He named it New South Wales because to him the hills along the coast resembled those of south Wales.

> Notwithstanding I had in the name of His Majesty taken possession of several places upon the coast,

> I now once more hoisted English colours and in the
> name of His Majesty King George the Third took
> possession of the whole of the east coast . . . by
> the name New South Wales, together with all the
> bays, harbours, rivers, and the islands situated upon
> the said coast, after which we fired three volleys of
> small arms, which were answered by a like number
> from the ship.[11]

Cook was well aware that while he may have been the first
to chart the coast on the eastern side of the strait, the west
had long before been discovered by others:

> On the western side I can make no new discovery,
> the honour of which belongs to the Dutch navi-
> gators, but the eastern coast from the latitude of
> 38 degrees south, down to this place, I am confi-
> dent, was never seen or visited by any European
> before us.[12]

After leaving the top of Australia, the *Endeavour* began the
long journey back to England. So far, by the standards of
the times, the ship's crew had been healthy, thanks largely
to Cook's insistence on the cleanliness of the ship and his
correct belief that scurvy could be kept at bay with an
appropriate diet. However, the rest of the journey proved
to be a nightmare. Their first landing was on the island of
Savu. Next they stopped on 13 October 1770 at the capital
of the Dutch East Indies, Batavia, where they loaded fresh
supplies and repaired the ship for the long voyage back
to England. Ships regularly restocked at Batavia, and
when Cook arrived, there were already sixteen other ships
at anchor, mainly Dutch but also from other European
countries and one English East India Company trader. In
Batavia many of Cook's men became sick, and by early

November Cook complained that the illness had spread so widely that they 'could not muster above 20 Men and Officers that were able to do duty'.[13] A week later only twelve or fourteen were able to work.

When the *Endeavour* left for Cape Town after three months, most of the *Endeavour*'s crew had contracted dysentery. Cook described Batavia as the unhealthiest place in the world:

> Batavia is certainly a place that Europeans need not covet to go to; but if necessity obliges them, they will do well to make their stay as short as possible, otherwise they will soon feel the effects of the unwholesome air of Batavia, which, I firmly believe, is the Death of more Europeans than any other place upon the Globe of the same extent. Such, at least, is my opinion of it, which is founded on facts. We came in here with as healthy a Ship's Company as need go to Sea, and after a stay of not quite 3 months left it in the condition of an Hospital Ship, besides the loss of 7 Men; and yet all the Dutch Captains I had an opportunity to converse with said that we had been very lucky, and wondered that we had not lost half our people in that time.[14]

After sailing for two months across the Indian Ocean, Cook recorded in his journal on 27 February 1771 that a further twenty-three men had died directly as a result of dysentery contracted in Batavia. On 28 March they arrived at Cape Town, where twenty-eight of the crew were carried ashore and hospitalised.

At Cape Town and on the last leg of their voyage, more men died, including the ship's master, Robert Molyneux, and his loyal deputy, Lieutenant Zachary Hicks, who had been the first on board to see the east coast of Australia.

After a brief stop at St Helena, the *Endeavour* reached England on 12 July 1771, having been away a few weeks short of three years. During the voyage, a total of thirty-eight of the original ninety-four who sailed had died.

On arriving back in England, the socially superior Joseph Banks and his scientist colleagues attracted more interest and publicity than Lieutenant James Cook, who rated barely a mention in the press even though he was the commander of the vessel. However, Cook's achievements were acknowledged within the Admiralty, which recorded that it 'well approve[d] of the whole' of his voyage.[15]

After Cook's voyage, the British showed little further interest in Australia until almost ten years later. In 1779, the House of Commons established an inquiry to find a workable solution to the problem of escalating convict numbers in Britain. By the second half of the eighteenth century, the prison population of Britain was rapidly growing. The early days of the Industrial Revolution, rapid urbanisation, rural displacement and an expansion of the number of offences that attracted custodial sentences all contributed to the spiralling problem. In the early part of the century, the British had sent a total of more than 40,000 convicts to work on plantations in Virginia, but this practice slowed then stopped after the American War of Independence began in 1775. Now a new answer had to be found.

The committee heard from a number of witnesses who argued for the establishment of a convict colony overseas. They had varying opinions on where it should be located, including in Gibraltar and along the west coast of Africa. It also heard from Duncan Campbell, a wealthy private London shipowner who had transported convicts to North America but recently 'declined contracting them upon the revolt of the colonies of Virginia and Maryland'. The committee concluded that the prison arrangements were failing:

> In short, your committee must observe, that the whole arrangements of the prisons, as far as they are informed, is, at present, ill suited, either in the economy of the state, or morality of its people, and seems calculated for the safe custody of the persons confined, without due attention to their health, employment, or reformation.[16]

The committee recognised that it was no longer feasible to send convicts to America and recommended that somewhere else be chosen in 'any part of the globe that may be found expedient'.[17]

At the time the House of Commons committee convened, Cook was far away from England, supposedly on his way back from his voyage in search of a passage linking the Pacific and Atlantic oceans. What was not yet known in London was that Captain Cook had in fact already been killed in Hawaii. So the most prominent witness to appear before the committee was Joseph Banks, and in Cook's absence he was to be a major influence on the ultimate decision to send the first fleet of convicts to settle in Botany Bay.

Banks had by now become president of the Royal Society, at the relatively young age of thirty-five, and was heavily involved in the development of London's Kew Gardens. In London he had the ear of the government, the Admiralty and the King. He was regularly consulted on a wide range of matters, including botany, earthquakes, farming and exploration. He was a trustee of the British Museum, a member of the Society of Antiquaries and a member of many London clubs, including the Society of Dilettanti.

When he appeared before the House of Commons and was asked where the convicts might be sent, Banks had no hesitation in recommending Botany Bay:

Joseph Banks Esq. being requested, in case it should be thought expedient to establish a Colony of convicted felons in any distant part of the Globe, from whence escape might be difficult, and where, from the fertility of the soil, they might be able to maintain themselves, after the fifth year, with little or no aid from the mother country, to give his opinion what place would be the most eligible for such settlement, informed your committee, that the place which appeared to him best adapted for such a purpose, was Botany Bay, on the coast of New Holland, in the Indian Ocean, which was about seven months voyage from England, that he apprehended there would be little possibility of opposition from the natives, as during his stay there in the year 1770, he saw very few and did not think there were above 50 in the neighbourhood, and had reason to believe the country was very thinly populated, those he saw were naked, treacherous, and armed with lances, but extremely cowardly, and constantly retired from our people when they made the least appearance and resistance. He was in the bay in the end of April and the beginning of May 1770, when the weather was mild and moderate, that the climate, he apprehended, was similar to Toulouse in the South of France . . . the proportion of rich soil was small in comparison to the barren but sufficient to support a very large number of people; there were no tame animals, and he saw no wild ones during his stay of ten days, but he saw the dung of what were called kangaroos, which were about the size of middling sheep and difficult to catch. . . and he did not doubt oxen and sheep, if carried there, would thrive and increase, there was a great plenty of fish . . . The grass was long and luxuriant, and the eatable vegetables, particularly a sort of wild spinach; the country was well supplied with water; there was an abundance of timber and fuel sufficient for any number of buildings, which might be found necessary.[18]

But Banks's glowing report about Botany Bay to the parliamentary committee was strangely at odds with his own, less enthusiastic, journal entries of the time. Cook had also said that the land visited by the *Endeavour* was uncultivated and produced virtually nothing fit to eat. However, he was not in a position to shape events in England, while Banks had become a figure of great influence. And Banks the botanist stood to gain from any settlement established on the east coast of Australia. He had collected many botanical specimens when he'd visited Botany Bay and would benefit from any ships returning with more specimens. His influence would also result in British ships being modified to have sheds installed on their decks for the storage of botanical samples.

Despite the committee's deliberations and Banks's recommendations, the decision of where to send the convicts was not made for another six years. It seems that many of Britain's ruling elite, including King George III, held the forlorn hope that the American insurrection could be put down and the transport of convicts to America resumed. However, after continued public agitation and widespread concern that overcrowded gaols would result in prison breakouts – or the outbreak of contagious diseases in the wider community – the home secretary, Lord Sydney, announced in 1786 that convicts would indeed be sent to Australia:

> The several gaols and places of confinement of felons in this kingdom being in so crowded a state that the greatest danger is to be apprehended, not

only from their escape, but for infectious distempers, which may hourly be expected to break out
among them, His Majesty, desirous of preventing by
any possible means the ill consequences which might
happen from either of these causes, has been pleased
to signify to me his royal commands that measures
should immediately be pursued for sending out of
this kingdom such convicts as are under sentence or
order of transportation . . . His Majesty has thought
it advisable to fix upon Botany Bay.[19]

The man chosen to lead the expedition to Botany Bay
and become the first governor of Britain's new colony of
New South Wales was Captain Arthur Phillip. Plucked
from semiretirement at his Hampshire farm at nearly fifty
years of age, like James Cook before him Phillip was an
example of how men from relatively modest backgrounds
could progress through the ranks of the British navy in a
way that was far less likely at the time in the army, where
class and connections were still dominant.

Phillip was born on 11 October 1738 in Bread Street,
London. His father, Jacob, had come to England from
Germany as a language teacher, and Phillip was said to have
spoken a number of foreign languages, including German as
well as passable Spanish and Portuguese. When Phillip was
twelve, his father died, and he was admitted to the Greenwich boys' navy college, which had been established in the
early eighteenth century for the sons of navy men who had
died or been killed at sea. Phillip had some help getting into
the school. His mother had previously been married to then
became the widow of a navy officer, Captain Herbert, who
was from a well-connected family, which included Lord
Pembroke. During his lifetime, Pembroke was a Member
of Parliament, a Privy Councillor, a major general in the
army and a knight of the Order of the Garter.[20]

At fifteen Phillip was indentured on a merchant ship that regularly sailed to Greenland and Europe, before he transferred to the Royal Navy as a captain's servant in 1755. The next year he was promoted to able seaman and served on a number of ships that saw action during the Seven Years War against the French. In 1760, aged twenty-two, he was promoted to master's mate and began steadily climbing the navy's promotional ladder.

Towards the end of the Seven Years War, he was pensioned off from the navy at half-pay, which was fairly standard practice when England was not at war or when hostilities subsided. He became a farmer near Lyndhurst, in Hampshire, where he married a widow, Margaret Charlotte Tybott. The couple had no children, and over the next forty years there was an almost total absence of reference to his marriage in any of his reports, letters or journals.[21]

In 1774, with the approval of the Admiralty, Phillip became the commander of Portuguese warships in the renewed war between Portugal and Spain. He was to serve for three and a half years and left in 1778 with high praise from the Portuguese for his bravery.[22]

Back in England, Phillip was appointed to a number of British navy ships, until 1784, when he was again paid off from further service. However, his 'retirement' abruptly came to an end when he was appointed to sail the first fleet of convicts to Botany Bay, on the other side of the globe.

The first fleet that sailed from Portsmouth in May 1787 was at the time the largest overseas migration the world had seen. Crammed onto eleven tiny ships (the largest was barely thirty metres long) were more than 1400 people, including nearly 800 convicts and several hundred seamen, navy officers, marines and some wives and children. The ships also carried enough food for the long voyage and for two years' subsistence after arrival, as well as all the tools and equipment necessary to start building a new life at Botany Bay.

The convicts loaded onto the transports were not chosen with any regard for their fitness for the long voyage or their suitability for building a new settlement once they got there. The youngest was John Hudson, who was nine years old when convicted for theft; and the oldest was Dorothy Handland, who, according to Arthur Bowes Smyth, the surgeon on the female convict transport *Lady Penrhyn*, was eighty-two years old when the fleet sailed. She was a dealer in rags and old clothes and had been convicted of perjury before being sentenced to seven years' transportation. Handland survived the journey to Botany Bay but is believed to have hanged herself from a gum tree in Sydney Cove in 1789.[23] Only those too frail to walk were excluded from consideration, and fourteen pregnant women convicts were boarded who would give birth during the voyage. Almost sixty per cent of the convicts had been sentenced for stealing food or other goods of relatively little value.

The fleet began its eight-month voyage in the early hours of Sunday, 13 May 1787. After sailing south from the English Channel for three weeks, it reached its first stop, at Tenerife, in the Spanish-controlled Canary Islands.

Despite the appalling conditions experienced by the convicts, who were cramped for many months below decks, only sixty-nine people died on the voyage, most of them while the ships were waiting to leave Portsmouth and before the stop at the Canary Islands. Because of better food and better care, the health and survival rates of the convicts on the first fleet were much better than those of the subsequent fleets. Shortly after leaving the English Channel, Arthur Phillip ordered that all but the worst convicts be released from their chains and allowed daily on deck while the ships were safely out to sea. With the urging of the fleet's chief surgeon, John White, the quarters below decks were regularly cleaned and aired, and at every port the limited convict diet was supplemented with fresh fruit and vegetables. Arthur Bowes Smyth, who described the convicts as an 'abandoned set of wretches', said that the death rate would have been even lower if the convicts had not been sent on the voyage in such poor health to start with. 'Few marines going out of England would [be as] amply provided for as these convicts are, and the surgeons and officers of the different ships pay such strict attention to keeping them and their berthing well aired and perfectly clean,' he wrote. Had the convicts 'all embarked in that perfectly healthy state', he firmly believed, 'very few, if any would have died hitherto'.[24]

However, the conditions below deck were undoubtedly extremely unhealthy. The convicts were regularly punished for breaking the strict rules on board – but that did not do anything to deter promiscuity during the passage. Even before the ships left Portsmouth the marines had broken a hole in the bulkhead to reach the convict women, and no amount of flogging could deter them on the eight-month voyage.[25]

After stocking up with fresh water, fresh food and some wine at Tenerife, the fleet headed via the Cape Verde Islands across the Atlantic and the equator, to reach the Portuguese colony of Rio de Janeiro on 6 August. In Rio they loaded more fresh food, including oranges, which were in season and known to be effective against scurvy. They also loaded 115 'pipes', or 65,000 litres, of rum for the marines, seamen and officers for the remainder of the voyage and to last them for the first few years in the colony. Taking such a large volume of liquor aboard required a major reorganisation of the ships' stores.

Before leaving, they also loaded plants and seeds for replanting in Botany Bay, including coffee, cocoa, banana, orange, lemon, guava, tamarind and pear.

The stop in Rio lasted a month, during which time the convicts were mainly kept secure below decks, and on 14 September they set off again across the Atlantic, to the Cape of Good Hope, on the southern tip of South Africa. A month into the voyage a planned mutiny was discovered on the largest of the convict transports, the *Alexander*. The convicts responsible were chained below deck, and the seamen who were found to have helped the plotters were flogged.

The fleet reached the Dutch-controlled port of the Cape of Good Hope on 13 October. After an initially frosty reception from the local Dutch authorities, the fleet replenished its stock of water and food for the last long leg of more than 10,000 kilometres across the Great Southern Ocean to the coast of New South Wales.

As they had done in Rio, the fleet took aboard more plants, including fig trees, bamboo, sugar cane, quince, apple, strawberry, oak and myrtle. The carpenters built wooden stalls on the decks of the already overcrowded ships, and more than 500 animals were brought aboard, including cows, bulls, pigs, horses, ducks, chickens, sheep, goats and geese.

Finally, on 13 November the fleet left civilisation behind and began the long haul, which would take more than two months in the worst sailing conditions they had yet encountered. Soon, in the high seas and strong winds, the livestock began to die; and by late November there was an outbreak of dysentery, first among the convicts then spreading to the marines. The epidemic lasted for six weeks, but despite the large number of serious cases, only one marine – and no convicts – died.

Only two weeks after leaving the cape, Arthur Phillip decided to split the fleet by taking the fastest four ships ahead. He intended to look for the best location on the New South Wales coast and start constructing the new settlement before the bulk of the fleet arrived. He may have suspected that Botany Bay might not be the best place to settle and wanted the time to explore other possible sites. Joseph Banks's journals would have been available to Phillip, the navy and the government, so Phillip may have been aware of Banks's earlier, more negative, assessment of Botany Bay, as well as the glowing reference he gave of it to the House of Commons committee.

Phillip left the slowest seven ships under the command of his deputy, John Hunter. Both divisions of the fleet were to experience the toughest sailing. It was summer in the southern hemisphere, but they were sailing at high latitudes, where it was icy cold, the seas high and the weather bad.

The four faster ships made heavy weather of the sailing and didn't reach Botany Bay until the afternoon of 18 January, and they were surprised to see Hunter's seven ships appear one by one over the next forty hours. When Hunter had been left with the seven slower ships in the Southern Ocean he took the decision – and the risk – to sail them to even higher latitudes, where the seas were rougher but the westerly winds stronger, and thus he was able to arrive at Botany Bay almost as quickly as Phillip.

It had been a remarkably successful voyage. They had sailed to the other side of the world without the loss of any ships and with fewer deaths than most of the later convoys that would bring convicts to Australia over the next fifty years.

The joy at surviving the voyage in such good shape was, however, short-lived: they quickly realised that Botany Bay was unsuitable for settlement. Over the next few days

Phillip and his officers searched the coast line in small boats but could not find sufficient fresh water, fertile soil or shelter for their needs:

> We set out to observe the country, [which] on inspection rather disappointed our hopes, being invariably sandy and unpromising for the purpose of cultivation . . . Closer to us was the spring at which Mr Cook watered but we did not think the water very excellent, nor did it run freely. In the evening we returned on board, not greatly pleased with our discoveries.[26]

After only three days of scouring the shores of Botany Bay, Phillip decided to set out in search of a more suitable site. He sailed off in three small boats with John Hunter, Judge David Collins and a number of other officers. They reached the mouth of Port Jackson in the early afternoon of 21 January and rowed through the one-and-a-half-kilometre gap between the north and south headlands. That night they pitched their tents on a small beach on the south side of the harbour, which is now called Camp Cove.

Arthur Phillip knew nothing of what to expect when he sailed between the Port Jackson heads. Eighteen years before, when Cook had left Botany Bay to resume his exploration, he had headed north-north-east out to sea and saw – but did not enter – the heads of a harbour:

> Having seen everything this place [Botany Bay] afforded we at daylight in the morning weighed with a light breeze . . . [and] steered along the shore N-N-E and at noon we were by observation . . . about two to three miles from the land and abreast the bay of harbour wherein there appeared safe anchorage, which I called Port Jackson.[27]

Phillip was by now in a great hurry. Still crammed aboard the eleven ships in Botany Bay waiting for the order to unload were more than 1400 people, many of them sick, who had not set foot on dry land for more than a year. The fleet had long exhausted its fresh food, and scurvy was breaking out. Also, many of the 500 animals loaded aboard at the Cape of Good Hope had already died, and more were dying each day. The fresh fodder was long gone, and while waiting in Botany Bay the marines were sent ashore to cut whatever grass they could find.

Phillip was aware he needed to find somewhere better to settle as quickly as possible. Late on the second day, some six kilometres deeper in Port Jackson, he discovered a sheltered bay about 800 metres long and 400 metres wide, which had fresh water running into it. He decided that it was here the settlers would build the new colony. He was to describe it as the 'finest harbour in the world' and named the site Sydney Cove, after the home secretary, Lord Sydney.[28]

Phillip and his small party returned to Botany Bay on the evening of 23 January and gave instructions for the entire fleet to prepare to sail from Botany Bay, where they had been anchored almost a week. While the British would continue for decades to refer to Botany Bay as the site of their penal colony, no convicts actually landed or settled there.

On the morning of 24 January, strong headwinds were blowing and the English decided to wait until the following day to try and sail out. While they waited, they were shocked to see the sails of two ships trying to enter the bay but being thwarted by the same strong winds. At first it was thought the ships were British, but by noon Phillip's men saw through their telescopes that the ships were flying French colours.

They were *L'Astrolabe* and *La Boussole*, under the command of Captain Jean François de Galaup, Comte de La Pérouse. They had been on a remarkable voyage of exploration for nearly three years, having left Europe two years before the first fleet, in June 1785.

It took two more days for the eleven British ships to work their way out of Botany Bay and past the French ships then sail the twelve kilometres north into Port Jackson. The first ship of the fleet to reach Sydney Cove was the nimble *Supply*, which arrived with Arthur Phillip on board on the evening of 25 January. Early the next morning Arthur Phillip was rowed ashore and landed on the spot he had chosen a few days earlier. Here a flag was planted and possession claimed on behalf of His Majesty King George III. A toast was proposed to the King and Queen and to the success of the colony. A *feu de joie* was fired by a party of marines and the whole group gave three cheers. Only a few marines, seamen and officers participated in the ceremony on what was to become Australia Day, and about forty convicts witnessed it from the deck of the *Supply*.

Later in the day the remainder of the fleet reached Sydney Cove, and the unloading of the supplies, which would take several weeks, began.

A week after the landing, Arthur Phillip sent Lieutenant Philip King – who spoke French fluently – to pay a courtesy call on the French ships they had passed on their way to Sydney, which were now anchored in Botany Bay.

King, Lieutenant William Dawes and a marine escort were rowed to Botany Bay, where they were 'received with the greatest politeness and attention' by La Pérouse and his fellow officers. King discovered that he was not the first of the English to visit: a number of convicts had already walked the twelve kilometres overland from Port Jackson but had been refused the opportunity of escaping with the French ships.[29]

King offered assistance to the French, who thanked him and made exactly the same offer to help the English. La Pérouse said he expected to be back in France in fifteen months but had enough supplies on board to last three years. During the meeting, King learned of the Frenchmen's remarkable voyage since they left Brest three years earlier. They had sailed around Cape Horn and up the Pacific coast from Chile to California and Kamchatka in eastern Siberia, before sailing south to Easter Island; Macau, in China (where they sold furs they had caught in the north Pacific); Manila, in the Philippines; the Friendly Islands (Tonga); the Sandwich Islands (Hawaii); and Norfolk Island. King was told how on Mauna Island, in the Navigation Islands (Samoa), less than two months before, on 11 December, a number of French officers and crew were massacred and others injured, including the captain of *L'Astrolabe*, Captain de Langle, eight officers, four seamen and a boy. The French had lost twenty-one crew when two of their small boats had been destroyed in big surf off the Alaskan coast eighteen months before, in July 1786.

When the French ships had been in Kamchatka they had been told the English intended to establish a colony in Botany Bay, so when he arrived, La Pérouse was surprised to see nothing except the English fleet trying to leave. He had thought 'a town might have been established and a market established'.[30]

After a pleasant visit, King said goodbye to his French hosts and returned to Sydney. Over the next few weeks there was little further contact between the English, who were unloading their fleet and trying to establish their new home, and the French, who were preparing for the next leg of their expedition.

Before the French left, Phillip's deputy, John Hunter, paid them another informal visit; and Monsieur de Clonard brought to Sydney letters from La Pérouse and asked that the English forward them to the French ambassador to London. The letters were later to provide the only indication of when La Pérouse had left New South Wales. Within two weeks, the French had quietly left Botany Bay with the two commanders, Phillip and La Pérouse, never having met. *L'Astrolabe* and *La Boussole* were never seen again and were eventually believed to have sunk off the coast of the New Hebrides (Vanuatu) with all crew.

Meanwhile, the English were struggling to adjust to their new environment. In addition to the hot summer winds, which were like a 'blast from a heated oven', they were confronted by tumultuous summer storms like none they had ever encountered in England.[31] They also had difficulty clearing the dense Australian bush that came down to the water's edge, and found that the English wood-cutting tools were not strong enough for the gnarled hardwoods of Australia.

The settlers had encountered local Aboriginal people on the first day they had landed in Botany Bay and again when they first came to Port Jackson. On both occasions there had been no violence, which gave Phillip and his colleagues confidence that the Aboriginals would not give them any trouble. In the instructions given to Phillip, the British government had made it clear that it wanted good relations with the locals 'and to conciliate their affections, enjoining all our subjects to live in amity and kindness with them'.[32]

Over the first few months of the new settlement, there remained little contact between the British and the locals, but as the year progressed there were a number of incidents where both whites and blacks were killed, which would spark increasing hostility between the European and the Aboriginal people. This hostility would shape the relationships between the Aboriginal people and not only those who arrived with the first fleet but also the settlers who came over the next two centuries.

Within a few months, the struggle to establish the settlement developed into a full-blown crisis as attempts to grow food locally failed and stocks declined. Sydney Cove may have been superior to Botany Bay in that it had a stream of fresh water and a good harbour, but the surrounding soil proved equally lacking in fertility. The seeds and plants brought from Rio de Janeiro and the Cape of Good Hope were sown but fared badly.

Before the coming of winter, Phillip wrote to England to say:

> The great labour in clearing the ground will not permit more than eight acres to be sown this year with wheat and barley. At the same time an immense number of ants and field mice will render our crops very uncertain. Part of our livestock brought from the Cape, small as it was, has been lost and our resources in fish is also uncertain.[33]

Only a few months later, Phillip had to write again to England to report that the first harvest had been an almost total failure and had yielded only enough food to support the colony 'for a few days'. Consequently none of the grain was fed to the settlers but was instead saved as seed for the following year's sowing:

> It was now found that very little of the English wheat had vegetated and a very considerable quantity of barley and many seeds had rotted in the ground, having been heated in the passage and some much injured by weevils. All the barley and wheat likewise, which had been out aboard the Supply at the Cape were destroyed by weevil.[34]

Despite the immediate problems, Phillip tried be optimistic about the long-term prospects of the colony by saying that he thought it would eventually 'prove the most valuable acquisition Great Britain ever made'.[35] The head of the marines in Sydney, Major Robert Ross, strongly disagreed with the governor and wrote a letter at the same time as Phillip, saying the colony would never work:

> With respect to the utility of settlement upon this coast . . . it never can be made to answer the intended purpose or wish of Government, for the country seems totally destitute of everything that can be an object of a commercial nation, a very fine harbour excepted, and I much fear that the nature of the soil is such as will not be brought to yield more than a sufficient sustenance for the needy emigrants whose desperate fortunes induce them to try the experiment.[36]

Life in the colony was harsh and getting worse. Hundreds of convicts already living on reduced rations were crowded into poor accommodation made of canvas or strips of bark. For several years they would not have beds to sleep in, tables to eat at or chairs to sit on. Clothing was also wearing out and replacements running short. As the first winter came, many of the settlers, including the marines, had worn out their shoes and were forced to go about their business barefoot.

News of the crisis in Sydney reached London on the ships of the first fleet, which returned to England early in 1789. The government reacted to the news that the settlement was struggling by sending a ship loaded with additional supplies to relieve the hungry colony. In September 1789 the *Guardian*, commanded by twenty-seven-year-old captain Edward Riou, left Portsmouth with almost 1000 tons of supplies. It made good time, arriving on 24 November in Cape Town, where it stayed only three weeks to restock food and load aboard some additional livestock for Sydney. Leaving the Cape on 11 December, it sailed south in the Great Southern Ocean to catch the strong westerly winds, but on Christmas Eve it smashed into a giant iceberg. The ship listing badly, with part of the top deck already under water, about half the crew managed to scramble onto five small boats, while Captain Riou and the remaining crew stayed on board pumping to keep the *Guardian* afloat. Out of the five small boats only one survived, and its fifteen inhabitants were picked up about 400 kilometres off the coast of Natal by a passing French ship on its way from India to Cape Town.

On 21 February, almost two months after hitting the iceberg, the *Guardian* was still listing and being pumped by a desperate crew, when it was seen drifting in the Indian Ocean south of Madagascar by a Dutch ship on its way back to Europe from Batavia. The Dutch ship helped tug the *Guardian* to the Cape of Good Hope, where in a gale the following April it was torn off its moorings and broke up.

Finally, in Sydney, at 3.30 in the afternoon on 3 June 1790, two and a half years after the arrival of the first fleet and when all hope had gone, the signal flag was broken out on Port Jackson's South Head: a ship's sail had been sighted.

It was the *Lady Juliana*, the first ship of the second fleet, bringing more convicts and, more importantly, food. Over the next few weeks another four ships would arrive bringing vital provisions to Sydney. The convicts on board had suffered an appallingly high death rate during the voyage. On the second fleet hygiene, diet and exercise of the convicts were largely ignored and many were chained below deck for the entire voyage.

The journey of the second fleet was an infamous episode in the early history of Australia and one of the worst chapters in seafaring history. Of the 1038 who were loaded on board the *Surprize*, *Neptune* and *Scarborough* in England in 1789, nearly a quarter died before they reached Sydney. Of the remaining 756 who arrived alive, almost 500 were hospitalised in hastily erected tents. A further 124 died during their first few days in the colony.

Whereas the first fleet had been under the control of the navy, the second fleet was managed by private contractors, who were paid irrespective of whether the convicts lived or died. Arthur Phillip wrote a letter of complaint to London about the treatment of the convicts. He said that while he did not want to 'dwell on the scene of misery . . . it would be want of duty not to say that it was occasioned by the contractors having crowded too many on board those ships, and from their being too much confined during the passage'.[37]

While food rationing would continue, the second fleet, with its stores and provisions, had averted almost certain disaster for the first-fleet settlers.

Slowly but surely, with the arrival of more ships with provisions from England, and the success of harvests on Norfolk Island and on farmland opened up to the west of Sydney, the colony would eventually produce enough food to survive.

*

In March 1791, the colony was party to a voyage of discovery of a different kind when convict Mary Bryant, her husband and their two children took a single-masted, six-oared rowing boat with seven others and sailed 4000 kilometres to Timor. Initially, they masqueraded as shipwrecks, but after two months Mary Bryant's husband,

William, admitted their true identity and they were immediately locked up by the local Dutch authorities. A month
later the British navy captain Edward Edwards arrived in
Batavia with his crew in small boats after their ship the
Pandora was wrecked in the Torres Strait. The *Pandora*
had been hunting down the mutineers from the *Bounty*.
On being handed the runaway convicts, Edwards clapped
them in irons and took them back to England for trial.

On the way back, William Bryant, his son and three
of the others died of various diseases before Cape Town,
and then Mary's daughter, Charlotte, died off the West
African coast. Mary Bryant and four others were jailed
in England on their return but, following a campaign for
their release involving the London diarist James Boswell,
all of the surviving prisoners were pardoned.

A year later, on 11 December 1792, Arthur Phillip finally
left on the *Atlantic* to return to England from Sydney. He
had wanted to leave earlier, having first requested to be
relieved more than two years before. However, the government, well aware that the settlement was still struggling,
had rejected his application, saying it was extremely important for him to remain at his post for the time being.

Throughout his governorship, Phillip had been almost
totally preoccupied with the establishment and survival
of the fledgling colony, so in the five years since his
arrival little had been done to extend British knowledge of
the land they had claimed. When Phillip went home, the
detailed exploration of New South Wales had extended
only a short distance to the north of Sydney to Brisbane
Waters, and to Botany Bay to the south. To the west,
expansion was blocked by the Blue Mountains, which
would not be crossed for another quarter of a century.
And while Arthur Phillip was struggling in Sydney,
unbeknown to him, the French had sent two more ships
on an expedition to explore Australia.

CHAPTER 4

ANOTHER FRENCH EXPLORATION

*L*a Pérouse had entrusted his last dispatches, addressed to the French Minister of Marine, to the English in Sydney shortly before leaving Botany Bay on 7 February 1788. Six months later they were taken back to Europe by Lieutenant John Shortland, who was on one of the first returning convict transport ships, the *Alexander*, which reached England at the end of May the following year. After being given to the French ambassador in London, the letters reached Paris in the middle of 1789.

When La Pérouse had not arrived back in France by the end of 1789, the French authorities became anxious, and by early the following year they were convinced his ships had been wrecked – probably somewhere outside the commonly used routes of the eastern Pacific.

On 14 January 1791 the Société d'Histoire Naturelle petitioned the parliament to send an expedition to search for La Pérouse, and on 9 February the National Assembly passed a resolution 'that in the name of humanity, and the arts and sciences . . . the King be requested that there be equipped one or more ships . . . with the mission of searching after M. De la Pérouse'.[1] The King approved the plan. The French Revolution had already begun, and he had been forced out of Versailles to be a virtual prisoner in the Tuileries. In the early days of the Revolution, France was at war with practically all its neighbours and was in a financially desperate situation. However, the plight of La Pérouse was able to unite the widely disparate French opinions of the times. La Pérouse was a war hero and well known for his earlier battles against the British in North America. He was also popular as an explorer, particularly as at the time the English dominated world exploration. So widespread was the concern that La Pérouse was lost that King Louis XIV, on the day before his execution, in January 1793, is said to have asked, 'Is there any news of La Pérouse?'[2]

Jean François de Galaup La Pérouse was born into an established rural family in Albi, in the south of France, in 1741. He entered the French navy at fifteen, and three years later he was wounded and captured off the north-west coast of France during the battle of Quiberon Bay, which was decisively won by the English in November 1759. Released by the English, La Pérouse returned to the navy and was promoted to captain. He later distinguished himself fighting the English in Canada. He was at the English siege of Fort Louisburg in 1781, when James Cook was fighting on the other side, and the following year he successfully captured two English forts on the coast of Hudson Bay.

In 1783, before the beginning of the French Revolution, he was appointed by King Louis XVI to lead a huge expedition around the world. Its aims included completing the discovery of the Pacific, which James Cook – who La Pérouse greatly admired – had extensively sailed on his three great voyages before being killed in Hawaii in 1779. The expedition was also to explore opportunities for French trade, open up new maritime routes and enrich French scientific knowledge and collections.

La Pérouse was ordered to explore the north and south Pacific but first to explore the coast of New Holland. Had he chosen to follow his instructions to the letter, he would have been the first to completely chart Australia, fifteen years before Nicolas Baudin and Matthew Flinders.

For the expedition, La Pérouse was given two 550-ton storeships that were converted to frigates: *L'Astrolabe* and *La Boussole*. They were supplied with the latest scientific equipment for the ten scientists chosen for the voyage, who included an astronomer, a mathematician, a geologist, a botanist, naturalists and two artists.

Over the next two and a half years La Pérouse sailed across a large part of the known and still unknown world. Leaving Brest on 1 August 1785, he sailed to the south Atlantic, and around Cape Horn in January the following year. After several weeks ashore on the Chilean coast he reached Easter Island in April 1786, the South Sandwich Islands in May and Hawaii later in the month, where he became the first European to land on Maui. In late June he reached Alaska, where the following month twenty-one members of his crew were drowned when two long boats were lost in heavy seas.

In August and September 1786 the French sailed south along the Spanish Californian coast, then crossed the Pacific in one hundred days, going to Manila, where they stayed for seven weeks, and on to Macau, where they sold the furs of animals they had caught in Alaska. From there, they sailed north to Japan and along the Russian coast to Kamchatka, arriving in September 1787.

The French then began their voyage to the South Pacific, and in December 1787 they reached the Navigation Islands, as they had been named by the French explorer Bougainville (they are now called Samoa). It was while on the Navigation Islands that the French were attacked by locals and eleven of the crew of *L'Astrolabe* – including its captain, Fleuriot de Langle – were killed.

At the end of the following January they finally reached Botany Bay, where they encountered the English ships of the first fleet bringing convicts to settle to New South Wales.

Before contact was lost with La Pérouse, France had been kept informed of his remarkable expedition with a number of dispatches and maps he managed to send back from as far away as Alaska and Siberia, Macau and finally Botany Bay. The dispatches from Macau and Botany Bay had been sent by sea, but the only way his dispatches from Kamchatka, in Siberia, could be returned to France was overland. The letters were taken by Barthélemy Lesseps (uncle of Ferdinand, who later built the Suez Canal), who had joined La Pérouse's expedition as a Russian translator for the Siberian part of the expedition.

Lesseps began a remarkable trek back to France two weeks after *La Boussole* and *L'Astrolabe* left Kamchatka on 30 September 1787 to sail for Botany Bay. After crossing the Kamchatka Peninsula, Lesseps trekked 1200 kilometres around the northern shore of the Sea of Okhotsk and then, with dog sleds and horses, travelled another 4000 kilometres to Kirensk, in central Russia, which he reached the following July. From there he headed to the Urals, and he reached St Petersburg 6000 kilometres later, in September 1788, to hand over La Pérouse's dispatches. Lesseps was ordered to return to Paris, where he was greeted like a hero and presented to King Louis XVI at Versailles. His journey of almost 13,000 kilometres had taken more than a year.

La Pérouse, on the other hand, arrived in Botany Bay four months after leaving Siberia. When he left Botany Bay three weeks later, in February 1788, he wrote in his last dispatch where he intended to sail:

> I shall go up again to the Friendly Isles [Tonga], and I shall do absolutely all I am enjoined by my instructions regarding the southern part of New Caledonia, Mendana, Santa Cruz Island, the southern coast of Surville's Arsacides [Mendana, Santa Cruz Island and the Arsacides are in the current-day Solomon Islands] and Bougainville's Louisiade [Archipelago], to see whether this is part of New Guinea or separate from it. At the end of July I shall pass between New Guinea and New Holland, by a different channel to that of the Endeavour if there is one. During September and October I shall examine the Gulf of Carpentaria and the whole western coast of New Holland right to Van Diemen's Land, but so as to allow myself to go north again to reach the Isle de France [Mauritius] by the beginning of December.[3]

However, La Pérouse's last dispatch was not much help to those looking for his whereabouts, because he planned to sail over such a vast area of the southern hemisphere.

The man chosen to lead the search expedition for La Pérouse in September 1791 was Joseph-Antoine Raymond de Bruni D'Entrecasteaux. Fifty-five-year-old D'Entrecasteaux had already served in the French navy for forty years. He was born in Aix-en-Provence to a noble family, and after an education by Jesuit priests he joined the navy when he was fifteen years old. He fought in the Seven Years War against the British, during which time he became an accomplished navigator.

D'Entrecasteaux was very familiar with La Pérouse and his expedition. In 1785, as the Deputy Director of Ports and Arsenals, he had been involved with the preparation of *L'Astrolabe* and *La Boussole*. Later that year he was appointed commander of a French squadron to the East Indies and discovered a new route to China, through the Sunda Islands and Moluccas (Maluku Islands), that enabled ships to avoid the hazardous south-east monsoon season. On reaching Macau in 1787 he was disappointed that he had missed La Pérouse by two days – *L'Astrolabe* and *La Boussole* had called in to sell furs on their way to Botany Bay.

In addition to looking for La Pérouse, D'Entrecasteaux was also instructed to undertake the charting of the still unknown south coast of Australia as far as Van Diemen's Land.

For the expedition, D'Entrecasteaux was given two well-supplied ships, *La Recherche* and *L'Espérance*, the latter of which was to be captained by forty-four-year-old bachelor Jean-Michel Huon de Kermadec. Both French ships were about 350 tons, forty metres long and eight metres wide.

Because of additional crew, including the scientists and artists, each ship was fitted out to carry more than one hundred men, rather than the usual sixty. All the guns on the lower deck except three on each side were taken out to make way for cabins for the officers and scientists. On each vessel, an extra orlop deck – the lowest deck on a ship – was built across the deep hold, for the storage of extra supplies and extra crew.

La Recherche and *L'Espérance* took ten scientists on board, including two botanists and four naturalists, three of whom were doctors of medicine. One of the botanists, thirty-six-year-old Jacques-Julien Labillardière, had previously spent two years in London, where he had met Joseph

Banks and studied many of the exotic plants brought back from the Cook expedition to Australia. There were two artists, a mineralogist, a gardener and two astronomers, one of whom was thirty-four-year-old Claude Bertrand, who was already widely known in France for having been one of the first men to fly in a hot air balloon in 1784, only a year after the Montgolfier brothers.

The expedition also included the leading French hydrographer Charles-François Beautemps-Beaupré, whose maps – particularly of Tasmania – would set a new high standard and would be used for international shipping for many years.

It took eight months to prepare the ships from the date of the authorisation of the expedition in February 1791 till their departure from the port of Brest in September. The preparation was complicated by the turmoil during the early days of the French Revolution. In September 1791, just before the ship left, there was a mutiny at Brest, which was described as 'an island of metropolitan French radicalism in the midst of the conservative Breton country-side'.[4] Citizen D'Entrecasteaux took care not to appoint any crew who may have been involved in the mutiny, and everyone was obliged to recite the oath 'to be loyal to the nation, the law and the king'. (Despite the fact that all titles had been abolished by the National Assembly the previous year.)

However, there were republicans on both ships, particularly among the scientists. The sympathy of many officers and crew with many of the aims of the revolution would cause great difficulties for the royalists later in the expedition.

D'Entrecasteaux was instructed to top up provisions in Tenerife, the Cape of Good Hope and Batavia. The basic rations for the French seamen included salted beef or bacon, cheese, rice, dried peas and dried beans, hardtack biscuits, wine and brandy. Each of the two ships also took aboard six live sheep and fifty chickens, which were penned under the gangway amidships. To combat scurvy, the expedition followed closely the practices of La Pérouse, who had closely followed Cook, and they took with them a variety of substances including malt, lemon, sauerkraut, sorrel conserve and the powder from crushed root vegetables.

D'Entrecasteaux's instructions were to head first for Cape Leeuwin, on the south-west tip of Australia, where he was to begin his exploration of the south coast. This was also where La Pérouse was believed to have gone. However, D'Entrecasteaux's plans were abruptly changed when *La Recherche* and *L'Espérance* arrived at the Cape of Good Hope on 17 January 1792. Waiting for D'Entrecasteaux was the local French chargé d'affaires, with a letter from the French commander of Asian seas, Vice Admiral Marquis de Saint Felix, which had been sent by special frigate to D'Entrecasteaux from Mauritius.

The letter contained statements from two French merchant-ship captains, who said that while they were in Batavia the previous September they had heard English captain John Hunter say that he had seen natives in canoes near the Admiralty Islands, north of New Guinea, wearing clothing that he was sure was part of the French naval uniform:

> Letter from Citizen Saint Felix, Commander of the Indian Station.
> . . . I hasten to transmit to you, at the Cape of Good Hope two accounts relative to your mission, which have just been given to me by two French ships arrived from Batavia . . . Commander Hunter, as well as his crew, have seen, near Admiralty Island in the South Sea, men covered with European clothes,

which he judged to be French uniforms. You will also see that the Commodore had no doubt of their being the remains of the wreck of M. de la Pérouse, whom he had seen at Botany Bay.[5]

Hunter was returning to England from Sydney. He had just been in Cape Town but had left only two hours after D'Entrecasteaux dropped anchor, so he could not be questioned about the story.[6]

D'Entrecasteaux was sceptical of the claims, because Hunter did not appear to have mentioned to anyone while he was in Cape Town that he had seen natives wearing French uniforms in the Admiralty Islands.

The following year, when his journal was published, Hunter speculated that La Pérouse might have been seen by some local natives north of New Guinea, but said nothing about seeing French naval uniforms:

> One of them made various motions for shaving, but holding up something in his hand, with which he frequently scraped his cheek and chin, this led me to the conjecture, that some European ship had been lately among them, and I thought it not improbable that it might have been Mons. de la Pérouse [on] his way north-wards from New South Wales.[7]

Despite D'Entrecasteaux's scepticism, since the letter had been sent by special frigate and seemed to have the approval of the French governor of Mauritius, he postponed following his instructions and instead took the most direct route to the Admiralty Islands.

As a result, the exploration of the south coast of Australia, a 'special object of the French king's curiosity', would have to await a return voyage. Had things been different, D'Entrecasteaux would have denied Flinders his later achievement of being the first to sail the Bass Strait, and to chart the unknown coast.

While D'Entrecasteaux was still in Cape Town, he met Captain William Bligh, who was there with the *Providence* and the *Assistance* on his second breadfruit expedition. Bligh's first attempt to collect breadfruit from the south-west Pacific had been spoiled by the mutiny of the crew of the *Bounty* nearly two years before. With Bligh was the eighteen-year-old Matthew Flinders – but it is not known whether Flinders ever met D'Entrecasteaux.

La Recherche and *L'Espérance* left the cape four weeks later, on 16 February 1792. There had been dissent among the scientists while in port and a number had resigned. Blavier the mineralogist and the artist Chailly-Ely stayed behind, and the balloonist-astronomer Bertrand was discharged on medical grounds – but the others, including naturalists Jacques-Julien Labillardière and Claude-Antoine Riche and artist Jean Piron, were persuaded to continue with the expedition. The day after sailing, they found two stowaways, one of whom was a German prisoner who had escaped from an English convict fleet bound for Botany Bay. He explained that after escaping from one of the British ships while the fleet was in Cape Town, he had hidden in the hills behind the city, before managing to hide aboard *La Recherche*. The German was a skilled blacksmith and was welcomed by the French because he helped fill a gap in the crew caused by a French armourer being left sick at the Cape.[8]

After three weeks of heading into strong easterly winds, D'Entrecasteaux had made practically no progress on the direct route north-east to the Admiralty Islands and decided to change course and go the long way round. By heading south he would sail with the roaring forties to Van Diemen's Land, then north along the entire east coast of Australia to the north of New Guinea and the

Admiralty Islands. The new route would involve sailing more than twice the distance, an extra 5000 kilometres, over the next six months.

The trip across the Great Southern Ocean in strong winds and high seas was very fast and took less than four weeks, but according to D'Entrecasteaux, it exhausted everyone aboard. During one storm he himself broke a rib when he was flung sideways, and he was still laid up in his cabin when they sighted the Van Diemen's Land coast on April 1792.

The French spent five weeks on Van Diemen's Land, where they repaired and caulked the ships, collected wood and water, and caught plenty of fish. In contrast to the barren south coast of the mainland, the beauty of Van Diemen's Land was enchanting to D'Entrecasteaux:

> I shall attempt the vain task of conveying the feeling I experienced at the sight of this solitary harbour, placed at the ends of the earth, and enclosed so perfectly that one could think of it as separated from the rest of the universe. Here one meets at every step . . . trees of enormous height and corresponding width . . . crowned with foliage always green: some appear as old as the world; so interlaced and compacted as to be impenetrable . . . Nature in all its vigour . . . seems to offer the imagination something more imposing and more vivid than the sight of the same nature embellished by industry and by civilised man; wanting to conserve only beauty, he has destroyed the charm; he has removed the unique character, that of being always ancient and always new.[9]

While in Van Diemen's Land, the French saw smoke from fires and evidence of camp sites, but the local Aboriginal people proved to be shy and quickly disappeared into the bush as the French neared. In one of only a few encounters, the locals happily ate some bread and drank some water offered by the French but when invited would not eat their cheese. Its smell, conjectured Labillardière, 'had probably prevented them from eating it'.[10]

The French also conducted some useful surveying and discovered that Adventure Bay was not on the mainland of Van Diemen's Land but was in fact on an island, which D'Entrecasteaux would name Bruny Island, after himself. He also named the strait that separated the island and the mainland the D'Entrecasteaux Channel.

In May they left on the shortest direct route north for the Admiralty Islands. By the middle of June they had reached James Cook's Isle of Pines, on the southern end of the archipelago of New Caledonia, but found no evidence that La Pérouse had been there. On 9 July they reached the Treasury Islands (in the current-day Solomon Islands), and then began searching the south-west coast of Bougainville; by the end of July they had reached the Admiralty Islands.

There were so many islands in this area that Captain Kermadec of L'Espérance suggested that the two ships split up and search separately, but D'Entrecasteaux thought the risk of them losing each other in the archipelago too high. At the highly populated island of Vendola (Nauna) north of New Britain they found a well-established settlement with coconut palms and terraced root crops, and boats were sent from both ships with goods to give to the natives in the hope they might be able to shed light on the whereabouts of La Pérouse.[11]

Unfortunately there was no evidence that La Pérouse had been there, and the French lamented that they 'did not see in the possession of these islanders any effects which belonged to Europeans'.[12] The locals were so astonished at seeing the French that D'Entrecasteaux felt they were likely to be the first Europeans who had landed there and that La Pérouse could not have been wrecked on these islands.

By taking the longer route and being at sea for a greater period than originally planned, the French ran out of fresh food and 'the situation of [their] scorbutic [afflicted with scurvy] people ... was daily becoming more alarming and the number [of them] ... was increasing with rapidity'.[13] While the coconuts and other fruit the French had traded with the locals had helped, they had not had any other fresh food for more than two months, since leaving Van Diemen's Land. Disappointed at finding nothing of La Pérouse, they quit the islands and headed for the tiny Dutch settlement of Amboina (current-day Ambon, Indonesia), where they hoped to replenish their depleted supplies.

When they reached Amboina after a further thirty-seven days' sailing, it was the first time they had set eyes on a township since leaving the Cape of Good Hope seven months before. Amboina had been established by the Portuguese in 1513 as a port for the loading of spices. Nearly a century later it was taken by the Dutch and became the headquarters of the Dutch East India Company before the establishment of the larger centre of Batavia, after which it became a small trading outpost for cloves and nutmeg. The town had rudimentary wharves, an old fort overlooking a collection of houses, a number of gardens, a Calvinist church, a Malay Mosque and a Chinese pagoda.

The Dutch sold fresh food to the French, but only for cash – they would not take French Treasury notes. In their five-week stay at Amboina, the French loaded aboard live goats, pigs, geese, ducks and chickens, and fresh fruit and vegetables, including yams, bamboo shoots in vinegar, bananas and ginger.[14] While there, D'Entrecasteaux prepared a report, which he left to be taken by the next ship that came on its way back toward Europe. In it he acknowledged that the search for La Pérouse had so far been fruitless but that, although he had 'lost a year', the expedition had not been wasted. As an example of why, he cited the discovery of the D'Entrecasteaux Channel in Tasmania, which had been missed by Cook and other British explorers. He also said that he would now return to recommence the exploration of Australia that had been postponed when he went to look for La Pérouse:

> I have to make repairs and provisions for my ships, so as to be able to undertake the reconnaissance of the south coast of New Holland to which I am devoting all of the good season.[15]

After four months in the tropics, the ships headed for New Holland. By now they were infested with cockroaches, which crawled 'on every part of the body that was uncovered' as the French tried to sleep at night. The botanist Labillardière, on *L'Espérance*, said the roaches devoured everything, including the ink from his inkwell:

> The species of *blatta germanica* had multiplied to such a degree for several months passed since we had been under the tropics, that they incommoded us extremely. These insects did not content themselves with our biscuit, they also devoured our linen, paper, etc.: nothing came amiss to them. Their fondness for vegetable acids however astonished me; no sooner was a lemon cut than they quickly dispatched it; but what astonished me still more, was the rapidity with which they emptied my ink-horn when I forgot to put in the stopper. The caustic quality of the [ink] with which they gorged themselves, seemed to have no prejudicial effect on them.[16]

The ships made good time after Amboina and sighted
Cape Leeuwin seven weeks later, on 9 December. But the
trip had been difficult because the water they had loaded
in Amboina had become putrid, much of the food had
become infested, and the goats and chickens had begun to
die from the cold nights and lack of proper food.

Pressing east in boisterous winds, they spotted a large
bay where they might have taken shelter had they not
been too far downwind to tack around. The bay was
King George Sound (the site of today's Albany), on the
south-west coast of New Holland. It had been charted
and named by the English explorer George Vancouver
nine years before, on the first part of a four-year voyage
of discovery to the north Pacific. Vancouver had spent
three years as a midshipman on board the *Resolution*
on Captain James Cook's second great voyage, which
circumnavigated the world, and was also on the *Discovery*
on Cook's third and final voyage, to the north Pacific,
when Cook was killed at Hawaii on the way home.

For Vancouver's own expedition, he was given
command of the 340-ton *Discovery* and the smaller
135-ton *Chatham*. In April 1791 he sailed from England
to the Cape of Good Hope, then to the south-west tip of
Australia, where he found King George Sound. After navigating about 300 kilometres east from there, he was forced
by adverse winds to head south, under Tasmania. From
there he called at New Zealand, Tahiti and China, before
heading to the north Pacific, where he charted Vancouver
Island and the site of what is now Vancouver, in Canada.

D'Entrecasteaux's failure to stop at King George Sound
would prove costly, because doing so could have provided
him with the water and wood he needed to complete the
exploration of the south coast of Australia.

About 1000 kilometres further east, in high seas
and violent winds, *La Recherche* and *L'Espérance*

hazardously navigated their way through a large group of
islands and were lucky to find secure anchorage in a bay
D'Entrecasteaux named Esperance. D'Entrecasteaux was
also to name the Archipelago of the Recherche, a group of
islands that spread almost 200 kilometres along the coast
and more than sixty kilometres out to sea. Apart from the
discovery of the D'Entrecasteaux Channel in Tasmania
the previous year, the Archipelago of the Recherche and
Esperance were to be the most important finds of the
expedition.

The land around Esperance was not very appealing to
them, although the botanist Labillardière managed to find
a new species of flowering eucalypt. The French saw no
signs of local inhabitants in the country, which was dominated by sand dunes and sparse, lifeless bushes. While
they remained at anchor the crew caught some seals,
penguins and fish but, critically, could not find any significant watering holes.

With their stock of drinking water declining, D'Entrecasteaux again reduced the daily ration, to a level below
which he believed it could not be cut further. After six days
of fruitless searching for more potable water, the ships left
Esperance and resumed their exploration eastwards.

Being summer, the weather was hot and dry. The expedition had reached the point where the vast plateau of the
Nullarbor reaches the sea, forming a perpendicular cliff
that is between 120 and 180 metres high and runs more
than 600 kilometres to the east. Along this barren, steep
rampart, D'Entrecasteaux said, there were no inlets or
capes and nowhere to anchor to dig for water:

> The whole coast from west to east looked the same:
> limestone rock rising precipitously, the same height
> all the way, the layers perfectly horizontal, like the
> platform at the top. The greenery above was dark, a

disagreeable contrast to the whiteness of the chalk.
No birds emerged from this arid coast, no smoke,
everything suggested that this land of such frighten-
ing aspect was uninhabited; it seemed that its aridity
had banished men and birds.[17]

The going was slow, since the wind again turned easterly
and they were forced to tack. But D'Entrecasteaux hoped
that they would be able to reach the St Peter and St Francis
islands, which were still almost 1000 kilometres further
east. (These were the islands the Dutchman Pieter Nuyts
had named almost 200 years before and the furthest
point east along the south coast that any European had
reached.)

However, on 1 January 1793 Kermadec signalled from
L'Espérance that he now had only enough water left for a
direct passage to Van Diemen's Land. Bitterly disappointed,
D'Entrecasteaux decided to abandon the exploration that
might have allowed him to chart the unknown coast and
discover the strait that he believed separated Van Diemen's
Land from the Australian mainland, which would be
sailed by Flinders and Bass four years later.

But what D'Entrecasteaux had done, he had done well.
He had gone further than Vancouver, and his charts of
the coast were far better than the rough maps made by
Nuyts's skipper, François Thijssen, nearly two centuries
before. He was also the first to sail completely around
Australia, more than ten years before Matthew Flinders
did so in 1803.

Three weeks later, on 20 January, the two ships were
again safely anchored in southern Van Diemen's Land, at
Storm Bay, where they had last been ten months before.

They stayed in Van Diemen's Land for thirty-eight
days. During their stay, the botanist Labillardière said,
they found vegetables and trees planted by English captain

William Bligh, who had been there more than a year before, on his second expedition to the South Seas:

> Bligh had with him two botanists, who at a small distance from the shore sowed cresses, some acorns, celery, etc. We saw three young fig trees, two pomegranates, and a quince planted by them, which had thriven very well [and an] inscription, which we found on a large neighbouring trunk . . .: 'Near this tree, Captain William Bligh planted seven fruit trees, 1792, Messrs S&W, botanists'.[18]

The French also replenished their stock of water, wood and food, and completed a survey of the south Tasmanian coast, which included the discovery of the River du Nord, which the British later renamed the Derwent, where the city of Hobart now stands.

On 27 February 1793 D'Entrecasteaux recorded that they 'had too long [been] separated from those parts' where they 'could hope to find traces of M. de la Pérouse', and the ships again headed north to resume their quest to find the lost French explorer. They were never again to touch on Australia.[19]

To date those on the expedition had survived well, but over the next year things would degenerate.

After twelve days' sailing they reached New Zealand, and a few days later the Friendly Islands (Tonga), where the locals enthusiastically traded fruit and other food. Soon the seamen and the local women were trading for sex – D'Entrecasteaux and his officers proved incapable of stopping the women from coming out to the ships and climbing on board, even through the gun ports and the scuttles of the officers' cabins.

On New Caledonia in April 1793 they encountered some friendly locals, who had a plank in their canoe coated with varnish that Labillardière believed was definitely from a European ship:

> I was not a little surprised to see one of the planks of their canoe paid with a coat of varnish. It appeared to have belonged to some European ship, and of this I had no doubt when I discovered that white lead had formed a principal ingredient in the composition of the varnish. This plank undoubtedly came from a ship belonging to some civilised nation, which had been lost on their coast.[20]

The French then tried, but failed, to get a satisfactory explanation about the timber from the locals:

> I requested these savages to relate to us what they knew on this subject; they immediately set sail to the westward, promising to return next day and to bring back the information we required, but they did not keep their word, and we had not afterwards an opportunity of seeing them.[21]

On 6 May Captain Jean-Michel Huon de Kermadec, the forty-five-year-old commander of *L'Espérance*, died, having spent the previous ten weeks largely confined to his cabin 'exhausted by fever'. Kermadec was popular with the officers and crew of both ships, and his death caused 'deep regret to all persons belonging to the expedition'.[22] After he was buried at sea, command of *L'Espérance* passed to his deputy, the thirty-three-year-old aristocrat Lieutenant Alexandre d'Hesmivy d'Auribeau.

Five days later they reached the Santa Cruz Islands, where La Pérouse had said he planned to go. The islands are north of current-day Vanuatu and at the southern end of the Solomon Islands. As they passed some sixty kilometres

to the west of an island D'Entrecasteaux was to name
Recherche Island (later renamed Vanikoro in the Solomon
Islands), they had no inkling that near here La Pérouse
and his ships had, indeed, met their doom. (In 1826 Irish
sea captain Peter Dillon found swords at Vanikoro that
are believed to have belonged to La Pérouse. But it was
not until 1964 that confirmed wreckage of *La Boussole*
was found.)

By June they had passed Guadalcanal, in the Solomon
Islands, and then, in accordance with the original instructions for the expedition, they charted many of the islands
of the Louisiade Archipelago, New Guinea and New
Britain.

It was now nine weeks since they had had abundant
fresh food, and, as Labillardière recorded, scurvy began to
appear among the crew:

> We had been reduced for a long time to living on
> worm infested biscuit and salt meat which had
> generally deteriorated; also scurvy had already
> made ravages to our vessel.[23]

Now, at the north-west tip of New Guinea and with little
choice, D'Entrecasteaux headed towards Java, where
he hoped to refresh the ships. On the way it became
obvious to the crew that D'Entrecasteaux himself had the
symptoms of advanced scurvy, including swollen legs and
black patches of skin. Then on 19 July he became dangerously ill and was forced to his bed in his cabin. Later that
day he was 'seized by violent convulsions . . . fell into
unconsciousness and died at 7.30 in the evening'.[24]

The crew had not expected the sudden loss of their
captain. Despite the numbers of crew suffering from
scurvy, D'Entrecasteaux had been the first to die, and
usually officers had access to a more varied diet, even

when food stocks were low. Labillardière recorded in his journal:

> He sank under the violence of a dreadful colic which he had experienced for two days. For a little time past he had some slight symptoms of scurvy, but we were very far from thinking ourselves threatened with so great a loss.[25]

After a dignified burial at sea for D'Entrecasteaux, and with a growing number of crew sick, the ships, now under the command of d'Auribeau, sailed on to Waigeo Island, on the western end of Papua, where they managed to catch some turtles and fish and collect grapefruit, coconuts, pawpaws, marrows, yams, bananas, lemons and capsicums.

But the ships were now confronted with an outbreak of dysentery: thirty men were sick on *La Recherche* and twenty on *L'Espérance*, and another five men died as they headed for the Dutch settlement at the eastern end of Surabaya, which they reached on 19 October. Dropping anchor at Madura, d'Auribeau sent two small boats to pay respects to the local governor in the Dutch settlement, some forty kilometres away.

They learned from the Dutch that for the last eight months France had again been at war with Holland. The ships would be able to harbour and land their sick only if they handed over all their arms and submitted to a state of arrest. It was the first news the French had heard from home since they left Brest two years before. And they were shaken to hear that France was also at war with England, Austria, Spain and Russia; the King had been executed; and the French monarchy had been replaced by the republic.

The officers were still overwhelmingly royalists, and rather than allow the ships to be put into republican hands, d'Auribeau arranged for them to be sold to the Dutch to pay for food and treatment of the sick.

While they were in Surabaya, it became known to the crew that Louis Girardin, a servant on *La Recherche* responsible for serving meals to the officers, was a woman, Marie-Louise Victoire Girardin. It seems that her gender was known from the beginning by D'Entrecasteaux and possibly Kermadec, but had been kept from practically everyone else. She was about forty years old and had apparently been abandoned by a faithless lover after the birth of a child. To escape the wrath of her father, an established wine merchant of Versailles, she had appeared at Brest disguised as a man and successfully secured the job on *La Recherche*.

During the voyage, Girardin had been able to guard her secret but occasionally had to put up with suspicions and insults. On one occasion, she challenged one of the ship's pilots to a duel and was wounded in the arm. Then, one night in January 1794, Girardin had a romantic encounter with a young sub-lieutenant, Mérite, while he was on night-guard duty – and the secret was out. It is not clear how attached the two lovers became, but within a year both had contracted dysentery and died.

On 19 February 1794 d'Auribeau handed *La Recherche* and *L'Espérance* over to the Dutch. In striking the deal, the Dutch agreed to provide passage to Europe for all the French. It was also agreed that the proceeds of the sale of the ships would go towards paying off the debts the French had accrued at earlier Dutch ports they had visited.[26]

The French stayed nine months in Java while d'Auribeau organised the sale of *La Recherche* and *L'Esperance*. Shortly before the deal was finally signed, d'Auribeau also became ill with dysentery and died, as so many others had in disease-ridden Batavia, where he had gone to sign the deal. Command of the French expedition now fell to the twenty-nine-year-old aristocrat Elisabeth-Paul-Edouard Rossel, who, like his three predecessors, remained loyal to the monarchy despite the Revolution in France.

On 5 December 1794 the remnants of the D'Entrecasteaux expedition began their homeward journey via Batavia, where a further twenty-four crew died. Not all the French left; some decided to stay on in the Dutch East Indies, accepting enticing offers to work for the Dutch.

Those heading back to France sailed on a number of different ships. Rossel, the last leader of the expedition, was on a Dutch ship that left Batavia in December 1795. Between St Helena, in the North Atlantic, and the English Channel he was captured by the English and taken to London, along with more than ninety cases of the surviving documents of the D'Entrecasteaux expedition. Rossel remained loyal to the fallen French monarchy and happily stayed in self-imposed exile in England for seven years before he returned to France in 1802. His account of the D'Entrecasteaux expedition was published in 1808.

The D'Entrecasteaux expedition was successful in expanding the geographic knowledge of Australia, particularly that of south-east Van Diemen's Land and around Esperance, in Western Australia. However, it found no evidence of the lost explorer La Pérouse, which had been the primary purpose of the venture, and its discoveries came at a very high human cost. Of the original 219 crew, eighty-nine had died before they reached the French-controlled island of Mauritius, and when later fatalities are considered, the death rate, which included three of the expedition's leaders, probably exceeded forty per cent.

Seven years after the D'Entrecasteaux expedition, the French sent another major expedition, under the command of Nicolas Baudin, to explore Australia. Meanwhile,

before all the survivors of D'Entrecasteaux's venture had
arrived back in France, the English sent a ship to Sydney
with a young officer aboard who would become famous
for his exploration of Australia.

CHAPTER 5

MATTHEW FLINDERS

*M*atthew Flinders was born in Lincolnshire on 16 March 1774, the eldest son of a well-established local doctor and one of ten children, of whom only he, three sisters and his younger brother, Samuel, survived.

Flinders was slight like his father, but he appears to have made up for it with his doggedness and determination. As a boy Flinders was described as 'lively and healthy', and in his early years at school he was regarded as very bright, which encouraged his father to allow him to continue his studies.[1] For three years from the age of twelve, he studied Latin and Greek at Horbling Grammar School; then he started, but did not finish, studies to be a doctor. Flinders chose not to follow in his father's footsteps, saying many years later, '[I was] induced to go to sea against the wishes of my friends, from reading *Robinson Crusoe*.'[2] Daniel Defoe's *Robinson Crusoe* had been published in England sixty years before but was still very popular. Europe was in the Age of Enlightenment, which saw a plethora of scientific discoveries, rapid industrialisation and developments in philosophy, literature, music and the arts. At the same time, the British and their French rivals – who had replaced Portugal, Spain and the Netherlands as the dominant sea powers – were organising explorations of the remotest parts of the world. So the British Royal Navy was at the forefront of world exploration, and Flinders would no doubt have realised that if he joined, great opportunities would be open to him.

Flinders's cousin John, who had already spent eleven years in the navy, said he had 'slender hopes of attaining to a lieutenant's commission' and advised Flinders that he 'had little chance . . . of success in the Navy without powerful interest'.[3] Undaunted, Matthew threw himself into a year of studying trigonometry and navigation, and at the age of sixteen applied to join the navy. With the help of a female cousin who taught the daughters of Vice Admiral Thomas Pasley, Matthew Flinders was given an interview with him. Flinders first joined Pasley's ship the *Scipio* as a lieutenant's servant, before following Pasley onto the warship *Bellerophon*.[4] Pasley – who would later be made a baronet and lose a leg in a sea battle against the French – would become a valuable supporter of the young explorer Matthew Flinders.

After serving on the *Scipio*, the *Bellerophon* and then the *Dictator*, seventeen-year-old Flinders transferred to sail with Captain William Bligh on the *Providence* on a two-year expedition to the South Pacific. Bligh was making a second attempt to collect breadfruit from the region after an earlier attempt had been thwarted by the mutiny on the *Bounty* two years before.

At thirty-six years old, William Bligh was already a vastly experienced captain and navigator. The son of a boatman, he had been signed up for the Royal Navy at the age of seven. When he was sixteen, he joined the *Hunter* as an able seaman, until, having served on a number of ships, he was made a midshipman. In 1776, at twenty-two, he was appointed master on Captain Cook's ship *Resolution*, which, accompanied by the *Discovery*, embarked on the great navigator's third and final expedition to the north Pacific. It was on the way home in February 1779 that Cook was killed in Hawaii.

Bligh was appointed commander of the *Bounty* in 1787. His instructions were to sail to the South Pacific to collect samples of the breadfruit plant and take them to the West Indies, where it was hoped the fruit could be grown as a cheap and nutritious source of food for the slaves working on sugar plantations. The English had first been made aware of the breadfruit by the English pirate William Dampier a hundred years before, and later by Captain Cook on his first voyage to the South Pacific, in 1768.

It was after collecting the breadfruit, on the way to deliver them to the West Indies, that the *Bounty*'s crew mutinied. Bligh and eighteen of his loyal crew were put over the side of the *Bounty* into a small cutter with a sextant, compass and timekeeper; and somehow, without maps, they managed to safely reach Timor, 4000 kilometres away. Meanwhile the mutineers sailed back to Tahiti, where some of them decided to stay, while Fletcher Christian and the others continued east to the uncharted Pitcairn Island, where they scuttled the *Bounty* and established a new settlement.

After he reached England, Bligh was acquitted – and exonerated – at a court martial. Then, partly thanks to the familiar patronage of Sir Joseph Banks, who had become highly influential in the appointment of commanders of exploration expeditions, Bligh was given another chance to collect breadfruit from the Pacific islands.

For the second expedition, he was given two ships, the *Providence* and the *Assistant*. The *Providence* was a new 400-ton, three-decked ship designed for heavy cargoes. It had twenty-eight guns and a crew of 200, including twenty marines to keep order – security Bligh did not have on the much smaller *Bounty*. The accompanying *Assistant* was a quarter the size of the *Providence* and carried a crew of only twenty-seven.

Matthew Flinders was excited about the opportunity of an adventure in the South Seas and was helped with a transfer to the *Providence* by his old captain of the *Bellerophon*, Thomas Pasley, who wrote to wish the seventeen-year-old well:

> I have little doubt of your gaining the good opinion
> of Captain Bligh if you are equally attentive to your
> duty there as you were in the *Bellerophon* – all that
> I have to request in return for the good offices I have
> done you, is that you never fail writing me by all
> possible opportunities during your voyage.[5]

The *Providence* and the *Assistant* sailed from Deptford, on the mouth of the River Thames, on 2 August 1791. After making what was a fairly routine stop at the Canary Islands to restock fresh water and provisions, they headed for the Cape of Good Hope and arrived in October. Among the many ships in the harbour was the *Waaksamheyd*, which had been chartered in Sydney by Arthur Phillip to take home to England his deputy, Captain John Hunter, and his crew.

There is no record of the very young and junior midshipman Flinders meeting the far more senior Hunter, who four years later became his staunch supporter. However, while Flinders may not have met Hunter, Bligh certainly did – and he was not very impressed by the deputy leader of the expedition that had established Britain's penal colony in New South Wales. In a letter sent from Cape Town to his friend and mentor in London Sir Joseph Banks, Bligh wrote that Hunter did not have the qualities necessary for his current position:

> I may pronounce with some certainly that the present second in command [of New South Wales] . . . is not blessed with a moderate share of good knowledge to give such stability to the new settlement.[6]

Bligh, of course, had no idea that within four years Hunter would be sent back to New South Wales to become Arthur Phillip's replacement and that Bligh himself would follow him into the same office ten years later.

Captain Bligh left the cape two days before Christmas, and after six weeks' sailing across the Great Southern Ocean his ships reached Van Diemen's Land on 9 February 1792. It was Flinders's first time in Australian waters but Bligh's third, as he had been with Cook sixteen years before to Van Diemen's Land on the *Discovery*, and again on the *Bounty* in 1789.

The ships gathered fresh drinking water and firewood, and botanists James Wiles and Christopher Smith planted some fruit trees and collected some new specimens of plants, before Bligh ordered the ships to sail on 24 February 1792. Flinders had by then become good friends with Wiles and Smith, and on this trip he learned a great deal from them about botany that would be useful to him in later explorations.

Bligh had no orders to sail north to visit the convict colony that had been established four years before in Sydney; instead he went east-south-east, circumventing New Zealand, and headed directly for Tahiti to collect the breadfruit plants. He would have been apprehensive about returning to Tahiti, because he had attributed the cause of the mutiny on the *Bounty* to the good times his crew had spent there:

> The women are handsome . . . and have sufficient delicacy to make them admired and beloved. The chiefs have taken such a liking to our people that they have rather encouraged their stay among them than otherwise, and even made promises of large possessions. Under these and many other attendant circumstances equally desirable it is therefore now not to be wondered at . . . that a set of sailors led by officers and void of connections . . . should be governed by such powerful inducement . . . to fix themselves in the midst of plenty in the finest island in the world where they need not labour, and where the allurements of dissipation are more than equal to anything that can be conceived.[7]

Before reaching the islands, Bligh ordered all the ratings (ordinary seamen) be examined for venereal disease, which he did not want spread among the locals. Bligh recorded in his journal that five men were infected, but the figure could have been higher and may have included officers, who were not subject to the compulsory medical checks. The seventeen-year-old Matthew Flinders may not have been infected when he arrived, but the pay book of the *Providence* shows that he was twice charged for treatment for venereal disease, which was thirty shillings, or the equivalent of two weeks' pay.[8] The most common venereal disease at the time was syphilis, and the most regular treatment involved applying mercury like an ointment to the affected area. Seafarers were regular users of prostitutes in the various ports they visited, and by the

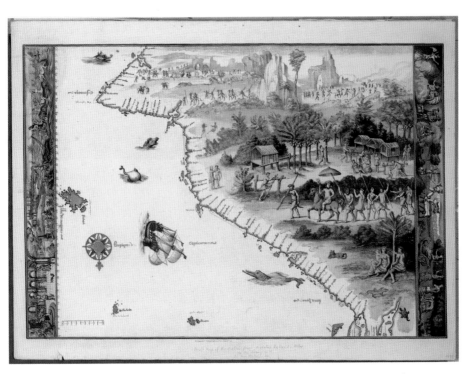

This map by Frenchman Nicholas Vallard, published in 1547, is one of a number of so-called Dieppe maps, named after the French port city where they were drawn. Some historians believe the maps, including this one (with south at the top), resemble the Australian coastline and provide evidence that the Portuguese had charted much of the coast up to one hundred years before the first Dutch landing in the north of Australia in 1606. Others, however, disagree, saying that the features on the Dieppe maps could also be applied to coastlines in Asia.

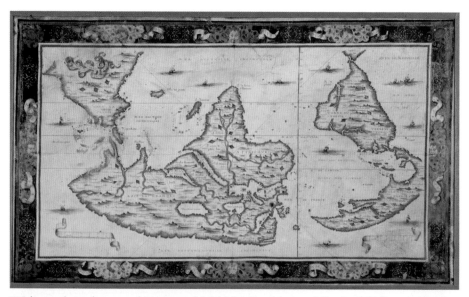

With south at the top, this map of 1566 by Frenchman Nicolas Desliens provides an interesting view of how Europeans saw the world – and the unknown great south land – in the mid-sixteenth century.

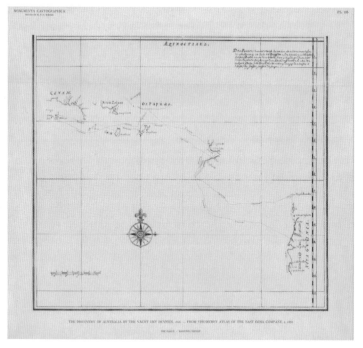

The track of the *Duyfken* in 1606. Dutchman Willem Janszoon sailed for about three hundred kilometres down the eastern side of the Gulf of Carpentaria on the Dutch East Indies ship the *Duyfken*. At the time, Janszoon was unaware he was the first European on Australian soil, instead assuming he had landed on the New Guinea coast.

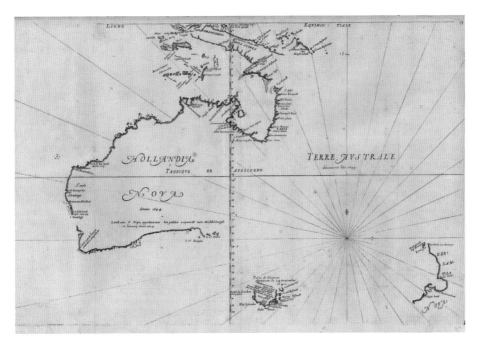

'Hollandia Nova' by Melchisédech Thévenot, 1663. This map shows the extent of Dutch charting of Australia until Abel Tasman's expeditions in 1642 and 1644. Much of the south coast and all the east coast is undiscovered, and Van Diemen's Land is thought to be part of the mainland. Also, New Guinea appears to be connected to New Holland because the Spanish have kept secret the discovery in 1606 by Luis Váez de Torres of the strait named after him.

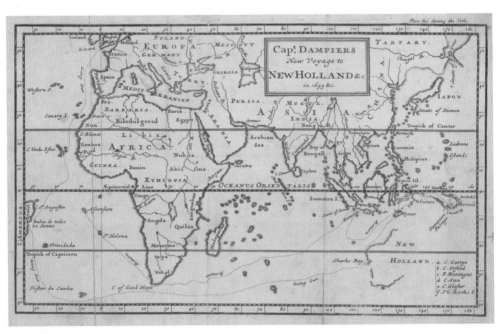

Map of William Dampier's second circumnavigation of the world in 1699. In 1688 Dampier became the first recorded Englishman to reach the Australian mainland. He returned there in 1699 as the commander of a British naval expedition.

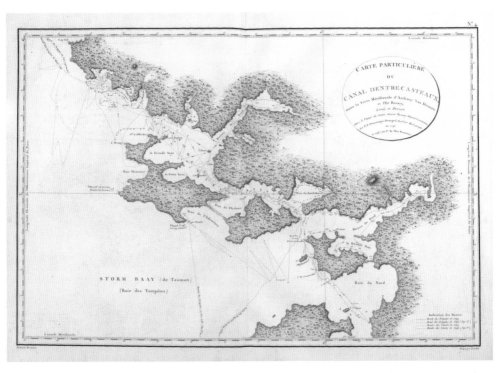

Map of the south-east coast of Tasmania drawn by Charles-François Beautemps-Beaupré on Bruni D'Entrecasteaux's expedition, 1792. The charts of Van Diemen's Land by D'Entrecasteaux's cartographer Beautemps-Beaupré were of such high quality that they were used by European countries for many years.

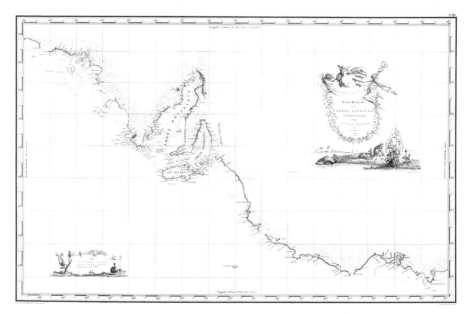

Map of the 'unknown' south coast by Louis-Claude Freycinet. The French expedition led by Nicolas Baudin explored the Spencer Gulf and the Gulf of St Vincent after Matthew Flinders had done so. After Baudin's death, his maps were eventually completed by Freycinet. On these French maps, the gulfs were named Bonaparte Golfe and Golfe Josephine, to Flinders's great annoyance.

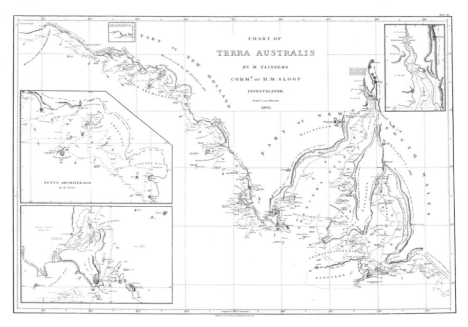

Matthew Flinders was the first to chart the southern coast of Australia and to confirm the west and east coasts of the continent were part of the same land and not separated by water. However, his first complete map of Australia was not published until 1814, three years after Freycinet's.

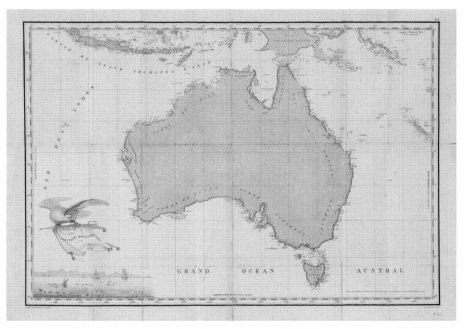

Louis-Claude Freycinet's completed 'Carte Générale de la Nouvelle Hollande', 1811.

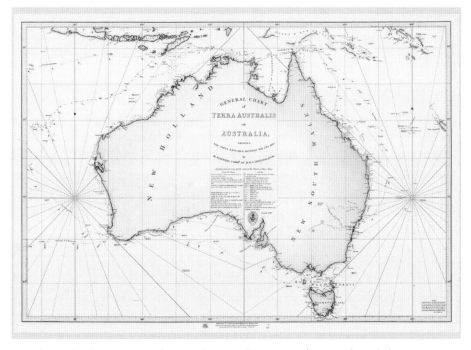

Matthew Flinders prepared a nearly complete map of Australia while imprisoned by the French on the island of Mauritius in 1804. The completed map reached England the following year but was not published until 1814, well after Flinders had returned to London and added the details and place names.

In 1606 Dutchman Willem Janszoon was sent to search 'the vast land of Nova Guinea and other east and south lands'. He was the first known European to land on Australian soil, on what is today the Cape York Peninsula. However, he was unaware he'd discovered a new continent; he thought the land was an extension of the New Guinea coast.

LUIS VAES DE TORRES 1606

Artist's proof. H "Torres passing New Guinea"

Also in 1606, Spaniard Luis Váez de Torres was the first European to sail through the strait that separates Australia from New Guinea. The Spanish kept the discovery a secret from their European rivals for 150 years.

end of the eighteenth century were a major cause of the spread of sexually transmitted diseases around the world.[9]

The two ships anchored in Tahiti's Matavai Bay on 4 April 1792. Bligh quickly established a fenced garden on the island, where several thousand small breadfruit and other plants were put into pots, tubs and boxes. When Bligh left Tahiti three months later, the plants loaded on board the *Providence* completely filled the great cabin – and both sides of quarterdeck, leaving only a narrow passage down the middle for the crew to walk through.

Next Bligh headed for the Cook Islands, Tonga and Fiji, which Flinders described as 'the most beautiful islands' they had yet seen.[10] In late September they reached the Torres Strait, at the northernmost tip of Australia, where Bligh had been in an open boat two years before, after the mutiny on the *Bounty*. It was while sailing through the South Pacific and the Torres Strait that Matthew Flinders drew his first maps, which were signed by his captain, William Bligh, and initialled by Flinders.[11]

They passed close to the point where a year before, in August 1791, the *Pandora*, which had been sent to capture the *Bounty*'s mutineers, had been wrecked on the Great Barrier Reef when trying to pass through the strait.

While they were in the Torres Strait, the *Providence* and the *Assistant* were attacked by Aboriginals in four sailboats. The British repelled them with gunfire, but Flinders was impressed by his first real encounter with the indigenous Australians:

> No boats could have been manoeuvred better, in working to windward, than were these long canoes by the naked savages. Had the four been able to reach the cutter, it is difficult to say whether the superiority of our arms would have been equal to the great difference of numbers, considering the

ferocity of the people, and the skill with which they
seemed to manage their weapons.[12]

Because of adverse winds, the sailing was slow and Bligh
cut back the ration to one pint of drinking water per day
per man to ensure there was enough water for the breadfruit plants. His men were reportedly so thirsty that they
'would lie on the steps, and lick the drops of the precious
liquid from the buckets, as they were conveyed by the
gardener to the plants'.[13] Many of the crew thought Bligh's
actions unfair, and on one occasion someone switched the
water for the breadfruits with seawater, which sent Bligh
into a rage.[14]

They reached Timor in October and spent the next
eight days stocking up on fresh water and food. The stop
at the notoriously unhealthy port resulted in a number of
crew contracting dysentery, which caused the death of the
quartermaster and two other crewmen.

From Timor the two ships crossed the Indian Ocean,
rounded the Cape of Good Hope and headed north
through the Atlantic, where they stopped briefly at
the British-controlled island of St Helena, which years
later would be the last residence of the exiled Napoleon
Bonaparte.

On 17 December the *Providence* and the *Assistant* finally
arrived at Kingstown – on the island of St Vincent, in the
West Indies – where they unloaded the first of the breadfruit cargo. Over the next two months they dispatched
more plants to a number of British-controlled West Indian
ports. Botanist James Wiles stayed on in Jamaica, where
he took the job of supervisor of the government's botanical
gardens. He gave Matthew Flinders a letter authorising
Flinders to collect his back pay when he reached London
and to hand it over to his father. The other botanist,
Christopher Smith, stayed on board the *Providence* to

take the balance of more than 1000 plants back to Kew
Gardens, in England.

While they were still in the West Indies, news arrived
in February 1793 that England had declared war on
France, and the *Providence* and *Assistant* were immediately assigned to the local Royal Navy command. Over
the next four months they patrolled the Caribbean, escort-
ing convoys and hunting down French ships.

In June, following the arrival of reinforcements, Bligh was
finally ordered to sail home. The ships and their remaining
crew arrived at Deptford on 7 August. Having been away
for two years and five days, Flinders had come back safely,
to the relief and gratitude of his father, who wrote in his
diary, 'By the Mercy and Divine Providence of God – my
son hath safe returned from his long and perilous voyage.'[15]

To date this had been Flinders's most extensive expedition by far; he had gained valuable experience and vastly
expanded his skills in navigation, surveying and seaman-
ship. But he was unimpressed by his commander, Captain
Bligh. Flinders must have discussed Bligh with his father,
who recorded in his diary after his son returned that Flinders
'was not on the best of terms with [Bligh], which was an
unpleasant circumstance'.[16] Many years later, Flinders
complained that Bligh had looked at him 'with an unfavourable eye', but he never explained why Bligh disliked
him.[17] He also accused Bligh of taking the credit for his
own achievements and wrote that he hoped in future he
would 'not be placed under his immediate orders, since the
credit, if any [which] should be due to my labours, would
be in danger of being monopolised'.[18]

Flinders and his colleagues came back to a Europe in
turmoil following the Revolution in France. Wars had
already broken out between France and many of its neighbours: the Austrian Netherlands (current-day Belgium);
and Savoy, Nice and the papal fiefdom of Avignon (in

current-day France). Very soon all the old monarchies of Europe – Britain, Austria and Prussia – were in a coalition to fight the new republic.

Flinders took several weeks' leave and had his first meeting with the legendary Sir Joseph Banks, at Banks's country estate, Revesby Abbey, which was only thirty kilometres north of Flinders's home town of Donington, in Lincolnshire. Flinders was carrying to Banks the letter from his good friend James Wiles in which Wiles asked for his back pay from Banks. While history doesn't record how Flinders and Banks got on or what they discussed, it would have been a good opportunity for the young sailor to impress the great botanist.

By October, Flinders was back at sea on Captain Pasley's *Bellerophon* as part of the English Channel fleet under the command of Admiral Lord Richard Howe. By the end of the year Flinders had been involved in skirmishes during which 'a few shots were exchanged', but no major battles.[19] This was about to change. In April 1794 Captain Pasley was promoted to rear admiral, and he appointed Flinders as his aide-de-camp as the *Bellerophon* went into a famous naval battle against the French on 1 June 1794. Known to the British as 'the Glorious First of June' as well as the Battle of Ushant, the clash of the two fleets 700 kilometres west of the island of Ushant, on the French north-west coast, was the largest naval battle of the revolutionary wars.

During the fighting, the *Bellerophon* was badly damaged and Flinders witnessed Captain Pasley being struck by a cannonball, which took off his right leg.

Initially both sides claimed victory but had to withdraw their battered fleets to their own ports. However, the French fleet was seriously diminished, and the English were able to maintain an effective blockade of the English Channel for the duration of the war. After the battle, Flinders witnessed the celebrations back at Portsmouth, where two weeks later King George III came down from London to present Admiral Howe with a diamond-studded sword.

After the tumult died down, Flinders had to think of his future. He was now twenty years old and quite accomplished. He had sailed for two years around the world with Captain William Bligh and had fought in the thick of it against the French in the Glorious First of June battle. But he was still only a midshipman and lacked the requisite six years of sea duty to be considered for promotion to lieutenant.

But he was lucky, because preparations were under way to take Captain John Hunter to Australia to become the replacement governor of New South Wales. Over at the Woolwich and Deptford shipyards, the *Reliance* and the *New Brunswick*, which was renamed the *Supply*, were being refitted for the long voyage to New South Wales. Flinders's good friend Henry Waterhouse had been appointed second captain to John Hunter on the *Reliance*, and he managed to secure for Flinders the position of first mate for the voyage.

*

In February 1795 fifty-eight-year-old bachelor Captain John Hunter boarded the *Reliance* in Portsmouth for his second voyage to New South Wales. Hunter had been back in England for three years. Over the next five years, as governor he would be responsible for significant new explorations of the east coast – about 1000 kilometres to the north and an even greater distance to the south, including Van Diemen's Land.

Also sailing on the *Reliance* were three young officers who would become close friends: Matthew Flinders, George Bass and Henry Waterhouse.

While Hunter was the most senior officer aboard, the command of the *Reliance* was given to twenty-five-year-old Waterhouse, who was also making his second voyage to New South Wales. The son of a page to the Duke of Cumberland, Waterhouse had joined the navy at a young age and served on a number of ships, including the *Bellerophon*, where he had first met Matthew Flinders.

Waterhouse was a veteran of Arthur Phillip's first fleet to Sydney and had been on Manly Beach in 1790 when Phillip was speared. Waterhouse had helped row the severely wounded and bleeding governor for several hours back to Sydney Cove for medical treatment. Waterhouse would prove to be a loyal friend to Flinders while they were in New South Wales but he did not have much enthusiasm for exploration and was happy to return to England in 1800.

At more than six feet tall, George Bass was a physically imposing twenty-four-year-old when he joined the *Reliance* as the ship's surgeon. The son of a Lincolnshire farmer who had died when he was six, Bass became apprenticed as a doctor before serving on a number of navy ships from the age of eighteen. It was not uncommon for the ship's doctor to be underqualified, as the job was far from attractive. But it would allow the enthusiastic Bass to travel to the South Seas and the Pacific, which had fascinated him since he read about them as a boy. In addition to his books and medical instruments, Bass boarded the *Reliance* with his thirteen-year-old servant boy, William Martin, who would later go with Bass and Flinders on some of their early explorations in New South Wales.

Bass impressed his boss, John Hunter, who said that the young man 'had so much ability in various ways out of the way of his [medical] profession'.[20] In addition to having studied medicine, Bass was a self-taught naturalist with a strong interest in botany and zoology. He wrote the first taxonomic description of the wombat and the white-capped albatross, and said he went to Australia with the 'intention of exploring more of the country' than any of his predecessors.[21] Bass shared Flinders's fascination with exploration and had collected many books about voyages in the Pacific.

At twenty-one, Matthew Flinders was two and three years younger than George Bass and Henry Waterhouse respectively. On the *Reliance* he would be making the second of three voyages that would take him to Australia. Flinders was excited about going to the Great South Land again, and later he said the appointment suited his 'passion for exploring new countries and . . . presented the most ample field' for his 'favourite pursuit'.[22]

The man who would send Flinders on his first famous exploration, John Hunter, had been born in Leith, Scotland, in 1737, the son of a shipmaster. He had gone to sea as a sixteen-year-old captain's servant before becoming a seaman and then a midshipman. He passed his exams to become a lieutenant in 1770 – but, as a man without a fortune, his rise was long and slow, and he was not given his first commission for another decade, in 1780. During his naval career he served in a variety of places, including North America during the War of Independence, the West Indies and the East Indies.

In 1787, when Arthur Phillip was appointed to take the first fleet of eleven ships to settle the convict colony in Botany Bay, Hunter was appointed his deputy and given command of the flagship *Sirius*. A year after reaching Sydney in 1788, and with the colony desperately short of food, Phillip sent Hunter on the *Sirius* via Cape Horn to the Cape of Good Hope to fetch a shipload of grain. Hunter returned to Sydney in May 1789 after a difficult seven months' voyage, having circumnavigated the globe.

He was again given command of the *Sirius* the following year, and it was wrecked on Norfolk Island. The loss of the flagship was a terrible blow to the fledgling convict settlement, as almost all the other vessels of the first fleet had by then returned to England. The only ship left in Sydney was the *Supply*, which, at twenty-one metres long, was a small vessel. Hunter and the crew of the *Sirius* were stranded on Norfolk Island for eleven months before being rescued and taken back to Sydney in December 1790.

Four months later, in March 1791, Hunter was among the first officials to leave the new colony to go home to England via Batavia and Cape Town – which was where he met Captain William Bligh – arriving at Portsmouth in April 1792. On his arrival he was exonerated at a court martial for the loss of the *Sirius*.

Hunter arrived home to find England again at war with France and went to sea on the flagship *Queen Charlotte*, commanded by Admiral Sir Roger Curtis, who was sailing against the French in the English Channel.[23] After Arthur Phillip had finally been given permission to come home, it was Admiral Sir Roger Curtis and Lord Richard Howe who helped promote Hunter to win the appointment as the second governor of New South Wales.

*

Before Matthew Flinders set off on his second long voyage to the other side of the world, this time with Hunter, he was granted three weeks' leave. At home, in Donington, he was reacquainted with one of his sisters' friends, Ann Chappell, whom he would marry six years later, when he finally returned from New South Wales. Ann Chappell was a small, slim young woman with dark curly hair. She was three and a half years older than Flinders and lived in the town of Spilsby, close to where the Flinders family lived.[24] Her father, John, had been a ship-owner sea captain who traded in the Baltic Sea out of the port of Hull. He had died at sea when Ann was four years old and after his death her mother married the Reverend William Tyler, who was the rector of Brothertoft, about twelve kilometres from Flinders's home in Donington.

When Flinders boarded the *Reliance* in September 1794, he arranged with Henry Waterhouse for his eleven-year-old brother, Samuel, to join the crew as a volunteer, in which role he would earn six pounds a year. While it was not uncommon for boys to go to sea at such a young age to learn the ropes, Flinders's father noted rather sadly in his diary that not only would this voyage be much longer than Matthew's earlier two-year expedition with William Bligh, but he would now be saying goodbye to two sons:

> My son Samuel having for some time expressed the desire for the sea – and Matthew wishing to take him and Captain [Waterhouse] being consulted and willing to take him also, I have advanced £30 to Matthew to fit him out and he is gone with him and is to go on the voyage – Pray Heaven bless them both . . . he is very young (12 in November).[25]

By the end of the year, the *Reliance* had been moved from the mouth of the Thames to Portsmouth, on the south coast, where the loading of supplies for the long voyage to Australia was completed. Also with Captain John Hunter on board, on a return voyage to Sydney, was the Aboriginal man Bennelong, who had been taken to London two years before by the returning governor Arthur Phillip. Shortly after the arrival of the first fleet, Phillip had conscripted Bennelong in Sydney to help the British communicate with the Aboriginal people, with whom relations were already deteriorating. Bennelong was believed to have been about twenty-five at the time.

Bennelong had adapted more readily to the white man's environment than most of his people, and for much of the time seemed happy among the English. As marine lieutenant Watkin Tench observed, Bennelong wore the white men's clothes and enjoyed their food, particularly the grog.

> He became at once fond of our viands [food] and would drink the strongest liquors, not simply without reluctance, but with eager marks of delight. He was the only native we knew who immediately showed a fondness for spirits.[26]

Bennelong had arrived in England in May 1793 on the *Atlantic* with an Aboriginal boy named Yemmerrawannie, two freed convicts, four kangaroos and several dingoes. The two Aboriginal men were a novelty in England but were by no means unique, as the practice of bringing back people from the New World for exhibition in Europe was by then long established.

One of the few newspaper reports of their arrival gave an unflattering account of the Australians:

> Governor Philip [*sic*] has brought home with him two natives from New Holland, a man and a boy, and brought them to town. The Atlantic has on board four kangaroos, lively and healthy, and some other animals peculiar to that country. From the description given [of] the natives of Jackson Bay they appear to be a race totally incapable of civilisation, every attempt at that end having proved ineffectual . . . no inducement, and every means have been perseveringly tried, can draw them from a state of nature.[27]

The two Aboriginal men were taken to see St Paul's Cathedral, the Tower of London, the theatre and the beach, and for a boat ride on the Thames. They were taken to the tailor and fitted out with silk stockings and blue and buff striped waistcoats, and were presented to Colonial Secretary Lord Sydney.[28] It is also believed they were presented to King George III, but there is no surviving record of the encounter.

Yemmerrawannie became ill towards the end of the first year, and he died five months later, on 18 May 1794. He was buried at the Eltham Anglican church, in southeast London. While the cause of his death is not known for sure, it is thought to have been tuberculosis.

While Bennelong seems to have been reasonably happy in London, he increasingly wanted to go home after the death of Yemmerrawannie and was eventually able to secure passage on the *Reliance*. Even while the ships were still in port and waiting for orders to go, Captain Hunter expressed concern at the declining health of Bennelong:

> Disappointment has much broken his spirit, and the coolness of the weather here has so frequently laid him up that I am apprehensive his lungs are affected – that was the cause of the other's [Yemmerrawannie's] death.[29]

Indeed, when Bennelong finally reached Sydney he was drinking heavily; and once the ship landed, he constantly fell into fights, including with the man who had taken up with his wife during his absence in England. By the early nineteenth century he was living on the north side of Sydney near current-day Ryde, in Wallumedegal country. He died a rather sad figure in 1813, at about fifty years old.

*

The *Reliance* eventually left Portsmouth on 16 February 1795, part of a huge convoy protected by the warships of Lord Howe's English Channel fleet until it had passed the threat of attack by French warships. Once out in the Atlantic, the convoy began to split up as the ships headed off to different destinations.

The *Reliance* and the *Supply* headed first for Tenerife, in the Portuguese-controlled Canary Islands. Flinders had been to Tenerife three years before, when he had sailed on the *Providence* with Captain Bligh. He had observed then that the locals were 'courteous to and appear happy to see strangers' and that fresh fruit was 'fine and in great plenty'.[30] This time, from the island he sent home a letter to two of his sisters and his sweetheart, Ann Chappell, reassuring them about the wellbeing of his younger brother, Samuel, who had turned twelve a few months before they left England:

> My little Samuel on board the *Reliance* stood the gales and the wind exceedingly well, he is in high spirits and has lost no part of that enterprising spirit which brought him on board with me, I hope he will make a good sailor, a good officer, and a good man, which last is the groundwork of the other two and the foundation of all happiness.[31]

After leaving Tenerife, they sailed across the Atlantic to Rio de Janeiro, where Flinders was given permission to land on the small island in the bay to practise navigational calculations. In Rio, his friend Henry Waterhouse gave him an unexpected, but not exceptional, promotion to acting lieutenant, which was made permanent six months later.[32]

Leaving Rio, Hunter decided against the usual stop at the Dutch-controlled port at the Cape of Good Hope.

The French had recently invaded the Netherlands, and he feared they may also seize this strategic Dutch-held port at the southern tip of Africa.

Thus on 7 September 1795, after a voyage of seven months, the crew of the *Reliance* sighted Sydney Heads and the settlement where Matthew Flinders would start the explorations that would make him famous.

CHAPTER 6

GEORGE BASS AND MATTHEW FLINDERS

*W*hen Matthew Flinders reached Sydney for the first time, in 1795, the tiny convict settlement was less than eight years old, with a population of barely 3000 people. It had only one reasonable road, directly west to the more fertile farming lands of Parramatta and Toongabbie, and the rest were rough tracks or paths. There was now a brickworks, but most of the dwellings were still crude constructions of timber and bark. With the limited amount of fertile soil around Sydney and the failure of the early harvests, the settlement was still heavily dependent on ships arriving from England with food and other provisions.[1] The colony had no treasury and no official local currency, and the only coinage was that brought in by individuals. Clothing and other provisions supplied through the government stores were brought in by trading ships and paid for with British treasury bills, which traders could later redeem from the British government.

After the departure of Arthur Phillip, under first Francis Grose and then William Paterson as acting governor, the local military had increasingly taken control of the colony's economy. By the time John Hunter arrived, the marines dominated most trade and monopolised imports, particularly of grog, which they then resold locally at exorbitant prices. Hunter would be the first of a line of governors, which included William Bligh and Lachlan Macquarie, who tried to break the stranglehold on commerce held by the New South Wales Corps.

As Matthew Flinders noted on his arrival, not only was Sydney still a small place but practically nothing was known of the coast of New South Wales beyond about a thirty-kilometre circumference:[2]

> On arriving at Port Jackson, in September . . . it appeared that the investigation of the coast had not been greatly extended beyond the three harbours; and even in these, some of the rivers were not altogether explored. Jervis Bay, [to the south] . . . and to the north, Port Stephens had lately been examined . . . but the intermediate portions of the coast, both to the north and south, were little further known than from Captain Cook's general chart; and none of the more distant openings, marked but not explored by that celebrated navigator, had been seen.[3]

Only a month after arriving in Sydney, Flinders and his friend George Bass proposed to Governor Hunter that they undertake an exploration of the rivers and bays south of Sydney. With Hunter's blessing, on 26 October the two young men embarked on what was probably the smallest expedition in British exploration history – to survey Botany Bay, twelve kilometres south of Sydney, which had been the original destination of the first fleet of convicts.

England was again at war with France, which gave it little opportunity to focus on the exploration of the country surrounding its tiny convict colony on the far side of the world.[4] While he was governor, John Hunter had tried to rally support in England for more exploration but was told by Sir Joseph Banks that it was out of the question:

> The situation in Europe is at present so critical and His Majesty's Ministers so fully employed in business of the deepest importance, that it is scarce possible to gain a moment's audience on any subject, but those which stand foremost in their mind and colonies of all kinds, you may be assured, are now put in to the background.[5]

Also there was a shortage of shipping in Sydney, and ship-building was restricted for fear vessels would be stolen and used by convicts to escape. So the only boat available to Flinders and Bass was a dinghy from the *Reliance* that was less than three metres long and two metres wide. Naming the tiny boat *Tom Thumb*, Bass and Flinders sailed south from the Port Jackson heads, rounded Cape Banks and came across Botany Bay to the Georges River, which opens into the south-west of the bay. Pushing another thirty kilometres up the river, where they were able to sail the tiny *Tom Thumb* further, they found a wooded area and what appeared to be fertile soil. On their return they wrote a report of their favourable findings. Encouraged, Governor Hunter visited the area, and two years later he established a town he named Bankstown, after Sir Joseph Banks.

On his return, Flinders was assigned to duty back on the *Reliance*, where the sailors lived as there was a shortage of houses in the Sydney settlement. In January the following year he sailed on the *Reliance* to take supplies to the settlement on Norfolk Island, about 1000 kilometres to the north-east.

When Flinders reached Norfolk Island he met Philip King, who was on his second tour of duty as the governor of the tiny island settlement. On his first tour, when he had been sent by Arthur Phillip from Sydney to establish a British presence, King had done what many officers in the early days of the colony did and had taken up with a convict woman, Ann Inett, who had borne him two sons. She had been convicted in 1786 in the Worcester Court for stealing a petticoat, two aprons, a pair of shoes, five handkerchiefs, a silk hood and other clothing with a total value of a little under a pound.

After two years on Norfolk Island, King returned to England, where he married a woman called Anna Josepha Coombe. On this second tour back to the island, he brought Anna with him and went on to have three children with her: Philip, Maria and Elizabeth. Nevertheless, he continued to care for his first two boys, Norfolk and Sydney, both of whom eventually became officers in the navy.

When Flinders and King met on Norfolk Island, neither man knew that seven years later they would both be back in Australia and their collaboration would be critical for the completion of the navigation of the continent.

Back in Sydney from Norfolk Island, Flinders once more teamed up with his friend George Bass and – again with John Hunter's blessing – they left on 25 March on a second expedition to explore a river that was believed to enter the sea south of Botany Bay but did not appear on Cook's maps. This time they took a slightly larger boat that had recently been built in Port Jackson for the governor. Nonetheless, it was only about twelve feet long, so they again named it *Tom Thumb*.[6] Over the next five days – in high seas in which the little boat was almost sunk and their provisions nearly lost – Flinders first charted Port Hacking River and, further south, what he named Tom Thumb Lagoon, which would later become Lake Illawarra, south of current-day Wollongong.[7]

The charts Flinders drew were taken back to London early the following year by Major William Paterson, who was returning to England after six years in the colony. Three years later, while Flinders was still in Australia, his maps were included in the publication of an atlas of New South Wales.[8] For Flinders, who was still only twenty-five, this was recognition and prestige that mattered.

Back in Sydney, he again returned to work on the *Reliance*, while Bass made an unsuccessful attempt to become the first European to cross the Blue Mountains, to the west of the settlement of Sydney. The first attempt to cross the mountains had been made in the second year of settlement. There had always been speculation as to what lay on the other side, including the possibility of a giant inland sea or a strait that separated the land mass of New Holland in the west and New South Wales in the east. But now there was a more pressing need to cross. The Sydney basin, which extended about one hundred kilometres to the north, west and south, had only a limited amount of fertile soil; and it was hoped more could be found on the other side to support the colony's anticipated growth in population.

For his attempted crossing of the mountains, Bass took two reliable seamen and used boathooks to climb the steep rock faces and ropes to descend into ravines. After fifteen days he returned, fatigued, to Sydney, having found no food or water and declaring the mountains impassable.[9]

Bass's failure, and the failure of other attempts, led to the widespread belief that the Blue Mountains could never be breached. As late at 1812, after Flinders had returned to England, he told a House of Commons committee that the mountains 'cannot be penetrated' from Port Jackson.[10] It was not until 1813 that the range was successfully crossed, by Gregory Blaxland, William Charles Wentworth and William Lawson.

Any hope of further exploration by Flinders and Bass in 1796 was dashed when Governor Hunter ordered both men to go with Henry Waterhouse on a long voyage on the *Reliance*. There was still a serious shortage of farm animals in New South Wales, so the *Reliance* and the *Supply* were ordered to the Cape of Good Hope to fetch cows, sheep, horses and goats. Hunter was familiar with the route, having been ordered by Arthur Phillip to sail there himself to fetch grain on the *Sirius* eight years before, in 1788, when the fledgling convict colony was starving at the end of the first year of settlement. The voyage would involve circumnavigating the globe by sailing east below the southern tip of America to Africa, then back across the Great Southern Ocean.

After leaving Sydney in September 1796, the *Reliance* and the *Supply* sailed east and under New Zealand, crossed the South Pacific past Cape Horn, then the south Atlantic, to reach the Cape of Good Hope in fewer than four months, arriving on 16 January 1797. Flinders had now completed six years of sailing and was eligible to apply for promotion to full lieutenant. In Cape Town, after Flinders successfully sat an examination, Henry Waterhouse recommended his promotion to the British commander of the cape, Rear Admiral Thomas Pringle. The results of the examination were sent back to the Admiralty in England, and Flinders's higher rank was approved the following year.

The *Reliance* and the *Supply* stayed for ten weeks in Table Bay, where they were refitted, repaired, and loaded with livestock and a large quantity of feed to keep the animals alive during the journey back to Sydney. In addition to purchasing about 250 cows, bulls and sheep, and dozens of horses and goats for the colony, the officers also bought animals for themselves. While there is no record of Flinders buying any livestock, George Bass bought himself a cow and nineteen sheep, and Captain Waterhouse some sheep. As the limited deck space was needed for the colony's purchases, many of the privately bought animals had to be accommodated in the officers' cabins.

The ships left the cape on 11 April 1797, and both struggled in the high seas. At one stage, the *Supply*'s captain, William Kent, said it was leaking so badly he feared it would sink.

Back in New South Wales, some of the officers sold their animals at a profit and others farmed them. Henry Waterhouse established his sheep on a farm west of Sydney between Bankstown and today's suburb of Strathfield, and later sold some to John Macarthur, an officer in the New South Wales Corps who was largely responsible for the early development of Australia's sheep industry.

With '31 cows, five mares, and 27 ewe sheep, all of them in good health' on board, the *Supply* returned to Sydney on 16 May, still some weeks before the arrival of *Reliance*. The next night, news came of another ship having been wrecked about 800 kilometres south of Port Jackson.[11]

On the night of 17 May a small boat fishing off the coast of Sydney brought back to Port Jackson three men the crew had seen waving for help from a beach about thirty kilometres south of Sydney. The three had walked more than 500 kilometres and explained they were the only survivors of seventeen who had set out to find help after the *Sydney Cove*, which was on its way to Sydney, had 'sprung a dangerous leak' and run aground on the Furneaux Group of islands, off the north coast of Van Diemen's Land, more than three months before.[12]

The three-masted *Begum Shaw* had been built in Calcutta for the carriage of rice. However, it was later bought by English traders, who renamed it the *Sydney Cove* and sent it with a cargo of food and spirits to sell to the fledgling colony in New South Wales. The cargo included tea, rice, sugar, salted meat, leather, tar, vinegar, candles, cloth, shoes, porcelain, 7000 gallons of rum, and livestock housed in specially built pens below deck. The *Sydney Cove* had left Calcutta on 10 November 1796, while Flinders and Bass were still on the *Reliance* in the south Atlantic on their way to Cape Town for livestock.

On 13 December the *Sydney Cove* had been damaged by heavy seas in the Great Southern Ocean and began taking water. On Christmas Day more damage was reported, and throughout January the ship required constant pumping. By the beginning of February the water was up to the lower deck hatches and the ship was in imminent danger of sinking. The ship's captain, Gavin 'Guy' Hamilton, managed to navigate his way into a sheltered cove of one of the Furneaux Group of islands. He successfully beached the stricken men on a small island, which would subsequently be called Preservation Island, and the salvaged cargo was taken ashore. The rum, however, was stored out of reach of the crew on a nearby islet, later named Rum Island. The entire crew survived the shipwreck, but four men died while the cargo was being transferred to the shore. The survivors were now marooned nearly 750 kilometres from Sydney.

On 28 February, nearly three weeks after the ship was beached, Captain Hamilton decided to send the ship's longboat to Sydney for help. The seventeen men who crowded into the little open boat were First Mate Hugh Thompson; the supercargo (who was responsible for the protection of the ship's cargo), William Clark; three European seamen; and twelve lascars, or Indian sailors.

The longboat headed across to the mainland but was wrecked off what is now Ninety Mile Beach, on the south-east coast of the Australian mainland, nearly 500 kilometres from Sydney.

With only limited supplies and no ammunition, the shipwrecked crew began the long walk north along the coast to fetch help from Sydney. After nearly three months, all but three – William Clark, seaman John Bennett and one of the lascars – had perished. On 15 May – when they had no provisions left and were about thirty kilometres short of Sydney, near Port Hacking – they were lucky enough to attract the attention of the fishing boat that was able to take them to Sydney.

Immediately after Clark and his colleagues recounted their story in Sydney, Governor Hunter sent the schooner *Francis* and the sloop *Eliza* to rescue the remaining survivors of the *Sydney Cove*. When the rescuers reached Preservation Island on 23 June, they found the *Sydney Cove* beyond repair and began to ferry its crew to Sydney. However, on the way back, the *Eliza* was separated and sank, with the loss of its crew and eight of the survivors of the *Sydney Cove*.

After reaching Sydney, the *Francis* would make two more trips to Preservation Island to salvage the stricken cargo of the *Sydney Cove*. Matthew Flinders managed to be aboard on the last trip and used it as an opportunity for exploration, as Hunter had given him 'directions to make such observations among the islands that he could'.[13] By now Governor Hunter had formed a strong and favourable view of Flinders's abilities, and also those of his good friend George Bass.

*

As the rescue of the *Sydney Cove* crew and cargo unfolded, Governor John Hunter decided it was time to properly chart the hazardous south coast, including Van Diemen's Land, and he gave the job to George Bass.

Bass left Sydney on 3 December 1797 on a longboat with a crew of six seamen chosen from the *Reliance* and the *Supply*. They had provisions for six weeks, but by fishing and shooting animals along the coast they planned to be able to stay away for some weeks longer.

Four hundred kilometres south of Sydney, Bass discovered Twofold Bay, which later became a prominent port for whaling ships and the site of the town of Eden. Sailing south, he passed Point Hicks where, nearly thirty years before, Captain James Cook had begun his exploration northward along the New South Wales coast.[14]

While passing the south-eastern tip of the continent, Bass came across seven escaped convicts who were stranded on a small offshore island. They had been part of a group of escapees who had stolen a boat in Sydney and were heading for the wreck of the *Sydney Cove*, which they hoped to plunder before returning to England. However, the convicts could not find the *Sydney Cove* and, running short of supplies, had left their seven colleagues on the island while they slept. For seven weeks they had survived by catching petrels and the occasional seal. Bass agreed to help them on the way back from his expedition.

He then sailed almost 1000 kilometres south of Sydney along the coast to where no European had sailed before. He charted as far as Wilsons Promontory, which he reached on New Year's Day, and then Westernport, which he reached on 4 January 1798.[15] It was here that he encountered strong currents and the Venturi effect – the speeding up of the flow of a fluid when its movement is constricted. As Bass realised, this is characteristic of a tidal current pushed between two bodies of land.[16] While not conclusive, it strengthened his belief that water separated Van Diemen's Land from the rest of New South Wales.[17]

Bass was now running short of supplies and decided to return to Sydney. On the way he called in on the seven convicts he had seen on the outward journey. He had enough room in his small boat to take back an old man and someone who was sick. He took the other five across to the mainland and left them a musket and ammunition, some hooks and lines for fishing, and a pot for cooking. He gave them directions as to how to walk to Sydney, but there is no record of any of them surviving.

After eighty-four days away, George Bass arrived back in Sydney on 25 February 1798, and an appreciative Governor Hunter granted him one hundred acres (forty hectares) of Crown land at Bankstown on the Georges River – the area Bass and Flinders had explored two years earlier.

By now Governor Hunter was also convinced that Van Diemen's Land was separate from the mainland, and to prove it conclusively he decided to send Flinders and Bass on their most important expedition yet: to circumnavigate Van Diemen's Land. However, it was now approaching the southern hemisphere winter, so it was not until September that Hunter ordered the two young explorers to prepare for the expedition.

Since Arthur Phillip had sailed with the first fleet to the east coast of Australia more than a decade before, the standard route to New South Wales from Europe had been south, under Van Diemen's Land, then north. For some years, different navigators speculated that a sea might separate Van Diemen's Land from the mainland. Governor John Hunter himself suspected it when in 1789 he was on his way back from an emergency voyage to Cape Town for food on the *Sirius* and experienced a strong easterly current and high seas, which led him to conjecture 'either a very deep gulf, or a straight [*sic*] . . . may separate Van Diemen's Land from New Holland'.[18] Hunter was well aware that a strait could significantly reduce the distance, time – and danger – of the journey between England and Sydney.

He wrote to the Admiralty in England telling them of his intention to send the expedition, adding that he already had charts from Flinders, and now Bass, which indicated Van Diemen's Land may be separate from the mainland.

> From this little sketch it will appear . . . that the high land in latitude 39 degrees . . . is the southern extremity of this country, and the land that is called Van Diemen's Land is a group of islands . . . probably leaving a safe and navigable passage between; to ascertain this is of some importance, I am endeavouring to fit out a decked boat of about fifteen tons burthen for that purpose, in which to send the two officers [Flinders and Bass].[19]

The boat chosen was a small sloop, the *Norfolk*, which had been built on Norfolk Island from local pine by Captain John Townson, who later became Philip King's successor as commandant of the island. When Bass and Flinders left Sydney on 7 October 1798, they were accompanied by a merchant ship, the *Nautilus*, which was heading south to hunt seal, for their skins. After six days of severe weather, they sheltered in Twofold Bay, where Bass had been the previous year on his exploration of the south coast on the whaleboat. On 14 October they sailed on, and a week later they reached the Furneaux Group of islands, and Cape Barren Island, where in early November George Bass became the first European to record seeing a wombat.

At Cape Barren Island, Captain Charles Bishop of the *Nautilus* set up camp and began hunting seals, while Flinders continued his westward journey, into strong headwinds, along the north coast of Van Diemen's Land. Bishop pitched tents on the island alongside fresh water 'about a mile' from the anchorage, and he planted a garden that 'produced some tolerable vegetables'.[20] Over the next few months the seal-hunting expedition proved extremely successful and Bishop got 9000 sealskins and several tons of oil, which he took to sell in China.[21]

Meanwhile, Flinders and Bass sailed south, where they named Cape Portland and Waterhouse Point, on the north coast of the island of Van Diemen's Land. Pressing further west than Bass had the year before, they found the mouth of a river, which would later be named the Tamar (the site of Launceston, where a British colony would be established by William Paterson six years later, in 1804). After leaving the river and re-entering the open sea, the little *Norfolk* was battered by powerful north-westerly winds and Flinders was forced to go back to Cape Barren Island, where he and the crew met up with the seal hunters from the *Nautilus*:

> We tried to beat back to the westward; but finding too much sea, bore away to speak to the commander of the Nautilus; that through him, Governor Hunter might be informed of our discoveries thus far, and of the delays experienced from the western winds. I was happy to find Captain Bishop proceeding successfully in the whaling business.[22]

As soon as 'a fair breeze' began to blow, Flinders made a second attempt at sailing westwards. While they headed along the coast, 'another gale sprung up from the north west' and 'it was happy circumstance' that they managed to reach their newly named port, Dalrymple, near current-day Launceston, where they took refuge. According to Flinders, the river provided 'an excellent place for refreshment', and they found fertile soil, kangaroos, black swans, ducks and plenty of other birds.[23]

On 4 December they resumed their westerly course, into the face of a strong north-west wind; they kept well off shore to avoid being blown onto the rocks. As they followed the coast in this north-westerly direction, Flinders began to fear that it might be only a large inlet and part of the southern coastline of New South Wales:

> This trending of the coast so far to the north made
> me apprehend, that it might be found to join the land
> near Western Port, and thus disappoint our hopes of
> discovering an open passage to the westward.[24]

Then, at the end of the first week of December, they noticed as they reached the north-west coast of Van Diemen's Land that the tide began coming from the west. They also saw that the shoreline tended to the south rather than to the north, in the direction of the New South Wales coast. Flinders was now satisfied they had at last confirmed that a strait separated the island from the mainland, and he named it the Basses Strait after his friend. He described how he and Bass 'hailed it with joy and mutual congratulation, as announcing the completion of our long-wished-for discovery of a passage into the Southern Indian Ocean':[25]

> This we considered to be strong proof, not only of
> the real existence of a passage betwixt this land and

New South Wales, but also that the entrance to the Southern Indian Ocean could not be far distant.[26]

After sailing around the island's mountainous north-west corner, named Cape Grim by Flinders, they sailed for the next four days southwards along the west coast, which he described as possibly the most inhospitable in the world:

> The mountains . . . were amongst the most stupendous works of nature I have ever beheld, and, at the same time, are the most dismal and barren that can be imagined . . . as there is no known place of shelter upon this coast, it becomes extremely dangerous to approach it . . . Judging from appearances, the west coast of Van Diemen's Land is as dreary, and as inhospitable a shore, as has yet been discovered.[27]

By now the *Norfolk* had been away for nine weeks, and with declining provisions Flinders made haste and reached the south-west cape of the island in four days. In the last few days of the year they landed in the same bays that had sheltered Abel Tasman more than 150 years before, as well as Cook, Hayes, Furneaux, Bligh and D'Entrecasteaux. On Christmas Day, in small boats, they explored the Derwent River; it had been named by British navigator John Hayes, who had reached there by the old southern route five years before, in 1793.

Early in the New Year, with its provisions almost exhausted, the *Norfolk* headed out of Adventure Bay and 1000 kilometres up the east coast of Van Diemen's Land, across the recently charted strait, to reach Sydney on 11 January 1799.

Bass and Flinders had made a momentous discovery, which would be of enormous benefit to ships sailing in the Southern Ocean and to those making the voyage from the Old World. Governor Hunter agreed with Flinders's suggestion to name the body of water separating Van Diemen's Land from the mainland after George Bass, and it became Bass Strait.

Shortly after the celebration of their success, Bass was granted sick leave, and in May 1799 he abruptly left the colony with the successful sealer Charles Bishop, whom he would join in business the following year, having left the navy. Despite Bass's genuine enthusiasm for exploration and botany, he was also attracted to the idea of making money. He arrived back in England in July 1800 and on 8 October married Elizabeth Waterhouse, sister of his and Flinders's old shipmate and friend Henry Waterhouse, the captain of the *Reliance*. After Bass's departure, he and Flinders remained good friends and corresponded, but they would never meet again.

Within months of his marriage, Bass, in partnership with Bishop, became the managing owner of the merchant ship *Venus*, which he sailed in January 1801 with goods he intended to sell in Sydney. On reaching Port Jackson, he had only limited success as a trader but entered an agreement to bring pork back to the settlement from Tahiti at an attractive profit. He now appeared to be emerging as a successful trader and had also secured some fishing concessions in New Zealand.[28]

In early 1803 Bass arranged to sail beyond Tahiti to the coast of Chile to buy other provisions, which he planned to sell at a profit in Sydney. He left Port Jackson on 5 February 1803 and was never seen again. To this day his fate remains unknown.

*

Meanwhile, back in Sydney, Governor Hunter was eager to continue the exploration of the colony. Now that the coast to the south of Sydney had been successfully explored, he wanted to chart more of the north coast of New South Wales. So in July 1799, Flinders was sent to explore Moreton Bay (the later site of Brisbane), some 900 kilometres north of Sydney. Captain James Cook had observed the bay as he sailed past it in May 1770 and named it after the 14th Earl of Morton, the then president of the Royal Society – but it was later misspelt from the early maps.

Sailing again on the small *Norfolk* from Sydney on 8 July, Flinders reached Moreton Bay a week later. He surveyed the area and concluded there was no major river flowing into it: he had completely missed the Brisbane River. He also failed to identify the 450-kilometre-long Clarence River, some 300 kilometres south of Moreton Bay, reporting that there were no major rivers along the coast that would allow any significant penetration of the interior of the country:

> However mortifying the conviction might be, it was then an ascertained fact, that no river of importance intersected the East Coast between the 24th and 39th degrees of the south latitude.[29]

The failure to identify these important rivers would not be Flinders's last major oversight. Later he would fail to notice Australia's most important river, the Murray, which enters the sea via Lake Alexandrina, in the south of Australia. However, grateful for his exploration effort, Governor Hunter rewarded Flinders with a land grant of 300 acres, or 120 hectares – three times the amount he had given Bass – in Bankstown, west of Sydney.

*

Flinders appears to have been a popular figure in the five years he was in Sydney. He was socially acceptable to all sections of the colony's small and fractious elite: as well as being a favourite of Governor Hunter, he regularly dined with the head of the New South Wales Corps, William Paterson, and his wife, Elizabeth. Paterson had been acting governor of New South Wales for the nine months before the arrival of John Hunter in 1795. Paterson shared Flinders's passion for exploration and botany but, like many of his ilk in the colony, had developed a heavy reliance on alcohol.

Flinders regularly wrote to Ann Chappell, but it is not known if he struck up any relationships with women while in Sydney, where it was common practice for officers to take up with the convict women, many of whom bore their children, as Ann Inett had to Philip King.

Flinders was also close to John Macarthur, a marine lieutenant who had become a successful and dominant businessman in the colony.

Macarthur was born in 1767 at Stoke Damerel, near Plymouth, and was the son of a draper. In 1789, as a lieutenant in the army with only limited prospects, he signed up with the New South Wales Corps and sailed on the second fleet of convicts, arriving in Sydney with his wife, Elizabeth, in June 1790. After accepting the position of superintendent of public works, he had significant influence over the economy of the settlement, including the allocation of convict labour. Within a few years Macarthur had quit the marines and become very powerful, with interests in sheep farming, rum and most of the colony's commerce.

When John Hunter was appointed governor, Macarthur was already extremely influential. The two men regularly clashed, and Macarthur sporadically complained to London about what he saw as Hunter's ineffectiveness.

Macarthur would be a thorn in the side of every governor for twenty years, from Arthur Phillip to Lachlan Macquarie, and would play a dominant role in the overthrow of Governor William Bligh in January 1808. However, Flinders and Macarthur had a cordial relationship, and Flinders was also friends with Macarthur's wife, Elizabeth, an intelligent and cultured woman with whom he would correspond for many years.

Also in 1799 Flinders adopted a kitten that he named Trim, after the eponymous character in Laurence Sterne's novel *Tristram Shandy*. Flinders would later write a glowing biographical tribute to the cat, which he said possessed superior intelligence, had no dread of water and learned to swim. Trim was popular with everyone. He would climb the masts and ropes to the top of the ship with the sailors and 'was admitted upon the table of almost every officer'.[30] He was a big cat – about twelve pounds, or five kilograms – and had black fur 'with the exception of his feet, which seemed to have been dipped in snow . . . and a white star on his breast'. Flinders became deeply attached to the cat, which would sail on all his explorations until it died ten years later in Mauritius.

By the beginning of 1800 Flinders was coming to the end of his term in New South Wales. He was twenty-six years old, and he had been in the navy for ten years and away from England for five. When he had arrived in Sydney in 1795, only about thirty kilometres of the coast around Sydney had been extensively surveyed. When he left for England, about 1000 kilometres to the north and the south had been charted by him, and he had also circumnavigated Van Diemen's Land.

However, Flinders was despondent about spending the rest of his life in the navy. On 12 February 1800 he received a wonderful gift from his old friend the botanist Christopher Smith in Calcutta, which included six dozen bottles

of Madeira wine, a dozen new shirts, a dozen new towels
and two silk handkerchiefs. Two days later a very grateful
Flinders wrote to thank Smith and express bitterness at
watching traders come and go from Sydney making their
fortune, while his own financial prospects remained bleak.
He said he was thinking of leaving the navy and following
his good friend George Bass into commercial trading:

> The thing is, my dear friend, I am tired of serving
> for a pittance, and as it were living from hand to
> mouth, while others with no better claim are making
> hundreds of thousands. The examples which have
> occurred in this place have opened my eyes a little to
> my own interest; and besides, I want to be my own
> master, and not be subject to the caprices of whom-
> soever the Lords above may please to set over me.[31]

CHAPTER 7

EXPLORING THE
UNKNOWN COAST

*I*f Flinders had been considering leaving the navy before he departed Sydney, he seems to have changed his mind on the voyage back to England. At the tiny port of Jamestown – on the island of St Helena, in the Atlantic – he met with Lieutenant Colonel Robert Brooke, the local governor, and discussed with him his plans to return to explore the remaining unknown southern coast of New Holland.[1]

Some years later, he explained why he decided to stay in the navy and become an explorer, rather than follow his good friend George Bass into private business to make a lot of money:

> I have too much ambition to rest in the unnoticed middle order of mankind. Since neither birth

nor fortune have favoured me, my actions shall speak to the world. In the regular service of the navy there are too many competitors for fame. I have therefore chosen a branch which, though less rewarded by rank and fortune, is yet little less in celebrity. In this the candidates are fewer, and in this, if adverse fortune does not oppose me, I will succeed: and although I cannot rival the immortalised name of Captain Cook, yet if persevering industry, joined with what ability I may possess, can accomplish it, then will I secure a second place.[2]

On 27 August 1800 Flinders and the *Reliance* finally reached England, after an absence of five and half years. After arriving at Portsmouth, the ship then sailed on to the Nore, on the mouth of the Thames, where Flinders wrote an affectionate letter to Ann Chappell, who was now approaching thirty years of age and surely thinking that her chances of marriage were diminishing.

My Dear Friend,

. . . I learn that you are in the land of the living, and at present on a visit at Boston [in Lincolnshire]. My imagination has flown after you so often and many a time, but the Lords of the Admiralty still keep me in confinement at the Nore. You must know, and your tender feelings have often antici- pated in me, the rapturous pleasure I promised myself on returning from this Antipodean voyage, and an absence of six years.

As you are one of those friends whom I consider it indispensable to see, I should be glad to have some little account of your movements . . . then I shall take that opportunity of coming to Lincolnshire.[3]

The following month, the Flinders brothers were paid off and together went on leave to the family home, in Donington. Within days, eighteen-year-old Samuel left to join the *Almene* and, having passed the necessary exams, was promoted to lieutenant. Before going on leave, Flinders had already been promoting his plan to return to Australia. On 6 September he wrote to the influential Sir Joseph Banks seeking his support:

> It cannot be doubted, but that a very great part of that still extensive country remains totally unknown . . . The interests of geography and natural history in general, and of the British nation in particular, seem to require, that this only remaining considerable part of the globe should be thoroughly explored . . . If His Majesty should be so far desirous to have the discovery of New Holland completed, as to send out a vessel . . . for the execution of it, and . . . the execution of it be committed to me, I should enter upon it with that zeal which I hope has hitherto characterised my service.[4]

Banks did not respond to Flinders for two months, then in a short note of apology on 16 November he explained he had 'been prevented by bad health' from writing earlier and invited Flinders to his townhouse at 32 Soho Square.[5]

Banks was impressed with the young Flinders and enthusiastically backed the venture with all of his considerable influence at all levels of the British government. After 'a voluminous proliferation of letters, orders, memoranda and diplomatic exchanges', approval was given by the end of the month for Flinders to undertake the expedition.[6]

Banks's efforts to persuade the government to sponsor the expedition were made easier because of Britain's fear of France. Not only were the two countries again at war, but Britain feared French attacks on her empire. Only two years before, Napoleon had embarked on the invasion of Egypt, and he harboured ambitions for control of India – and soon would begin the planning for the invasion of England. The English East India Company was concerned that the French might establish themselves somewhere on the Australian coast, which they could use as a base to menace British trade.[7]

British suspicions of the French were made even more immediate by the application the previous June by L. G. Otto, the French representative in London, for passports for two French ships to explore Terra Australis. The ships were *Le Géographe* and *Le Naturaliste*, commanded by the well-known navigator and naturalist Nicolas Baudin, who may not have been known to Flinders at the time but would certainly have been well known to the British authorities.

Despite the fact that England and France were at war, communication between the scientific elites of the two countries remained open, and they would both have known that they were committing rival expeditions with essentially the same quest.

Meanwhile, Matthew Flinders was well aware of the important role Banks played in his appointment and eagerly acknowledged the value of the patronage. While he was back in England, he finalised and published a small volume about his exploration of Van Diemen's Land and the Bass Strait, which he dedicated to Sir Joseph Banks:[8]

> Your zealous exertions to promote geographic and nautical knowledge, your encouragement of men employed in the cultivation of sciences that tend to this improvement, and the countenance you have been pleased to show me in particular, emboldened me to lay the following observations before you.[9]

Flinders received his commission on 16 February 1801 and began preparing for the voyage. At twenty-six, he held only the rank of lieutenant, which was not unusual for the commander of such an expedition. Both Cook and Bligh had been only lieutenants when they were assigned to their famous voyages, though both had been older than Flinders: Cook was forty and Bligh thirty-two.

The ship chosen for the expedition was the three-masted *Xenophon*, which was renamed the *Investigator* for the expedition. At 334 tons and with a crew of seventy-five, the ship was much larger than the tiny vessels Flinders had previously used for exploration in Australia. The *Investigator*, a ship built in the North Country, had been bought some years before by the navy. It had recently been repaired and its hull given a new copper sheath, which led Flinders to comment that it was 'the best vessel which could, at that time, be prepared for the projected voyage to Australia'.[10] However, within a year Flinders would form a dramatically different view of the ship and the repairs done to it.

The vessel was prepared for the voyage at Sheerness, on the mouth of the River Thames. Flinders was told he could fit her out in whatever manner he 'should judge necessary, without reference to the supplies usually allotted to vessels of the same class'.[11] He was also able to select his own crew. Some of the older crew members of the *Xenophon*, and those who did not want to volunteer for the expedition, were discharged, and some younger crew from other ships who wanted to go took their place.

The preparation of the *Investigator* was made easier by the support of the local resident naval commissioner at Sheerness, the colourful forty-one-year-old Isaac Coffin. Coffin would serve in the navy for forty years: he started as an able seaman in 1771 and eventually retired as a vice admiral in 1808. Regularly at odds with his superiors, he was, during his career, charged, court-martialled and dismissed, but eventually reinstated, to the navy.

Flinders said that the master attendant at Sheerness navy dockyards, Joseph Whidbey, had also given 'valuable advice and assistance in the selection of stores' for the preparation of the *Investigator*.[12] Whidbey had been master on the *Discovery* during George Vancouver's exploration of the north Pacific between 1792 and 1796, and he had been the first to chart sections of the Alexander Archipelago, in southern Alaska.

Over the following months an array of state-of-the-art astronomical and surveying equipment was brought abroad, including a number of Troughton's sextants, Earnshaw's and Arnold's chronometers in their sturdy wooden boxes, timekeepers, telescopes, compasses, pedometers, rulers, surveying chains, thermometers, barometers, and mapping and drawing equipment.

Absolutely vital to the expedition were copies of all the previously known maps by various seafarers and navigators who had charted sections of the Australian coast over almost 200 years. Most of the charts had been prepared under the direction of the sixty-three-year-old hydrographer Alexander Dalrymple, who was a dominant figure in the navigation of the South Seas and the Pacific for nearly half a century. Born in Scotland in 1737, as a boy Dalrymple had gone to England and joined the English East India Company. At the age of twenty-two, he made his first visit to China, and at twenty-eight he was elected a member of the Royal Society. In 1767 Dalrymple published *An Account of the Discoveries Made in the South Pacific Ocean, Previous to 1764*, which was based on a study of all the known maps and information of voyages over the previous two centuries. His book included the charts and records of explorers from the time of Torres and Janszoon.

Flinders also carried with him the maps and journals of Captain James Cook, who had surveyed the east coast of Australia in 1770, and the charts of his own explorations, including of Van Diemen's Land and his recently charted Bass Strait. Together, all this information showed that more than eighty per cent of the Australian coast had been seen by European sailors over the 200 years before Flinders set sail to try and complete the picture.

During the preparation for the expedition, Flinders went home to Lincolnshire and on 17 April 1801 married Ann Chappell. He took the stagecoach from London on a Wednesday night and arrived the following evening at Spilsby, in Lincolnshire, more than 150 kilometres away. The next day Ann and he were married. While he was away, the two had written regularly to each other. When Flinders was on the *Norfolk* in 1798 he named a small hill in the Kent Group of Islands Mount Chappell and called a small cluster of islands the Chappell Isles.

The marriage between Ann Chappell and Matthew Flinders was hastily concluded, as Flinders explained in a letter to his cousin Henrietta:

> Everything was agreed to . . . and just at this time I was called up to town [London] and found that I might be spared a few days from thence. I set off on Wednesday evening from town, arrived next day at Spilsby, was married next morning, which was Friday; on Saturday we went to Donington, on Sunday reached Huntingdon, and on Monday were in town. Next morning I presented myself before Sir Joseph Banks as if nothing had happened . . . We stayed in town till the following Sunday, and came on board the Investigator next day, and here we have remained ever since . . .[13]

In fact, the wedding was so quickly arranged that not even the Flinders family knew about it. When the newlyweds journeyed to Flinders's home in Donington the day after the marriage, his father expressed concern in his diary:

> With concern note that my son Matt came upon us suddenly & unexpectedly with a wife on Sat. April 18 & left us next day – it is a Miss Chapple [*sic*] of Partney [a town two miles north of Spilsby]. We had known of the acquaintance, but had no idea of the marriage taking place until the completion of his ensuing voyage. I wish he may not repent his hasty step.[14]

Flinders had promised his new bride that she could accompany him on the *Investigator* for the voyage to Australia and live at Port Jackson; and shortly after the marriage Ann had written to close friends to say farewell.[15] However, Flinders did not have permission to take her and was nearly dismissed from the venture when he was caught trying to smuggle his new wife on board the ship for the voyage to Australia. Flinders probably knew that his superiors would not take kindly to him taking his bride on the expedition; indeed, when he first suggested it to Ann, he confessed it may be a problem:

> It will be better to keep this matter entirely secret. There are many reasons for it yet, and I also have a powerful one. I do not exactly know how my great friends might like it.[16]

Navy wives were rarely given permission to travel with their husbands. Officers taking up appointments were sometimes allowed to take their families with them to the colonies and bring them home again – but no explorer, particularly on such a long voyage of discovery, had ever been accompanied by a woman. More importantly, Flinders had never sought, let alone received, permission for Ann to go with him.

It is not clear why Flinders thought he could get away with this arrangement, and there is no other example in his career of him displaying so little regard for the rules. In mid-May, during an inspection of the *Investigator*, Admiralty officers were alarmed to find Ann settled in the captain's cabin 'without her bonnet'.[17] When Sir Joseph Banks heard about the incident, he wrote to warn Flinders that to take his wife was a serious breach of navy regulations and that he had heard that Flinders would be sacked and replaced by one of the scientists aboard if he went ahead and took Ann to Australia:

> I have but just time to tell you that the news of your marriage, which was published in the Lincoln paper, has reached [me]. The Lords of the Admiralty have also heard that Mrs. Flinders is on board the Investigator, and that you have some thoughts of carrying her to sea with you. This I am very sorry to hear, and if that is the case I beg to give you my advice, by no means to venture to measures so contrary to the regulations and the discipline of the navy; for I am convinced by the language I have heard, that their Lordships will, if they hear of her being in New South Wales, immediately order you to be superseded, whatever may be the consequences, and in all likelihood order Mr. Grant to finish the survey.[18]

Flinders wrote back to Banks admitting that he had intended taking his wife, but only as far as Sydney, where he would leave her while he undertook the exploration survey. Given a choice between his new bride and the expedition, Flinders did not hesitate:

> It is true that I had an intention of taking Mrs. Flinders to Port Jackson to remain there until I have completed the purpose of the voyage . . . The Admiralty have most probably conceived that I intended to keep her on board during the voyage, but this was far from my intention . . . If their Lordships sentiments continue the same . . . I shall give up my wife for the voyage of discovery; and I would beg of you, Sir Joseph, to be assured that even this circumstance will not damp the ardour I feel to accomplish the important purpose of the present voyage.[19]

And so, after the stern words of rebuke from the Admiralty, Flinders decided he would leave Ann behind in England when the *Investigator* sailed. She had already waited five years for Flinders to come back to marry her and she would have to wait another ten years before she saw him again.

The ship had a total complement of seventy-five men. Flinders's first lieutenant was twenty-three-year-old Robert Fowler, and Flinders's eighteen-year-old younger brother Samuel was third lieutenant. Samuel Flinders had wanted to go on the voyage. Matthew had recommended him with some reservation: in a letter to his father, he said that any mistakes Samuel made on the voyage because of 'inattention or inexperience will be placed on my discredit'.[20]

The bulk of the crew included thirty-five seamen and fifteen marines, who were to help maintain order on board and ensure safety on land. The balance of the crew included the boatswain and the boatswain's mates, a gunner, a clerk, a cook and his mate, a carpenter, a sail-maker and four quartermasters.

In addition to the provisions loaded on to the *Investigator*, Flinders organised for another ship to take supplies to Sydney so he could restock for his continued exploration once he reached New South Wales. Flinders was aware that the convict colony was still struggling and would not be able to provide him with what he needed. On 14 May 1801 he sent a request to Evan Nepean, the Admiralty secretary, asking for further 'provisions for 90 men for six months' to be sent for him to Sydney, including salted 'beef and pork, peas, spirits, lime juice, essence of malt mustard, essence of spruce, molasses and sauerkraut'. [21] The request also included equipment that they would have difficulty procuring in Sydney: cables, a spare anchor, two barrels of tar, forty gallons of black varnish, fifty gallons of linseed oil and a complete set of replacement sails.

Sir Joseph Banks played a role in the preparation of the ship and the selection of most of the scientists, and very little he asked for was denied. At one point when he asked Nepean if a detail he had proposed for the *Investigator* had been approved, Nepean replied in a note, 'Any proposal you will make will be approved. The whole is left entirely to your decision.'[22]

The scientists on the expedition included natural-ist Robert Brown, a short, lean twenty-seven-year-old who had established an early reputation for himself when as an eighteen-year-old he had published an original paper on Scottish flora. Years later, in 1827, he would become famous for describing a phenomenon that became known as Brownian motion: the random movement of microscopic particles suspended in a liquid or a gas, caused by their collisions with molecules of the liquid or gas. The astronomer on the expedition, John Crosley, had previous experience surveying in the

North Pacific from 1795 to 97. He brought with him additional equipment, including chronometers and a pocket watch, which could be used by boat parties conducting separate surveys.

In the age before the camera, drawings and paintings were an extremely important part of the explorer's record, and the expedition included the forty-one-year-old natural history and portrait painter Ferdinand Bauer and the twenty-year-old landscape painter William Westall.

Bauer was born on 20 January 1760 at Feldsberg, Austria, the youngest of three sons of Lukas Bauer, court painter to the Prince of Liechtenstein. From 1776 he travelled with botanists John Sibthorpe and John Hawkins on their expedition through Greece and the Balkan Peninsula, and provided more than a thousand drawings and paintings for the ten volumes of the celebrated *Flora Graeca*, published between 1806 and 1840.

William Westall was studying at the Royal Academy School and had been taught to draw and paint by his older half-brother Richard, who was at the time the painting teacher of Princess Victoria, later Queen Victoria.

Most of the scientists on the expedition took with them a servant. However, the remaining two members of the scientific team were of a lower social class and did not have servants. The gardener, Peter Good, was a foreman at the Royal Botanic Gardens at Kew and had successfully transplanted plants brought back from India. His collection of more than one hundred Australian plants was later lost when, as part of the Flinders expedition, he was shipwrecked off the Great Barrier Reef. Good died the following year, while he was returning to England after being rescued. Twenty-six-year-old miner John Allen was the son of a coalminer in Derbyshire and had begun mining as a twelve-year-old. Young John had sufficient education to be able to read and write. He had been recommended to Sir Joseph Banks for the expedition by Banks's uncle, William Milnes, who said Allen was 'an ingenious lad' who understood 'blasting and boring and likewise the nature and construction of Engines'.[23]

When it was finally ready to sail, the *Investigator* would be loaded with twelve months' supply of food, the most basic of which was salted meat and hardtack. The notorious hardtack, which had been the basis of the seafarer's diet for several hundred years, was made from wheat or barley and baked brick hard, until it was devoid of moisture, like a biscuit. Normal bread would be edible for only about a week if stored in cool and dry conditions, and even less if it was damp and hot. Hardtack could last practically indefinitely but was less palatable, very hard to chew and often became infested with weevils. Flinders said the ship was also 'liberally furnished with antiscorbutic medicines' (those that stave off scurvy), which would have included spruce oil, lime, molasses, sauerkraut, malt and vinegar.[24]

In addition to plentiful supplies, the *Investigator* carried trinkets to placate the native peoples – or, as the Admiralty described them, a 'List of Articles for His Majesty's Sloop Investigator, to take on her Voyage of Discovery, for use, Presents to Natives, etc'.[25] These goods included looking glasses, or small mirrors, because the English had learned from earlier explorations that many of the Aboriginal and Pacific island people were fascinated when they saw a reflection of themselves for the first time. Other items included 500 pocketknives; one hundred combs; 200 strings of blue, red, white and yellow beads; one hundred pairs of earrings; 200 finger rings; 1000 yards of blue and red garter material; one hundred red caps; one hundred small blankets; one hundred yards of thin red baize; one hundred yards of coloured linen; 1000 needles; five pounds of red thread; 200 files; one hundred shoemaker's knives;

300 pairs of scissors; one hundred hammers; fifty axes; 300 hatchets; a quantity of other samples of ironmongery; a number of medals with King George III's head imprinted on them; and some new copper coins.[26]

Flinders's detailed, lengthy written instructions were not issued until 22 June 1801, almost six months after he was appointed to command the expedition and only a few weeks before the ship set sail. This was fairly common practice in the British navy at the time; and there would have been few surprises in the document, as Flinders would have been consulted on its contents.

The most important instruction was to explore the unknown coast and determine if a strait separated New Holland, in the west, from New South Wales, in the east:

> Whereas the sloop you command has been fitted and stored for a voyage to remote parts . . . you should proceed in her to the coast of New Holland for the purpose of making a complete examination and survey of the said coast, on the eastern side of which His Majesty's colony of New South Wales is situated . . . and on your arrival on the coast, use your best endeavours to discover . . . any creek or opening likely to lead to an inland sea or strait.[27]

Flinders was ordered to sail from England via Madeira to the Cape of Good Hope, then to King George Sound on the south-west of New Holland, which had been named by the English explorer George Vancouver nine years before. At King George Sound, Flinders was to restock with water and timber and repair the *Investigator* for the eastward exploration of the unknown coast. When he finally reached the only European settlement – almost 4000 kilometres away, at Sydney – he was to use it as his base and resume the survey of the Australian coast as soon as circumstances enabled him to do so:

> You are to repair from time to time, to Sydney Cove for the purpose of refreshing your people, refitting the sloop under your command . . . and [after taking] under your command the Lady Nelson tender, which you may expect to find at Sydney Cove, you are to recommence your survey.[28]

The sixty-ton sloop, the *Lady Nelson*, under the command of Lieutenant James Grant, had left England in March 1801, four months before Flinders. It had been part of an earlier plan to send a small vessel that would be suitable for surveying bays and rivers along the New South Wales coast. With the later decision to send the larger Flinders expedition on the *Investigator*, it was resolved that the *Lady Nelson* should be made available to Flinders and the *Investigator* when he arrived in Sydney, for the closer to shore exploration of the coast of Terra Australis.

After departing Sydney, Flinders was to finish surveying the south coast of Australia and commence charting the north-west coast, part of which had been explored by Englishman William Dampier more than one hundred years before:

> When you have completely examined the whole of the coast from Bass's Strait to King George the Third's harbour . . . you are to explore the north west coast of New Holland, where, from the extreme height of the tides observed by Dampier, it is probable that valuable harbours may be discovered.[29]

After exploring the north and north-west coasts, Flinders was to continue sailing east across the top of Australia to survey the Gulf of Carpentaria and then make his way to the Torres Strait off the north-east tip of the continent.

His instructions were to do much more than simply chart and map. Flinders needed to explore the topography of all rivers and report on soil fertility, the customs of the local peoples and astronomical observations. The ship's two artists were to paint landscape and portraits of the natives. The expedition was also instructed to collect animal specimens, both dead and alive, and 'plants, trees, shrubs, etc.', which were to be stored in the 'plant cabin' that had been built on the ship. He was also to collect any plants that might be 'suitable for the Royal Gardens at Kew':

> You are to be very diligent in your examination of the said coast, and to take particular care to insert in your journal every circumstance that may be useful to a complete knowledge thereof, noting the wind and the weather which usually prevail there at different seasons of the year, the production and comparative fertility of the soil, and the manners and customs of the inhabitants of such parts as you may be able to explore . . . [and] the true position of remarkable headlands, bays and harbours.[30]

The final part of the instructions was for Flinders to survey the east coast of Australia 'from Cape Flattery to the Bay of Inlets', which had not been studied in detail by Captain James Cook when he had sailed north thirty years before, in 1770.[31]

When the surveying was finally completed, Flinders was told, he was allowed to take his crew on leave to the Pacific islands. Contrary to the widespread belief that sexual fraternisation with the native women was officially frowned on, Flinders was given this instruction:

> In order to refresh your people, and to give advan-
> tage of variety to the painters, you are at liberty to
> touch at the Feejees, or some other of the islands in
> the South Seas.[32]

At the time Flinders was preparing to leave, the British
were aware that the French had already sent an expedition
to explore Australia, because, at the urging of Sir Joseph
Banks, they had given a passport to the French explorer
Nicolas Baudin.

Just as the French explorers applied for a passport
from the British, Flinders sought one from the French.
Despite the state of war, both countries offered freedom
of movement to the other's ships, as long as they were
engaged only in scientific discovery. The passport issued to
Matthew Flinders guaranteed the *Investigator* immunity
from attack by French ships while its object was to extend
'human knowledge and promote the progress of nautical
science'.[33] The protection of the passport was valid as
long as the *Investigator* 'did not announce her intentions
of committing any act of hostility against the French
republic and her allies and did not render assistance to
her enemies'.[34]

The terms of the passport were to become important
later when Flinders was arrested and then imprisoned by
the French. In addition to the passport, Flinders was given
instructions that the *Investigator*, while a British navy
ship, should not engage in any hostilities with the French.
If he met any French ship, he was to act as if the two countries were not at war.

> And with respect to the ships and vessels of the
> other powers with which this country is at war, you
> are to avoid, if possible, having any communication
> with them.[35]

Finally, on 27 May 1801 the *Investigator* left the Thames and headed for Portsmouth, on the English south coast, where its preparations would be completed and it would await orders to sail. For this part of the journey, Ann Chappell was on board with her husband; she was to be left at Portsmouth. Her presence went undetected, until early the following morning the ship ran aground and within two hours small boats were used to pull the undamaged *Investigator* off the sand. The incident, at the very start of the expedition, was embarrassing for Flinders. The situation was made worse when it was discovered that a prisoner he was charged with delivering to Portsmouth had escaped during the relaunching of the *Investigator* and that three of the crew had deserted. When Sir Joseph Banks heard the news of what had happened, he wrote to Flinders reminding him of the folly of taking his wife aboard:

> I was mortified to learn that you had been on shore
> . . . and I was still more mortified to hear that several
> of your men had deserted, and that you had lost a
> prisoner entrusted to your charge . . . I heard with pain
> many severe remarks on these matters, and in defence
> could only say that, as Captain Flinders is a sensible
> man and a good seaman, such matters could only be
> attributed to the laxity of discipline which always
> takes place when the captain's wife is on board.[36]

In a letter to his wife from his ship at the Nore two weeks before sailing, Flinders expressed his love for Ann and assured her that even though she would not be part of the voyage, his achievements as an explorer would reflect well on her:

> Rest confident, my dear, of the ardent and unal-
> terable affection of thy own MF, he does love you

beyond everything. I go, my beloved, to gather riches and laurels with which to adorn thee, rejoice at the opportunity which fortuitous circumstances give me to do it. Wilt thou not feel pride in thy M? who will have gone through so much, and with whose labours, individuals in all parts of the world will be acquainted as a useful member of society?[37]

Having loaded the last of their provisions and livestock – which included goats, sheep, pigs and poultry – they finally received their order to depart, and on 20 July the expedition sailed down the English Channel towards the Atlantic Ocean.

On the second day out, after Spithead, Flinders issued orders for the cleaning of the boat, which were similar to those of Captain James Cook more than three decades before. The decks were to be regularly washed, cleaned with vinegar and aired with fire in the stoves, and hammocks and clothing were to be aired on deck frequently.

On 3 August they anchored at Madeira to restock with water and food. They also bought wine; Flinders complained they had been 'charged at the enormous price' of more than five shillings a gallon.[38] Then, after only four days, the *Investigator* was on its way to the Cape of Good Hope. On 17 September it crossed the equator, and a month later anchored at False Bay, off Cape Town. During the voyage, the crew was fed the regular navy diet of oatmeal, rice, salted meat and hardtack, supplemented by lime juice; and on their arrival at the cape there were no cases of scurvy.

The *Investigator* stayed at the cape for fewer than three weeks while fresh water and supplies were loaded; the ship left on 5 November 1801 and headed into the vastness of south Indian Ocean.

As they left the port, Flinders recorded that they heard the British ships in the harbour fire their cannons 'to commemorate the escape from the gunpowder treason', which marked the failed attempt by Guy Fawkes to blow up the Houses of Parliament in London on 5 November 1605.[39]

This was the fourth time Flinders had sailed this route. He had first done so ten years before, in 1791, with William Bligh on the *Providence*. He'd next sailed with John Hunter on the *Reliance* in 1795, on Hunter's posting to Sydney. On the third occasion he was again on the *Reliance*, when it was sent from Sydney in 1798 via South Africa to collect livestock for the struggling colony.

Over the next few weeks, sailing as low as thirty-seven degrees, the ship covered almost 150 miles (about 240 kilometres) a day. On 6 December, a little more than a month after they left the Cape of Good Hope, they spotted the St Alouarn Islands, off the south-west tip of Australia, and then Cape Leeuwin.

Flinders did not attempt to land near Cape Leeuwin but headed further east. In three days, using George Vancouver's charts, he had reached King George Sound and the inner harbour, called Princess Royal Harbour, which he said was a well-chosen spot to prepare for the subsequent exploration of the unknown south coast:

> The first essential prerequisite was a place to secure shelter, where the masts could be stripped, the rigging and the sails put in to order, and communication had with the shore without interruption from the elements.[40]

The *Investigator* stayed in Princess Royal Harbour for four weeks, during which time the ship's leaks were mended and the crew was sent ashore to find firewood and water.

Flinders first alighted at Oyster Harbour, which had been named by Vancouver when he found an abundance of oysters there. While Flinders resurveyed the sound, the *Investigator*'s scientists collected botanical samples and made astronomical calculations, and landscape painter William Westall sketched the western side of the harbour.

Flinders's detailed notes provide his first picture of the desolate, arid country of the southern coast of the continent, where the basic stone was granite, the soil barren, and the most common tree the eucalypt, which, he observed in his journal, did not grow very large. The most common animals were kangaroos and emus, and there was an abundance of oysters and fish. Among the animals Flinders said they saw was a strange giant lizard, which he thought was similar to one described by Dampier more than a hundred years before:

> Amongst the reptiles was a variety of lizards; one of which, of the larger size, was met by Dampier on the West Coast, and is described by him 'as a sort of guano [iguana]', but differing from others in three remarkable particulars: for these had a larger and uglier head, and had no tail: and at the rump, instead of the tail there, they had a stump of a tail, which appeared like another head; but not really such, being without mouth or eyes. Yet this creature seemed, by this means, to have a head at each end; and, which may be reckoned a fourth difference, the legs, also, seemed all four of them to be fore legs, being all alike in shape and length, and seeming by the joints and bendings to be made as if they were to go indifferently either head or tail foremost. They were speckled black and yellow like toads, and had scales or knobs on their backs like those of crocodiles. They are very slow in motion and

when a man comes nigh them they will stand and
hiss, not endeavouring to get away. Their livers are
also spotted black and yellow; and the body when
opened hath a very unsavoury smell.[41]

As there were no rivers or creeks, they began to dig wells
for water, and while they were searching were surprised to
find evidence of a recently built camp:

Some person, but not Captain Vancouver, had
nevertheless been cutting wood there; for several
trees had been felled with axe and saw. Not far from
thence stood a number of bark sheds, like the huts
of the natives who live in the forests behind Port
Jackson, and forming what might be called a small
village; but it had long been deserted.[42]

As they continued the search for water, Flinders and his
men came across a small patch of ground that solved the
mystery of who had used saws and axes to build a camp:

We landed on the east side, and found a spot of
ground six or eight feet square, dug up and trimmed
like a garden; and lying upon it was a piece of sheet
copper, bearing the inscription 'August 27, 1800.
Chr. Dixon – ship Elligood'.[43]

So it seems that at least one other European ship had been
there before Flinders, and more recently than Captain
George Vancouver a decade before. Christopher Dixon was
the captain of the whaling ship the *Elligood*, which sailed
for the South Seas with another whaler, the *Kingston*, and
reached the south coast of Australia early in 1800. They
found King George Sound and took advantage of the
sheltered waters, abundant fresh water and available wood

supply. The ships were initially successful and caught a number of whales, before heading west then north up the Western Australian coast to continue fishing at Shark Bay. However, they began to run short of supplies and were forced to start the return journey to England via Madagascar and the Cape of Good Hope. As they sailed across the Indian Ocean, sickness spread through the ship and Captain Dixon of the *Elligood* and nine of his crew died and were buried at sea. The ship, subsequently captained by Job Anthony, reached the safety of Cape Town in May 1801, two months before Flinders left England on his expedition.

Back at King George Sound, still looking for water, Flinders saw evidence of human habitation, including smoke from fires. But the locals kept away, and it was not until a week after landing that they had their first encounter with the local Aboriginal people:

> Next morning (Tuesday 15 December), however, we were agreeably surprised by the appearance of two Indians, and afterwards of others, upon the side of the hill and behind the tents. They approached me with much caution, one coming first with poised spear, and making many gestures, accompanied with much vociferous parleying, in which he sometimes seemed to threaten us . . . and at others to admit of our stay.[44]

After the British traded some of the trinkets, including 'iron and toys', that had been brought for the purpose of appeasing the locals, Flinders said that after staying a short time, the Aboriginals left, 'apparently on good terms' with the British.[45] After the encounter, he commented on the similarities between the local people and those he had seen in Sydney, almost 4000 kilometres east:

It was with some surprise that I saw the natures of the east coast of New South Wales so nearly portrayed in those of the south-western extremity of New Holland. These do not, indeed, extract one of the upper front teeth at the age of puberty, as is generally practised at Port Jackson, nor do they make use of the Womerah, or throwing stick, but their colour, the texture of the hair, and personal appearance are the same, their songs run in the same cadence; the manner of painting themselves is similar, the belts and fillets of hair are made in the same way, and worn in the same manner. The short, skin cloak, which is of kangaroo, and worn over the shoulders, leaving the rest of the body naked, is more in the manner of the wood natives living at the back of Port Jackson than of those who inhabit the sea coast.[46]

However, one of the biggest differences according to his observations was that the locals appeared to live more by hunting than by fishing, whereas the Port Jackson Aboriginal people were heavily dependent on food from the sea:

None of the small islands had been visited, no canoes were seen, nor was any tree found in the woods from which the bark had been taken for making one. They were fearful of trusting themselves upon the water; and we could never succeed in making them understand the use of the fish hook, although they were intelligent in comprehending our signs upon other subjects.[47]

Before they left King George Sound, the ship's surgeon, Hugh Bell, took detailed physical measurements of some of the local males, including height, circumference of the head and the size of the eyebrows, nose, nostrils, chin, mouth, ears, jaw, arms, chest, pelvis, legs, feet, hands, fingers, feet and toes.

Also while at the sound, the English found an abundance of new plant specimens, and the principal botanist, Robert Brown, later wrote to Sir Joseph Banks to tell him that in twenty-four days they had collected about 500 plants, of which almost 300 were new species.

Finally, after four weeks – including Christmas Day, celebrated by the crew with a big dinner at which 'several got completely drunk' – and having been replenished with wood and water, the *Investigator* left King George Sound on 5 January 1802 to resume its exploration to the east.[48]

By 8 January they had reached the Archipelago of the Recherche, which D'Entrecasteaux had named after his ship a decade before. For three days they wound their way in high seas through the islands, then they scraped the bottom and were lucky not to puncture the hull of the ship. Eventually they found refuge in a sheltered cove, which Flinders named Lucky Bay.

Two weeks of sailing later, on 25 January, they neared the start of the Great Australian Bight, which was close to the furthest point east reached by D'Entrecasteaux almost a decade before, in 1793, when the French commander had been forced by a shortage of water to abandon his exploration of the south Australian coast and turn south to Tasmania.

In late January they came to the same high cliffs, stretching for hundreds of kilometres, that D'Entrecasteaux had seen a decade before:

> The length of these cliffs, from their second commencement, is thirty seven leagues, and that of the level bank, from near Cape Pasley where it was first seen from the sea, is no less than one hundred and

forty leagues. The height of this extraordinary bank
is nearly the same throughout, being nowhere less,
by estimation, than four hundred, nor any where
more than six hundred feet.[49]

By the beginning of February they had reached the group
of islands named by Pieter Nuyts in 1627 the St Francis
and St Peter islands, which was the furthest point east
along the south coast known to have been reached by
Europeans. Beyond was the unknown coast. In honour of
the Dutchman who had been there more than 170 years
before, Flinders named the whole group, including
St Francis and St Peter islands the Nuyts Archipelago:

> Upon the identity of the particular islands compos-
> ing this group, as compared with the chart of Nuyts'
> discovery there may possibly be some differences of
> opinion but there can be no doubt that the group
> generally is the same with that laid down by the
> Dutch navigator; and I therefore distinguish it from
> the others upon this coast by the title of Nuyts
> Archipelago.[50]

In the week the English stayed in the archipelago, more
flora and fauna samples were collected, including a new
species of kangaroo:

> At two o'clock, Mr. Brown and his party returned
> from the eastern island, bringing four kangaroos, of
> a different species to any before seen. Their size was
> not superior to that of a hare, and they were miser-
> ably thin, and infested with insects.[51]

Charting the coast, Flinders gave names to many of its
features, including Fowlers Bay, after his first lieutenant,

Cape Radstock, Coffin Bay, Point Drummond, Point Sir Isaac, Thistle Island and Cape Wiles.[52]

On 9 February – at the height of the hot, dry Australian summer – as they began sailing beyond where anyone had sailed before, they saw more frequent signs of Aboriginal settlement on shore:

> Many smokes were seen round Coffin Bay, and also two parties of natives, one on each side; these shores were therefore better inhabited than the more western parts of the south coast.[53]

On 20 February, Flinders said there was great excitement on the *Investigator* when they saw 'a tide from the north-eastward' and believed it might be part of a strait that separated New Holland and New South Wales:

> No land could be seen in the direction from whence it came; and these circumstances, with the trending of the coast to the north, did not fail to excite many conjectures. Large rivers, deep inlets, inland seas and passages to the Gulf of Carpentaria, were terms frequently used in our conversations of this evening; and the prospect of making an interesting discovery seemed to have infused new life and vigour into every man in the ship.[54]

The euphoria was short-lived, for only two days later disaster struck. The ship's master, John Thistle, had been rowed over to the mainland in one of the ship's small boats to search for fresh water. In the evening the boat, which was also carrying midshipman William Taylor and six other crew, was suddenly lost from sight. Lieutenant Fowler was immediately sent in another boat, but it was now 9.30 at night and dark, and no amount of yelling and firing of guns could locate the sailors in the first boat:

> Had it been daylight, there is no doubt that we should have picked up some or all of the people, but the hallooing and firing of muskets was ineffectual to procure any intelligence of their situation, and it was too dark to see anything. After the last boat had gone two hours I became anxious for her safety, and fired a gun for her return; it appeared that my fears had not been groundless, for she had narrowly escaped being swamped in a strong ripping tide.[55]

The search began again in earnest at daybreak the following morning and continued for the next three days, well after there was any realistic expectation of finding anyone alive, as only three of the eight missing seamen knew how to swim:

> The recovery of their bodies was now the furthest to which our hopes extended; but the number of sharks seen in the cove and at the last anchorage rendered even this prospect of melancholy satisfaction extremely doubtful.[56]

Finally, all that was found were some footprints on the beach, a sail and yard floating near the shore, and 'a bit of' John Thistle's gear. As the search was abandoned, Flinders lamented the loss, particularly of John Thistle, who had joined the expedition after returning to England only three weeks before the *Investigator* sailed, despite having been away from home for six years:

> Mr. Thistle was a truly valuable man, a seaman, an officer, and a good member of society. I have known

him since the year 1794, and we have been together since that time . . . In a voyage like the present, his loss cannot be otherwise than severely felt; and he is lamented by all on board.[57]

Much later Flinders said that his second-in-command, Lieutenant Fowler, recounted a remarkable story in which Thistle told of how he knew he would die:

> Whilst we were lying at Spithead [in England], Mr. Thistle was one day waiting on shore, and having nothing else to do he went to an old man, named Pine, to have his fortune told. The cunning man informed him that he was going out on a long voyage, and that the ship, on arriving at her destination, would be joined by another vessel . . . but he added, that Mr. Thistle would be lost before the other vessel joined. As to the manner of his loss the magician refused to give any information. My boat's crew, hearing what Mr. Thistle said, went also to consult the wise man, and after prefatory information of a long voyage, were told that they would be shipwrecked, but not in the ship they were going out in: whether they would escape and return to England, he was not permitted to reveal. This tale Mr. Thistle had often told at the mess table.[58]

(Not only was Thistle lost, but other aspects of the fortune teller's story would come true. Two months later they would have an unexpected encounter with another ship, and more than a year later most of the crew from the *Investigator* were shipwrecked on another ship on their way back to England.)

Flinders named the spot Cape Catastrophe, and on 25 February the *Investigator* continued with its exploration to the east. Names were given to Cape Donington and Boston Island, after local towns in Flinders's native Lincolnshire, and the Sir Joseph Banks Group of islands was named 'in compliment to the Right Honourable President of the Royal Society, to whose exertion and favour the voyage was so much indebted'.[59] Sailing further east, they rounded a cape and entered a harbour Flinders named Port Lincoln, after Lincolnshire.

Despite this being a fine harbour, they were disappointed it had 'no coastal run of fresh water'.[60] The shortage of drinking water was now reaching a point of crisis, and there was no chance of collecting rainwater, because in this part of the world there is practically no rainfall during the high summer months. Finally, after digging a number of pits, they found some brackish water and eventually loaded sixty tons aboard:

> A stratum of whitish clay was found at three feet below the surface and on penetrating this, water drained in, which was perfectly sweet though discoloured; and we had the satisfaction to return on board with the certainty of being able to procure water, although it would probably require some time to fill our empty casks.[61]

On 6 March they left Port Lincoln and resumed their search of the unknown coast, which now trended to the north, fuelling speculation that they might be entering a strait that separated New Holland and New South Wales, or at least led to a major river emptying into the sea. However, within days, Flinders's hopes of finding a way through to the Gulf of Carpentaria were fading:

> We had then advanced more than twenty five leagues to the north-north-east from Cape Catastrophe;

but although nothing had been seen to destroy the hopes formed from the tides and the direction of the Cape, they were yet considerably dampened by the want of boldness in the shores and the shallowness of the water; neither of which seemed to belong to a channel capable of leading us into the Gulf of Carpentaria, nor yet to any very great distant island.[62]

After they had sailed almost 300 kilometres, the sides of the gulf closed in. There was no strait and no major river. They then saw a wide opening that gave them 'a consolatory hope that it would terminate in a river of some importance', but the water continued to be salty as the sea ran into sand near current-day Port Augusta.[63]

Flinders finally gave up on finding water separating New Holland and New South Wales, noting in his journal: 'Our prospect of a channel or a strait cutting off some considerable portion of Terra Australis, was lost, for it now appeared that the ship was entering into a gulf'.[64]

Disheartened that 'nothing of particular interest [had] presented itself', on 13 March Flinders turned and headed back down the eastern shore to the mouth of the gulf, which he named Spencer Gulf, after George John Spencer, 2nd Earl Spencer, who was the great-grandfather of Princess Diana. Spencer had been a Member of Parliament and a Privy Councillor, and at the time of Flinders's voyage he was the First Lord of the Admiralty.

When they left the seventy-five-kilometre-wide mouth of Spencer Gulf and continued south, Flinders came upon a large island, which he named Kangaroo Island. His crew spent the next two days killing and butchering the abundant kangaroos, which weighed up to fifty-seven kilograms, and ate as much as they could:

The whole ship's company was employed this afternoon in skinning and cleaning the kangaroos; and
a delightful regale they afforded, after four months'
privation from almost any fresh provisions. Half a
hundredweight of heads, forequarters and tails were
stewed down in to soup for dinner on this and the
succeeding days; and as much steak given, moreover,
to both officers and men as they could consume by
day and by night.[65]

Crossing back to the mainland and to the east of Spencer
Gulf, Flinders reached what he named Yorke Peninsula
after the then British Secretary for War, Charles Philip
Yorke. From the tip of the peninsula, the *Investigator* spent
the next six days surveying the large bay, which Flinders
named the Gulf St Vincent. The aristocrat John Jervis, first
Earl of St Vincent, had joined the navy as a thirteen-year-
old able seaman in 1749 and had served in all of Britain's
major wars over the next fifty years, including the Seven
Years War, the American War of Independence, the French
Revolutionary Wars and the Napoleonic Wars. He had
become famous in 1797 when he defeated a large Spanish
fleet off Portugal's Cape St Vincent, from which he earned
his title.

Flinders noted that the country around Gulf St Vincent
'appeared to be generally superior' to the country around
the large Spencer Gulf; indeed the city of Adelaide would
be established there less than forty years later.[66]

Flinders named scores of places across southern
Australia after prominent British naval figures, which was
customary for British explorers at the time. They included
Cape Pasley, after Admiral Pasley; Cape Radstock, after
Admiral Lord Radstock; Point Sir Isaac and Coffin Bay,
after the Vice Admiral Isaac Coffin; the Gambier Islands,
after Admiral Lord Gambier; Point Marsden, after the

Second Secretary to the Admiralty; and Nepean Bay, after Evan Nepean, the Secretary of the Admiralty. In many other cases he named places after fellow officers and members of the *Investigator*'s crew: Point Bell, after the ship's surgeon; Purdie Islands, after the assistant surgeon; Point Sinclair, after a midshipman; Point Brown and Mt Brown, after the botanist Robert Brown; Cape Bauer, after the botanical artist Ferdinand Bauer; and Olive Island, after the ship's clerk.

He also named places after his family and friends, including Pearson Island, after his brother-in-law; Mount Arden, after his great-grandmother; Flinders Island, after his younger brother Samuel, who was, of course, on the *Investigator*; and Partney Island, after the town where his wife had lived.

The *Investigator* had now been exploring the south coast for more than three months and had covered almost 3000 kilometres, but it was still almost 2000 kilometres from the only settlement in Australia, at Sydney. Before resuming their exploration to the east, they crossed again to Kangaroo Island to shoot kangaroos and cut wood, and for the naturalists to 'pursue their researches'. But this time it seemed the kangaroos had learned to keep away from the intruders and had become shy, so very few were killed.[67]

It was now April and Flinders was growing concerned that he was running out of time. The *Investigator*'s stock of food was dwindling, and Flinders had to consider the arrival of the southern hemisphere winter. He was a very long way from Sydney, but he decided to cut short the exploration and head straight there:

> The approach of the winter season, and an apprehension that the discovery of the remaining unknown part of the south coast might not be completed

before a want of provisions would make it necessary to run for Port Jackson prevented me from
stopping a day longer at Kangaroo Island.[68]

But only two days after starting the 2000-kilometre
voyage, the *Investigator* had an amazing encounter with
another ship sailing in the opposite direction.

CHAPTER 8

NICOLAS BAUDIN

*O*n the morning of 8 April 1802, one of the lookouts aloft the *Investigator* called down that he could see a white rock that appeared to be the shape of a pyramid. In a few minutes they realised it was a ship, and soon after that it was flying French colours.

The ship was *Le Géographe*, captained by Nicolas Baudin, who had the year before been authorised by Napoleon Bonaparte to go on a similar quest to that of Flinders: to be the first to explore the unknown southern coast of Terra Australis.

It was in many ways remarkable that France had managed to maintain a commitment to enlightenment and scientific discovery while the country was experiencing decades of turmoil. The Bastille had been stormed in 1789, which was followed by the guillotining of King Louis XVI in 1793 and the period of the Terror. Then, during the fifteen years of the Napoleonic era, France was almost permanently at war with most of its European neighbours. In 1814 the monarchy was restored, first under Louis XVIII and from 1824 under his brother Charles X, but the new governments were often in conflict with many of the still-prevailing principles of the Revolution. Popular uprisings in Paris and the July Revolution, in 1830, saw Charles X abdicate and Louis-Philippe take his place.

Yet throughout the chaos and financial upheaval, France continued to send well-equipped and expensive scientific expeditions to explore Australia and the Pacific. This period later became known as the Age of Enlightenment, which was characterised by great intellectual developments in all fields, including science, art, philosophy, literature, architecture and music. This new cultural force, which swept across Europe and America, was prominent in France in the salons of the ancien régime and later during the Revolution and the age of Napoleon.

Until the Revolution, most of the commanders of French explorations tended to come from the aristocracy, whereas their British counterparts often came from families of more humble backgrounds. The first Frenchman believed to have seen Australia was Abraham de Bellebat Duquesne-Guitton, who, on his way to establishing a French presence at the court of the Kingdom of Siam (Thailand) in 1687, had sailed along part of the coast of New Holland near what became known as the Swan River and the later site of the city of Perth.[1]

A little more than eighty years later, in 1768, Louis Antoine de Bougainville was sent by King Louis XV to search the lands of the southern oceans. After sailing via Cape Horn and Tahiti and encountering the Solomon Islands, he reached – but did not penetrate – the Great Barrier Reef, off the north-east coast of Australia. When Bongainville returned to France in 1769 as the first Frenchman to have circumnavigated the world, Captain James Cook was on his way to discover the east coast of Australia.

Four years later, Marc-Joseph Marion Dufresne was sent to explore Terra Australis on the *Mascarin* and the *Marquis de Castries*, and he became the first European to land on Van Diemen's Land since Abel Tasman 130 years before. Marion Dufresne claimed the country for France, but the French did not establish any settlement there to protect their new territory.

Marion Dufresne is believed to have been the first European to make contact with the Tasmanian Aboriginal people, and Marion Bay on the south-east of the island is named after him. After leaving Tasmania, Marion Dufresne sailed for New Zealand, where he and twenty-six of his crew were killed and, according to the remaining crew, eaten by Maoris. In a punitive expedition that followed, the surviving French killed more than 200 Maoris, committing the largest single massacre in New Zealand history.

Also in 1772, while Marion Dufresne was sailing from Van Diemen's Land to New Zealand, another Frenchman was 4000 kilometres to the west, exploring the coast of New Holland. Thirty-four-year-old aristocrat Louis Aleno de St Alouarn was commander of the *Gros Ventre*, accompanying Captain Yves-Joseph de Kerguélen-Trémarec of the *Fortune* on an exploration of New Holland, when the ships became separated near the Kerguelen Islands, in the Great Southern Ocean. St Alouarn pressed on alone on the *Gros Ventre* and reached Cape Leeuwin, before sailing north along the coast to Shark Bay. On 30 March on Dirk Hartog Island he claimed ownership of the land on behalf of King Louis XV of France. He was in sight of Cape Inscription, where Willem de Vlamingh had claimed the same land on behalf of the Dutch 156 years before, in 1616.

On the way back to France, the *Gros Ventre* stopped off at Kupang, in Timor, then Batavia, where many of the crew became ill with dysentery. When the ship reached the French-controlled island of Mauritius in September, St Alouarn was hospitalised, and he died a month later, on 27 October.

The next French expedition to Terra Australis was in 1788, when Jean François de Galaup, Comte de La Pérouse reached Botany Bay after his three-year expedition to the north Pacific, before disappearing later that year. He was followed by Joseph-Antoine Raymond de Bruni D'Entrecasteaux, who was sent with *La Recherche* and *L'Espérance* to search for La Pérouse in 1792, resulting in the death of both ships' captains, D'Entrecasteaux and Jean-Michel Huon de Kermadec, during the expedition.

Sadly, Nicolas Baudin would share the same fate as nearly all his French explorer predecessors – Dufresne, St Alouarn, La Pérouse, D'Entrecasteaux and Kermadec – in that, having reached Australia, he died before reaching home.

*

Baudin had similar instructions to Flinders – to survey the unknown part of the southern coast and to explore whether a river or a strait separated New Holland from New South Wales:

> Citizen Baudin . . . will ascertain whether or not the country, completely new to Europeans, offers unknown species of animals and products inter-esting to botany and mineralogy. He will make a special search along the mainland coast to discover if there is some large opening to a large river.[2]

After charting the south coast, he was to explore north along the west coast of New Holland, including the Swan

River and Shark Bay, which had been recorded by earlier Dutch sailors and Englishman William Dampier. After the west coast, he was to complete the charting of the north coast and the Gulf of Carpentaria.

Had Baudin gone straight to the south coast, as his instructions specified, he would have arrived there before his English rival. However, he took a long time to reach Cape Leeuwin and then decided it was too near the southern hemisphere winter to continue east along the south coast, deciding instead to first explore north along the west coast.

Nicolas Baudin was forty-seven years old when he was appointed to lead the expedition. He was born on 17 February 1754 on Ré Island, about three kilometres from the French port of La Rochelle, on the Bay of Biscay. The son of a merchant and the third of thirteen children, he joined the French army at twenty years of age. A year later he sailed as quartermaster in the supply ship *Flamand* with 300 replacement troops for Ile de France – the former Dutch colony of Mauritius, off the East African coast – where he would return a number of times throughout his life. From there Baudin joined the French East India Company in Pondicherry, about 150 kilometres south of current-day Chennai, for a year and a half, before returning to France, where he joined the navy.

After five years on East India runs, he served in 1779 and 1780 on the *Minerva* against the British in the West Indies during the American War of Independence. Returning to France in 1792, he was appointed commander of the French naval ship the *Apollon* but was replaced by an officer from an aristocratic family, a practice that Baudin claimed happened all too frequently.[3] Bitterly disappointed, he left the navy and for the next five years commanded merchant ships, sailing regularly to the Caribbean and to the Indian and Pacific oceans. It was during this time that he demonstrated a flair for keeping animals

and plants alive at sea, and brought back from Africa
and Asia a number of exotic species, including ostriches
and zebras for Austrian emperor Joseph II's Schönbrunn
Palace gardens.

In 1796 he was appointed to bring a collection of animals
and plant specimens back from Trinidad to the National
Museum of Natural History in Paris. The expedition took
almost two years and was packed with incidents. After
leaving France, he and his men struggled to reach Tenerife,
where their ship was declared unseaworthy. A second ship
was found to be too small and was replaced by the *Fanny*, an
American vessel. On the way back to France from Trinidad,
loaded with plants and animals, the *Fanny* was intercepted
by a British warship, and Baudin was held and interrogated
before being allowed to resume his journey.

He arrived back in Normandy in June 1798 with a
collection that included seventy birds, 4000 butterflies
and other insects, shells, molluscs, fish, two hippopotamus skeletons and thousands of species of plants.[4] The
collection caused a sensation when it was paraded in the
streets of Paris on its way to the exhibition. Riding on this
acclaim, Baudin proposed to the French government that
he lead an expedition to explore the coast of New Holland
and New South Wales.

There was widespread support for Baudin in France,
who at the time would have enjoyed more recognition
for his achievements at home than the younger Matthew
Flinders did in England for his. In July 1798 the director
of the National Museum of Natural History, Antoine-
Laurent de Jussieu, wrote enthusiastically to the French
Minister of Marine, describing Baudin as 'an excellent
mariner'. He invited the government:

> to make further use of Captain Baudin's ability by
> sending him at the first opportunity on another

voyage in which the interests of natural history would not be forgotten. This excellent mariner can further render service to his country; he can combine geographic researches with those that interest us more particularly; the knowledge of the past and the knowledge of his former achievements make us believe he follows worthily in the steps of Bougainville, La Pérouse and D'Entrecasteaux.[5]

Baudin's proposed expedition pre-empted Flinders's by two years. It was supported by the organisation the Institute of France and at the highest levels of the French government, including Napoleon Bonaparte, who was particularly keen that the French be first to explore the world's last unknown coast. On 29 April 1800 the Minister of Marine reported:

> The First Consul was pleased with the plan presented to him and . . . he is disposed to order a voyage which will have for its main objective the exploration of the south west coast of New Holland where Europeans have not yet penetrated.[6]

At the time of his appointment, Baudin appears to have been popular and very highly regarded, and to have shown none of the erratic behaviour that would later characterise his leadership of the Australian expedition.

The French made a larger commitment to the number of scientists on their expeditions than the English. Flinders took only six men of science, while Baudin took twenty-two: three botanists, five zoologists, two mineralogists, three artists, five gardeners, two geographers and two astronomers. These were in addition to the naval officers who would be responsible for navigating, surveying and mapping.

As well as a number of young scientists who were keen to establish their reputations, Baudin took some older specialists who were already famous. Fifty-four-year-old André Michaux had been on a botanical expedition to Persia more than twenty years before and was responsible for successfully introducing a number of eastern species of plants to Europe. In 1785, with the authority of Louis XVI, he had gone to America to ascertain the kinds of native plants that would be useful back in France for building, medicine and farming. While in America he established botanical gardens in North Carolina and New Jersey. René Maugé, another on Baudin's voyage, was a celebrated botanist who had sailed with him on his earlier expedition to the West Indies.

The two ships provided by the French government for the expedition were the corvette *Galatée*, which was renamed *Le Géographe*, and the storeship *Menaçate*, which was renamed *Le Naturaliste*. Each weighed around 300 tons, which was about the same as Captain James Cook's *Endeavour*, Matthew Flinders's *Investigator* and the two ships fellow Frenchman D'Entrecasteaux had taken ten years before when he was sent to look for La Pérouse.

Baudin commanded *Le Géographe* and Emmanuel Hamelin *Le Naturaliste*. Hamelin turned thirty-two the week before the ships sailed from France. He came from a family with a long history of seafaring and had been at sea from the age of seventeen. Before joining the French navy, he had sailed on merchant ships carrying cargo and slaves to the West Indies, during which time he developed his skills as a hydrographer and navigator. In 1795 and 1796 he saw action in the French navy against the English in the Mediterranean. Hamelin was an experienced sailor but, unlike Baudin, had never been on a voyage of discovery or scientific exploration. He had, however, spent fourteen years in the navy and been on long voyages to Africa and the West Indies, where he'd learned the importance of naval hygiene and nutrition in staving off sickness among crews committed to long periods at sea.

Le Géographe was longer and sailed a lot faster than Le Naturaliste, but it was less suitable for exploring closer to the shore in shallow water. The different sailing speeds of the ships would later become a major problem, as twice Le Géographe would lose Le Naturaliste off the Australian coast.

The modifications made to Le Géographe and Le Naturaliste had many similarities to those made to Flinders's Investigator. To make room for plant samples, the number of guns on both ships' gun decks was reduced – from thirty on Le Géographe and twenty on Le Naturaliste to six on each. Additional cabins were also built for the large number of scientists who sailed on the expedition.

The expedition took a total of fifty-eight different maps supplied by the general depot of the French navy. They included all the known charts of the time: those of explorers D'Entrecasteaux, George Vancouver, Cook, Bougainville and St Alouarn; all the old Dutch charts; Matthew Flinders's map of Bass Strait; and the collection of Aaron Arrowsmith, the London mapper who had in 1790 made himself famous by creating a large chart of the world based on Mercator projection, a type of map-making grid that is valuable for navigation.[7]

Just as Flinders did, Baudin also took trinkets – ribbons, braid, small ornaments, nails and knives – to appease the natives. One of the last men to join the expedition before it left France was a twenty-three-year-old Chinese seaman named A Sam, who had been taken prisoner when the French captured an English East India Company ship on which he was working. Napoleon had personally ordered that he be returned to China. When the First Consul said he could go home, he was languishing in a French prison with what French doctors said was a melancholy that would kill him. Baudin was to take A Sam as far as Mauritius, where he was to be transported by the next available ship to China.

The French government gave Baudin even more elaborate instructions for his voyage than the English gave Flinders. Titled 'Plan of Itinerary for Citizen Baudin' and issued on 29 October 1800, his orders specified that Baudin was to survey those parts of the coast that had not yet been mapped, so that a complete chart could be produced:

> The aim of the Government in assigning to a special expedition the . . . Geographe and the Naturaliste [to] the command . . . of Captain Baudin . . . has been to examine in detail the south-west, west, north-west and north coasts of New Holland, some of which are still entirely unknown . . . By combining the work that will be done on these various parts with that of the English navigators on the east coast and of D'Entrecasteaux on Van Diemen's Land, we shall come to know the entire coastline of this great south land.[8]

Baudin was instructed to first head for Tenerife, then to the French-controlled Mauritius by the end of January 1802, 'without a stop' at either the Cape Verde Islands or Cape Town unless it was 'absolutely essential'.[9]

Le Géographe and Le Naturaliste, carrying a total of 251 men, left Europe nine months before Flinders, on 19 October 1800 – but in contrast to Flinders's quiet farewell from Portsmouth, Baudin's send-off from Le Havre was spectacular. Baudin said the farewell was a 'memorable event in the history' of France and involved crowds of people cheering and waving, a band playing, a salute from the cannons on the fort and a train of small craft following the two ships down the harbour and out to sea.[10]

Shortly after leaving Le Havre, Baudin faced the first British test of his passport. Waiting outside the harbour was an English warship, the *Proselyte*, which was stationed to attack French ships leaving the port for the open sea. When confronted, Baudin said he went aboard the enemy ship, where he was treated courteously and then allowed to pass:

> The captain received me politely and after he had read the passport from the English Admiralty, we were friends, and remained aboard his vessel about half an hour, and we drank to the success of the voyage.[11]

Heavily weighed down with extra men and more than a year's supplies, the ships pitched through the Bay of Biscay, where many of the men, some of whom had never been to sea before, suffered seasickness. Hamelin complained that because of the extra space taken for cabins for the scientists, and the extra provisions, there was not enough room for all the seamen to hang up their hammocks.

Two days after leaving, a stowaway who had been hiding on *Le Géographe* surrendered, and Baudin allowed him to stay and work as a member of the crew:

> During the morning a stranger by the name of Antoine Guth presented himself to the officer on duty . . . Upon questioning this stranger about his motives in stowing away, I discovered that, having no means of support in France, he was on the brink of destitution, and chosen to express himself to all kinds of adventures rather than remain any longer

in his poverty stricken position . . . I gave orders
that he should receive a ration, like the members of
the crew . . . [and] do whatever work on board it
was thought fit to employ him [to do].[12]

Within days, Baudin began complaining of the difficulty
of dealing with civilian scientists while maintaining order
and discipline among the officers and ratings:

I must say here, on passing, that those captains who
have serious scientists . . . aboard their ships, must
take them with a good supply of patience. I admit
that though I have no lack of it, the scientists have
frequently driven me to the end of my tether and
forced me to retire testily to my room. However,
since they are not familiar with our practices, their
conduct must be excusable.[13]

After sixteen days' sailing, they landed at Tenerife, in the
Canary Islands, and loaded aboard fresh water and food –
including fish, game, fruit and vegetables – before heading
off eleven days later. Sailing south past the Cape Verde
Islands but too near the African coast, they were becalmed
in the doldrums near the equator and forced to sail south-
west until they picked up winds that would take them
around the Cape of Good Hope and towards Mauritius.

They were already more than a month behind schedule
when they reached Mauritius on 15 March 1801, and
were pushed further behind when their stopover – which
in their written instructions was to be 'no longer than a
fortnight' – stretched to forty days.

Mauritius, or Ile de France as it was then known, had
been under French control since the early eighteenth
century. The Dutch had settled the island in 1598 and
stayed for more than a century, before leaving when the

Cape of Good Hope became strategically more important. One of the main sources of food on Mauritius then had been the flightless dodo, which was unafraid of humans and easy to catch, but it was extinct by the end of the 1600s. After the departure of the Dutch from the island, Guillaume Dufresne D'Arsel claimed the territory on behalf of France in 1715, and a few years later the French began to establish farms on the island. Almost a century later, in 1810, the island was taken from France by the British.

Baudin's visit to Mauritius got off to a bad start when his ships were kept out of Port Louis harbour for a day and a night because the local port authorities thought they might be enemy ships – even though they displayed French colours.

After finally being allowed to land, Baudin complained that he had great difficulty buying fresh bread or meat for his men, and that the local French administration was slow and unresponsive to the needs of the expedition. Emmanuel Hamelin, the captain of *Le Naturaliste,* said the locals were hoarding food and that because of the fear of an English attack there was a 'great stagnation in the trade' on the island.[14]

Despite the difficulties, by 5 April each ship had been loaded with firewood, fresh water, and wheat for the baking of bread. The ships had been careened and the Chinese prisoner A Sam handed over in good health for 'dispatch to his homeland at the first opportunity'.[15]

On 13 April the ships were ready to go but were delayed because of widespread desertions. A number of men were already missing, and their descriptions had been given to the local police. Later that night another six escaped from the ships by swimming ashore. Baudin wanted to move further away from the harbour to make it more difficult for the crew to abscond but the following night three more men escaped in the same way.

By now a total of forty of the crew from the two French ships were missing. Baudin threatened the local authorities that until they rounded up and handed over his men, who were hiding in and around Port Louis, he would keep the thirty native workers who had been assigned to help load the ships.

Two days later, twenty-two of the deserters were arrested when they joined a large crowd to watch the public execution of two natives. However, according to Baudin, fourteen 'were allowed to escape' because the local police were made up of 'publicans and canteen keepers' who profited from the French seamen being on the island. Some of the recaptured deserters who continued with the expedition later confessed they had been attracted by the promise of work around Port Louis harbour at higher rates of pay.[16]

Even more serious than the lowly seamen deserting was the high number of officers and scientists who refused to go on with the expedition. Some of the disaffected officers used the excuse of illness for not continuing:

> At eleven o'clock I went ashore and visited the hospital to see the officers and naturalists who . . . were to be found there. The Sisters of Charity . . . assured me that the gentlemen sometimes returned in the evening and even rather late. They usually spent the day in town . . . Most of the officers, supposed to be in hospital because of illness or need to relax, went walking on various plantations . . . I did not find a single soul.[17]

The next day Baudin complained that the men who were supposed to have been in the town hospital had deserted, 'not over the wall, but through the gate, with their baggage, with the permit of the local commissioner'.[18]

Such a loss of officers would have been unthinkable in the English navy at that time, when it would be close to inconceivable for an officer not to continue doing his duty. Baudin had already complained that many of his officers had taken rooms ashore and only appeared occasionally on board ship.[19]

From *Le Naturaliste* seven of the scientists stayed on Mauritius; and only the mineralogist, geographer and astronomer agreed to board *Le Géographe* for the next leg of the voyage. Among the scientists who jumped ship was the esteemed biologist André Michaux, who, Baudin said, could not agree that all the samples he would collect would be the property of the government:

> [I] had discussed with him in the most friendly fashion the inconvenience which would result but all to no avail; as he could not bring himself to agree to give up to the government the collections he would have made while he was serving with us.[20]

A factor in the high rate of defections was the great charm of Ile de France compared with the hardship and privation of life at sea, particularly for the scientists, who were not accustomed to life below decks. Ile de France had many attractions. For many years it was well known for its licentiousness and its attractive women (Baudin reported a number of cases of venereal disease), plentiful food, good wine, warm climate, clean air, green hills, forests, cascading waterfalls, comfortable beds and opportunities for walking in the countryside.[21]

Baudin said that despite the defections, the expedition would not be seriously weakened by their loss: 'I at least had enough to work the ships . . . and I was not distressed about the officers and scientists who had abandoned the expedition.'[22]

Finally, on 15 April, more than two months behind schedule, *Le Géographe* and *Le Naturaliste* left Port Louis and headed for the south coast of New Holland. In the original plan for the expedition, the search of the unknown coast was to take place in April, May and June, before the southern hemisphere winter had set in. However, the ships could not reach Cape Leeuwin until late May or early June, and Baudin knew that the end of June was a time limit 'not to be exceeded'. Notwithstanding the delay, he sent a letter from Mauritius to the Minister of Marine saying that, despite being late, he was determined to comply with his instructions:

> In my position it will be perhaps difficult to visit in this season the southern part of Van Diemen's Land and the strait that separates it from New Holland. However, in order to comply with the Government's wishes I am going to make my way to the D'Entrecasteaux Channel and, in spite of the little time remaining to me, endeavour to complete the work concerning that part of my orders before the height of the bad season.[23]

However, a month later, when *Le Géographe* and *Le Naturaliste* reached Cape Leeuwin on 27 May, Baudin had changed his mind and decided to abandon the quest to the south coast until the following spring and instead first explore north along the west coast of New Holland.

Of course, Baudin would have had no way of knowing at the time that Matthew Flinders was well advanced in the preparation of the *Investigator* and in a little more than six months would be at Cape Leeuwin in the right season to begin his own exploration of the southern coastline.

Much later, a zoologist on *Le Géographe*, François Péron, would write critically of Baudin, suggesting they could have carried out their original instructions:

> Our commander was afraid to make for Van Diemen's Land, and decided to begin his exploration with the reconnaissance of the north-west of New Holland, reserving until the following spring the voyage to the south. This important decision caused us much concern, because it was not strictly demanded by our situation at the time. The season, though already advanced, was not so advanced as to prevent us from doubling [sailing past] the South Cape. And as from there on we would have been moving towards warmer regions it appeared to us prudent to continue to respect the instructions of the Government, which we well knew were the result of the most learned deliberations and the most extensive knowledge of the subject.[24]

As the French ships headed north along the west coast, they rounded a cape, which Baudin named Cape Naturaliste (near current-day Bunbury). A boat was ordered to row to shore to report on the local conditions on land. The small boat was under the command of twenty-two-year-old Sublieutenant Henri Freycinet, who had sailed on the expedition with his twenty-one-year-old brother, Louis-Claude. The brothers were from a wealthy landowning family at Montélimar, on the Rhône, and had been in the navy for only six years but had both reached the rank of sublieutenant at an unusually early age.

After inspecting the shore, Henri Freycinet reported that he had found the same arid country and shortage of water that Dutch and other explorers had noted over the previous 150 years:

The number of trees I saw on the hills gave me hope of discovering some fresh water streams, but I searched in vain. The land, in spite of the large amount of growth, seems too sandy to be fertile, and the country appears to me to offer navigators no other resource than that of firewood.[25]

Two weeks later Baudin made his first journal entry that described a local Aboriginal man:

This man was black and naked from head to foot, except for a skin or a piece of bark covering his back. Judging by the colour of his beard, which was very long and grey, [he must] have been a very old man . . . Apart from the spears he was carrying, he had a fire brand, which leads me to think that as soon as they catch something, by fishing or other means, they cook and eat it.[26]

As *Le Géographe* and *Le Naturaliste* continued to sail north along the west coast, there were already major problems with their provisions. The salted meat and the vegetables from Mauritius had deteriorated, and the hardtack biscuits were infested with 'worms'.[27] The wheat loaded in Mauritius was almost exhausted, and fresh bread was baked and served only every ten days.

Still, after more than a week they sailed past Cape Naturaliste and into Geographe Bay, where the eager scientists went ashore to explore and to collect samples. It was here they first saw the white-tailed black cockatoo – *Calyptorhynchus baudinii*, or Baudin's black-cockatoo – the only Australian creature to bear Baudin's name.

On 7 June their first crew member was lost to the sea: a helmsman from *Le Naturaliste*, Thomas Vasse, was believed drowned when a small dinghy he was in with other sailors capsized in big waves. Years later, in 1804, French newspapers claimed he had managed to reach the shore, walked more than 400 kilometres and was picked up by a passing American whaler, which took him back to Europe, where he was arrested and jailed by the British when he was sailing through the English Channel. However, the story was subsequently rejected as a fabrication by survivors of Baudin's expedition.

A different story was told nearly forty years after that by a British settler, explorer, judge and Western Australian politician, George Fletcher Moore, who said he had been told Vasse survived but died later in the same area:

> Some natives of that neighbourhood recollect him. They treated him kindly and fed him but he lingered on the seacoast looking for his vessel. He gradually became very thin from anxiety, exposure and poor diet. At last the natives were absent for a time on a hunting expedition and on their return they found him dead on the beach, his body much swollen.[28]

Six days after the disappearance of Vasse, while exploring Geographe Bay, *Le Géographe* lost contact with *Le Naturaliste*. Despite several days' search, the two ships did not reconnect; they would not meet again for three months, 3000 kilometres away in Timor, having missed two pre-arranged rendezvous points.

The first agreed meeting point was Rottnest (Rats Nest) Island, about 200 kilometres further north and off the coast from the entrance to the Swan River. (Both Rottnest Island and the Swan River had been explored by the Dutch more than one hundred years before.) On 18 June, *Le Géographe* passed Rottnest Island, but Baudin said that 'extremely bad' weather prevented him from sailing between the island and the Swan River, where

Le Naturaliste was already anchored.[29] Instead, Baudin sailed around the western side of the island towards the next rendezvous point, about 800 kilometres further north.

While *Le Géographe* did not see *Le Naturaliste*, Hamelin's men at the top of the masts saw *Le Géographe* sailing past. Years later the mapper on *Le Naturaliste*, Louis-Claude Freycinet, wrote critically of Baudin for not coming to look for *Le Naturaliste* at the agreed point: 'We were all at a loss to conjecture why the commander, having himself fixed the rendezvous, did not come thither to meet us.'[30]

However, not everyone felt the same. François-Michel Ronsard, the engineer on *Le Géographe*, said they had no choice but to go west of Rottnest:

> We took the route towards the north, to reach the Swan River; we were there days without seeing land. The weather was not right for exploring the coasts, and we could not wait longer for fine weather in these parts, the season was too advanced. We had to sail outside Rottnest Island.[31]

It was around the time *Le Géographe* passed Rottnest Island that some of the French began to grumble about their commander's leadership. *Le Géographe* pressed on, arriving on 22 June at the second rendezvous point – Dirk Hartog Island, at the entrance of Shark Bay – which Baudin described as 'arid, disagreeable and dreary'.[32] With the help of some old Dutch charts, *Le Géographe* spent the next fortnight conducting a more detailed survey of Shark Bay, but did not wait any longer for *Le Naturaliste* before heading further north. The decision to move on without waiting longer again puzzled some of his colleagues, but in a letter Baudin wrote to the Minister of

Marine, he explained that he was in a hurry to explore the most westerly point of New Holland and the north coast as far as the Gulf of Carpentaria:

> Once we finished our work at Shark Bay I decided to head toward the northern part . . . in order to establish its most westerly position, thus delaying my reunion with the *Naturaliste* until we meet in Timor. Time was all the more precious to me in that I wanted to advance to the entrance of the Gulf of Carpentaria before going to Couping Bay [Kupang, in Timor].[33]

During the next thirty-eight days, *Le Géographe* sailed north past the Dampier Archipelago, before reaching and naming a number of islands, including the Rivoli Islands, L'Hermitage Island, Cape Leveque and the Lacepede Islands. Then, in early August and north of the current-day Kimberley region, Baudin came to and named the Bonaparte Archipelago, on the far north-west tip of Australia.

On 19 August – and still 1500 kilometres from the start of the Gulf of Carpentaria – he changed his plans again. Instead of continuing along the coast, he decided to head north for Kupang, in Timor, which was only a few days' sail away. By now *Le Géographe* had only enough firewood for another three or four days and enough drinking water for a week. They had no fresh food left, and ten of the crew were suffering from scurvy and two were already too ill to work. Baudin said the crew was delighted with the decision: 'This news had such an effect upon the sick on board, that several of them found strength enough to come up on deck in order to make sure that it was really true.'[34]

Baudin emphasised that he planned to return to the north-west coast the following year to complete a more comprehensive survey. Because the French hadn't issued Matthew Flinders his passport until 28 May 1802, seven months after Baudin had left Europe, he did not know that Flinders and the *Investigator* had left England a month before and were sailing towards the south coast of New Holland.

*

Meanwhile, *Le Naturaliste* was still almost 1000 kilometres further south. After spotting *Le Géographe* in the distance passing the western side of Rottnest Island, Hamelin had stayed inland around the island and the Swan River for twelve more days. In the fortnight *Le Naturaliste* spent there, Hamelin and his men had found plenty of food – including fish, seals, pelicans and wild celery – and firewood. For most of the time there were high winds and it rained heavily. On the Swan River they had copied the local Aboriginal people and dug wells for fresh water.

Before leaving Rottnest Island, Hamelin put a letter in a bottle under a small tricolour flag for Baudin, should he return. In it he reported on the survey work they had undertaken and said that storms had damaged much of his food supply. He explained that he was trying to save the sodden wheat by putting it out on sails to dry in the sun – when it was not raining – but that much of it was infested with mites. He mentioned that they had seen *Le Géographe* passing on 18 June and would now try to reach the second rendezvous at Shark Bay and, failing that, would sail on to Timor.

Le Naturaliste reached Shark Bay on 16 July – four days after Baudin and *Le Géographe* had left. Over the next seven weeks they extensively surveyed the area. By good fortune, practically all the work Hamelin did at Shark Bay complemented Baudin's a few weeks before.

Baudin had examined the northern entrance, the Bernier and Dorre islands, and the area around Peron Peninsula. Hamelin examined practically all the rest: the southern entrance, Dirk Hartog Island, the passage between the mainland and the island, and the waters to the east and west of Peron Peninsula.

On Dirk Hartog Island, the French found the inscribed pewter plaque left by Dutch explorer Vlamingh more than one hundred years before. The plaque commemorated Vlamingh's visit to the island and included the wording of an earlier plaque that had been left on the island by Dirk Hartog more than eighty years before. Believing it would have been sacrilegious to souvenir the plaque, Captain Hamelin had the Vlamingh plaque mounted on a new post, as the old one had rotted away.

(Louis-Claude Freycinet, the mapper on *Le Naturaliste* with Hamelin, had no such scruple. When he returned on his own expedition in 1818 he took the Vlamingh plaque and gave it to the Institute of France. In 1897 the French government told the Australian government that the plaque had been lost, but in 1940 it was found among some old copper engraving plates in a cupboard of the museum. It now sits in the maritime museum in Fremantle, Western Australia.)

After their time in Shark Bay, running short of fresh water and food, Hamelin ordered *Le Naturaliste* to head for Timor without doing any more coastal surveying. It appears that when *Le Naturaliste* reached Timor and reunited with *Le Géographe* at 10 am on 5 September, the two captains amicably discussed missing each other twice over.

The French found Timor to be very different from the barren wasteland of much of the coast of New Holland; and they enjoyed a range of fresh food, including vegetables and fruit, goats, chickens, fish and rice. The sick among the crew were quickly cured of their scurvy there, but soon they began to fall to the more serious affliction of dysentery, which had decimated many European crews in the Dutch East Indian ports before them.

Baudin had become ill shortly after arriving in Timor, and his fever worsened after the arrival of *Le Naturaliste*. At one point he thought he was dying, and he discussed with Hamelin the idea of his taking command of the expedition. Among the French who did die on Timor was thirty-two-year-old botanist Anselm Riedle, who had been with Baudin on his expedition to the West Indies seven years before. Baudin was deeply upset at the loss:

> Nobody knows how much I love him, how attached I am to him . . . I feel in advance how much the expedition will lose . . . No one on board can even partly replace him in this department.[36]

Baudin was too ill to attend the funeral but ordered that it be conducted with the honours usually afforded someone of much higher rank. During the service, flags on the ships were lowered; and a cannon was fired every half-hour for six hours. Twelve Dutch soldiers carried the coffin, which was buried alongside that of the English botanist David Nelson, who had died in Timor a decade before. Nelson had been with William Bligh on the *Bounty* and had survived the 5000-kilometre journey in an open boat after the mutiny, only to die when he reached Timor.

In Timor there were more rumblings of disquiet about Baudin's leadership, arguments between the officers and even a fight, during which the second-in-command of *Le Géographe*, Sainte-Croix Le Bas, was shot in the arm by the ship's engineer, François-Michel Ronsard.[37]

The French were treated well by the Dutch in Kupang. The local governor arranged housing on shore for the officers and the scientists and the sick crew. Baudin described how he was lavishly fed and entertained at the house of Madame van Esten, the widow of a former governor in a style that reminded him of 'a scene from a Paris opera'.[35] He said that the hostess was attended by more than one hundred beautifully dressed slaves, and that her guests were offered delicacies on fine silver and later escorted by torchlight back to their lodgings.

Finally, on the evening of 13 November – having replenished his ships and taken aboard more than 400 live chickens, goats, sheep and pigs – Baudin was ready to resume the exploration of the south of Terra Australis. Six sailors had already died before they sailed, and eleven more would perish at sea on the way to Van Diemen's Land.

Baudin planned to sail back down the west coast to Cape Leeuwin and take the westerly winds to Van Diemen's Land. He then proposed to sail up the east coast of Van Diemen's Land, loop back to the west through Bass Strait and explore the south coast from the east, as his original instructions prescribed – although he was a year later than planned.

Again, the French did not know that when they left Timor, Matthew Flinders had already been at sea for four months and was only three weeks from Cape Leeuwin, where he would begin his own exploration of the south coast – before the French could reach it.

*

The 6500-kilometre voyage of Le Géographe and Le Naturaliste from Timor to Van Diemen's Land demonstrated the critical importance of the winds to sailing ships. Because of contrary winds and calms, the first leg – of around 3600 kilometres, from Timor to Cape Leeuwin – took fifty-two days. By that stage, the Investigator was already well past Cape Leeuwin and preparing to leave King George Sound, 350 kilometres to the east. The next stage – of around 3000 kilometres, from Cape Leeuwin to Van Diemen's Land – took only eight days, as the French ships were driven by the strong westerly winds. Both ships dropped anchor in D'Entrecasteaux Channel on 13 January 1802. They were short of drinking water again. When Baudin ordered rationing, the zoologist François Péron said the restrictions were too severe and that, 'Some of our unhappy men were seen to drink their own urine.'[38]

After stepping onto dry land after nearly seven weeks at sea, the French spent five weeks around the D'Entrecasteaux Channel, where they replenished their stocks of firewood and water, and the scientists studied the surroundings and collected samples. They were on the lookout for English settlers, who they thought might have arrived by now (in fact, they did not start settling the area until a year later).

In addition to reprovisioning their ships, the French undertook some productive exploration around the island. Even though some survey work had been done by D'Entrecasteaux a decade before and by Flinders three years before, Baudin now comprehensively charted the Derwent River and the east coast of the island, from Cape Pillar in the south to Banks Strait in the north.

While they were in southern Van Diemen's Land, the French had a number of encounters with the local Aboriginal people, who, Baudin said, were generally friendly:

> These men were naked from head to foot. One, alone, wore a skin that covered his back and shoulders. They were paler in colour than the African negroes, and it is perhaps because they do not think of themselves as black enough that they daub various parts of their face with charcoal. Everyone was tattooed for about 6 inches below

the shoulders. The lines ran across and sometimes down. Furthermore there was nothing unpleasant about these men. Their expression was one of liveliness or even gaiety, and their glance was quick. Their noses were rather flat and their mouths wide.[39]

After leaving the D'Entrecasteaux Channel on 5 February, the ships began the survey of the east coast of the island and named a number of coastal features, including the Freycinet Peninsula, after the hydrologist on *Le Géographe*; and Point Mauge, after the zoologist René Maugé. (Maugé died off the east coast of Van Diemen's Land and was buried on nearby Maria Island. He had appeared to be recovering from being gravely ill with dysentery after leaving Timor, but his condition deteriorated as they sailed closer to Van Diemen's Land.)

While exploring the coast, *Le Géographe* lost one of its small surveying boats. On 7 March Baudin had ordered geographer Charles-Pierre Boullanger, with a crew of seven, to survey the coast from closer to the shore. Even though instructions were issued that *Le Géographe* was not to lose sight of the boat, it disappeared from view and by nightfall was lost. Throughout the night, Baudin ordered lights to be lit on the masts and rockets to be regularly fired, but still there was no sight of the dinghy. The next day they resumed the search, and very soon *Le Géographe* had also lost sight of *Le Naturaliste*.

On 10 March, *Le Géographe* encountered an English schooner named (coincidentally) the *Endeavour*, which was heading south on a sealing expedition. The *Endeavour*'s captain told Baudin that he had seen *Le Naturaliste* further north, but the English could not be persuaded by the French to postpone their seal hunt to help look for the lost dinghy. After five more days of fruitless searching,

Baudin set a course for the north of Van Diemen's Land, hoping to reconnect with *Le Naturaliste*.

A fortnight later, without *Le Naturaliste* and without Boullanger and his boat crew, Baudin finally began the voyage along the unknown coast from the east. As he admitted in a letter he later wrote to the Minister of Marine, he was again running short of time:

> Knowing that the season was beginning to advance and that there remained the work of exploring all the unknown coast of the south west of New Holland, I gave up the search for the *Naturaliste*, and even a visit to the northwest of Van Diemen's Land, so as to devote myself entirely to the task.[40]

By now Matthew Flinders on the *Investigator* had surveyed most of the south coast and was leaving Kangaroo Island, having already charted Port Lincoln and the Spencer Gulf.

Le Géographe headed north across Bass Strait to Wilsons Promontory, on the mainland, then past the entrance to Port Phillip Bay.

It was not until the beginning of March 1802 that Baudin passed the westernmost point of the southern Australian coast as previously seen by Europeans. At long last the French were starting a true voyage of discovery. They were now sailing west along a part of the unknown coast that no European had sailed before. By 30 March they had passed Cape Otway, and Baudin and his crew began to name certain features of the coast, including Guichen Bay (the site of current-day Robe), after Admiral de Guichen of the French navy.

However, the unique part of the expedition did not last long, because less than a week later *Le Géographe* encountered the *Investigator*, which was heading in the other direction.

The two ships sighted each other around mid-afternoon on 8 April. Flinders wrote:

> Before two in the afternoon we stretched eastwards again, and at four a white rock was reported from aloft to be seen ahead. On approaching nearer it proved to be a ship standing towards us, and we cleared for action, in case of being attacked. The stranger was a heavy looking ship, without any top gallant masts up.[41]

At first Baudin thought the *Investigator* was his second ship, *Le Naturaliste*:

> Shortly after, we sighted a ship which we thought at first could only be the Naturaliste, for we were far from thinking that there would be any other European in this region . . . Nevertheless we were greatly mistaken, for as we drew near her, we realized from her masts and size that she was not our consort.[42]

Flinders ran up a white flag but received no reply. Baudin recorded in his journal that the white flag was a signal to 'which we couldn't reply'.[43] Flinders said that he then replaced the white flag with an English flag and pennant, and Baudin responded with the French national colours.[44]

As the ships pulled alongside each other, Flinders asked for the identity of *Le Géographe* and Baudin replied 'French'. Baudin was surprised that Flinders knew who he was:

> As they spoke to us first, they asked what ship it was. I replied that she was French. They then asked if Captain Baudin was her commander. I was very

surprised, not only at the question, but having myself named as well.[45]

After the French commander had identified himself, Flinders removed his hat and his officers did the same. When Baudin and his staff returned the salute, Flinders ordered a boat to be rowed over to *Le Géographe* so he could meet Baudin.

Notwithstanding the civilities, the *Investigator* veered around as *Le Géographe* passed, 'so as to keep our broadside to her, lest the flag of truce be a deception'.[46] Each captain would have been wary of the other, as neither was aware that war between France and England had been suspended for six months, since the signing of the provisional Treaty of Amiens.

Because Flinders did not speak French, he took with him Robert Brown, the *Investigator*'s naturalist, to act as interpreter. Once aboard *Le Géographe*, they were received by an officer, who presented them to Baudin. He took them down to his cabin and surprised Flinders by meeting with them alone: 'No person was present at our conversations except Mr. Brown; and they were mostly carried on in English, which the captain spoke so as to be understood.'[47]

It might seem odd that Baudin, who spoke limited English, would meet with Flinders and Brown on his own ship but not invite any of the French officers to participate. It may have been that Baudin believed the meeting should involve only the two commanders and that Robert Brown was there solely in the event that a translator was needed. But stranger still, Baudin did not know he was meeting with Matthew Flinders, as he did not ask him his name.

Flinders began by asking to see Baudin's passport from the Admiralty; after reading it, he offered his own from the French Ministry of Marine, which Baudin returned without reading.

Baudin said he found Flinders 'extremely reserved' at their first meeting, which may have been because, at forty-eight years old, Baudin was twice his age and held a more senior rank than the twenty-four-year-old English lieutenant.[48]

The two commanders learned from each other that they had been exploring the south coast from different directions, Flinders from the west and Baudin from the east.

Flinders was the first to explore the south coast from Nuyts Archipelago to the point where they were now meeting. Baudin thought he was the first to have explored from Bass Strait to that point. But both would discover when they reached Port Jackson that much of the south coast Baudin had surveyed had in fact already been explored more than a year before by two British navy officers from Sydney, James Grant and John Murray. Grant and Murray – who had been sent on the sixteen-metre-long, sixty-ton *Lady Nelson* from England to Sydney – had been on the first to sail through Bass Strait from west to east since its discovery by Bass and Flinders three years before.

Flinders said that at their first meeting, Baudin asked little about Flinders's exploration and talked more about his own:

> It somewhat surprised me that captain Baudin made no inquiries concerning my business upon this unknown coast, but as he seemed more desirous of communicating information, I was happy to receive it.[49]

According to Brown's account of the meeting, Baudin went into some detail about his survey of the east coast of Van Diemen's Land and was critical of the accuracy of the English map, dated 1800, that he was using – not realising that he was discussing it with its maker.

Baudin also said he had discovered that what William Dampier thought was an island off Shark Bay on the west coast of New Holland was in fact a peninsula.

He told the Englishmen that the French had collected more than one hundred boxes of botanical samples, much of them from Mauritius. Brown later reported that he noticed in the captain's cabin rows of flowerpots filled with soil but no plants. Baudin also told Flinders that he intended to continue with his exploration to the west until the colder season forced him back to Sydney, where he hoped to replenish his ship.

The meeting lasted only about forty-five minutes, then Flinders and Brown left to go back to the Investigator. The next morning at around 6.30, Flinders, in full dress uniform, was rowed across with Brown for his second meeting with Baudin. Flinders said that the French captain was again alone, and more casually attired.

At this second meeting Baudin listened more while Flinders described his own exploration from Cape Leeuwin, which must have concerned Baudin, who would have now realised that he had been beaten in his quest to explore much of the south coast, despite having left Europe nine months earlier than the English expedition.

During the meeting, Flinders gave Baudin several new charts published by Arrowsmith in London and a memoir of his own explorations of Bass Strait, and the north and east coast of Van Diemen's Land. Baudin gave Flinders some of his charts, which Brown later said 'were finished and coloured but Captain Flinders thought that in their general appearance were rather below mediocrity'.[50] Having come from different directions, Flinders and Baudin each told the other that they had not seen any major rivers running into the sea on the coast they had both been skirting.

What they were unaware of was that barely twelve kilometres from where they were meeting, Australia's largest river system – later named the Murray – did indeed run into the sea. This oversight is understandable. The Murray – and all the other rivers that run into it, stretching back 2500 kilometres – empties into a huge lagoon, which was later named Lake Alexandrina, after the princess who later became Queen Victoria. The lake is hidden from the sea by a long, almost straight stretch of sand dunes; the release of water through the dunes is often quite small, and was particularly so at the time Flinders and Baudin were there.

In fact, on the morning of his encounter with Flinders, Baudin had been closely studying the very part of the coast into which the river flowed, but had seen nothing beyond the dunes: 'The entire stretch of coast that we have examined since yesterday consists solely of sand hills and inspires nothing but gloom and disappointment.'[51]

Baudin said he and Flinders exchanged stories of having lost boats and crews, and each promised to keep a lookout for survivors:

> I told him of the accident that had befallen my dingy and asked him to give it all the help he could if he had the chance to meet it; he told me of a similar misfortune that had happened to him, for he had lost eight men and a boat.[52]

Baudin also asked that should Flinders come across *Le Naturaliste* on his journey eastwards, he pass on an instruction to the captain to head back to Port Jackson when the 'bad weather set in'. Amazingly, it was not until Matthew Flinders asked the name of *Le Naturaliste*'s captain that Baudin finally asked Flinders his name:

> At parting the captain requested me to take care of his boat and people in case of meeting with

them; and to say to *Le Naturaliste* that he should
go to Port Jackson so soon as the bad weather set
in. On my asking the name of *Le Naturaliste*, he
bethought himself to ask mine; and finding it to
be the same as the author of the chart which he
had been criticising, expressed not a little surprise,
but had the politeness to congratulate himself on
meeting me.[53]

The second meeting took a little over an hour, and Brown
and Flinders were back on the *Investigator* and ready to
sail by 8.30 in the morning. After they parted at what
Flinders named Encounter Bay, *Le Géographe* headed in a
north-westerly direction.

After leaving Baudin, Flinders initially began sailing in
a south-easterly direction, in what he described as 'light
and unfavourable winds'.[54] He was now moving out of
unknown territory and along a coastline where others had
been before. Fewer than two weeks after leaving Baudin, he
reached Cape Otway, which was part of the coast already
charted by James Grant. A week after that, Flinders passed
an opening that he thought was Westernport but was in
fact Port Phillip Bay, which had been found only ten weeks
before, by Lieutenant John Murray, who had replaced John
Grant as commander of the *Lady Nelson*. (Murray had
named it King Bay, but Governor King later changed it to
Port Phillip Bay, after Arthur Phillip. It was on Port Phillip
Bay that the city of Melbourne would be established more
than thirty years later.)

Flinders anchored on the eastern side of Port Phillip
Bay and allowed the botanist Fowler to study the local
area for three days before they sailed up the coast to
Sydney, where they arrived on 9 May 1802. Flinders
had sailed more than 10,000 kilometres in more than six
months since arriving at Cape Leeuwin. Apart from John

Thistle and the seven other crew who had been lost, all hands were in good health when Flinders anchored in Sydney. He had charted a large part of the world's largest remaining unknown coast but had found no major river system and no strait separating New Holland and New South Wales.

*

Meanwhile, after his meeting with Flinders, Baudin pressed on with his westward exploration. But there was a limit to how far he could go. The southern hemisphere winter was approaching, *Le Géographe* was running short of provisions and scurvy had again broken out among the crew. Shortly before meeting Flinders, the French had harpooned nine large dolphins, which the zoologist Péron on *Le Géographe* said at least slowed down the rate of sickness:

> [The dolphins] seemed like a gift from heaven; for at this time the scurvy had begun its ravages, and the salt provisions, putrid and worm eaten, to which we had been reduced for several months increased daily the dreadful scourge.[55]

On 15 April Baudin completed his own survey of Kangaroo Island then crossed to Gulf St Vincent and the Spencer Gulf, which he surveyed, but not as far as Flinders had done. Pressing further west, he reached the Nuyts Archipelago, which Flinders had named.

Baudin was now becoming more isolated from his restless and disaffected crew. He was also aware of the growing disquiet among some of his officers and scientists, and alluded to the rift in his journal when on 17 April he cut the water ration again:

> As we still had plenty of work to do on the coast
> of New Holland and only had enough water for
> another two months, I judged it right to be cutting
> down on it in good time . . . instead of giving each
> man two and a half bottles of water, I gave him no
> more than two. Undoubtedly it was not a very great
> reduction . . . Nevertheless, it produced malcontents,
> not amongst the sailors, but in another quarter.[56]

Finally, in early May, he decided to abandon the quest and
to return the following year to try again. The reasons he
gave at the time included a shortage of water, no firewood,
fourteen crew already sick with scurvy, and too little food.
They were down to the last good cask of salted meat, and
the remaining dry sea biscuits 'had for a long time been
crumbling into dust, being riddled with worms and mites'.

> Some serious reflections, upon the position I was
> in, the weakness of my crew, which now consisted
> only of thirty men for the handling of the ship, our
> pressing need for firewood, the shortness of the
> days, and a host of other private considerations all
> decided for me to abandon the coast . . . and make
> for Port Jackson.[57]

Baudin considered returning to Timor or one of the other
Dutch East Indian ports but chose Port Jackson, because,
he said, it was 'infinitely preferable to the Moluccas, for
the sake of the crew's health'. He was no doubt remem-
bering the sickness that befell his crew on his previous
visit to Timor.

The trip to Port Jackson via the south of Van Diemen's
Land was a nightmare, with high seas, contrary winds
and rough weather. They were completely out of firewood and began to burn odd planks and used casks; the

scurvy was spreading; there was too little winter clothing, and much of it was too small to fit the sailors. To add to their woes, dysentery broke out anyway and began to kill people, including Baudin's cook.

Despite the protests of his increasingly sick crew, who Baudin said were convinced he wanted to bring about their deaths, he made the extraordinary decision to resume a detailed survey of the east coast of Van Diemen's Land before sailing north to Sydney.[58] He said that it would have been done the last time they'd been on the coast, but then they were looking for Boullanger and his crew:

> If I had not been unwell and obliged to keep to my cabin when we sailed along this coast in both directions trying to find our dinghy, this work would not have remained to be done.[59]

Baudin wrote in his journal that he 'needed only two days of good weather to complete the work'.[60] But he was not to have two fine days. Of the eleven days between 24 May and 4 June, the French could survey on only one of them. On several of the other days, they could not get close to the coast because of strong offshore winds. On the others, the winds were blowing strongly from the north-east or south-east, and Baudin no longer had enough fit crew to tack the ship.

On 4 June he realised he could do no more. It was by now impossible to sail the ship properly, as there were only 'four men able to remain on deck, including the officer of the watch', and Baudin had no choice but to make a straight run for Port Jackson. Confronted by adverse wind and weather, it took Le Géographe another three weeks to sail north along the New South Wales coast to Sydney, where the French discovered Flinders, who had already been at anchor there for more than a month.

CHAPTER 9

THE FRENCH AND ENGLISH RIVALS IN SYDNEY

*W*hen Nicolas Baudin sailed for the first time into Sydney Heads on *Le Géographe*, he was greeted by the sight of the *Investigator* at anchor. Matthew Flinders had been in Sydney since 9 May. Unlike the French, he was able to boast that after ten months at sea, his crew were in good shape:

> There was not a single individual on board who was not on deck working the ship into harbour; and it may be averred that the officers and crew were, generally speaking, in better health than the day we sailed from Spithead, and not in less good spirits. I have said nothing of the regulations observed after

we made Cape Leeuwin; they were little different from those adopted in the commencement of the voyage, and of which a strict attention to cleanliness and a free circulation of air in the messing and sleeping places formed the most essential parts. Several of the inhabitants of Port Jackson expressed themselves never to have been so strongly reminded of England as by the fresh colour of many amongst the *Investigator*'s ship's company.[1]

Flinders said that 'as soon as the anchor was dropped', he called on the governor of New South Wales, Philip King, who had replaced Flinders's friend and supporter John Hunter while Flinders had been back in England.

Hunter had been sacked. He had been given the letter ordering his return to England by King, who arrived in Sydney in April 1800, the month after Flinders had left to go home. The sixty-three-year-old John Hunter had struggled throughout most of his five years as governor, facing strong opposition from the military, which had gained overwhelming control of the colony's economy, including a monopoly on the lucrative rum trade. In the end, the British government had been swayed more by the private correspondence of disgruntled colonists than the dispatches from its governor, and the colonial secretary, the Duke of Portland, wrote a letter of dismissal to Hunter:

> Having now made all the observations which appear before me, it is with severe concern that I find myself obliged to add that I feel myself called upon by the sense of duty which I owe to the situation in which I have the honour to be placed to express my disappointment of the manner in which the government of the settlement has been administered by you in

so many respects – that I am commanded to signify to you the King's pleasure to return to this kingdom by the first safe convenience which offers itself after the arrival of Lieutenant King, who is authorised by his Majesty to take upon him the government of the settlement immediately on your departure from it.[2]

After handing over the governorship to King in September 1800, Hunter returned to England in May the following year and unsuccessfully requested a public inquiry into his dismissal, which he hoped would clear his name. Later he returned to naval service and was appointed rear admiral in 1807 and vice admiral three years later. He never married and passed his final years at his home in Hackney, London. He died on 13 March 1821, aged eighty-four.

Flinders was able to develop an equally good working relationship with Philip King, and King would become a strong supporter of his later explorations around Australia.

Philip Gidley King was forty-two years old and on his third tour of duty to New South Wales when he was appointed governor. Born into a modest family from Launceston in Cornwall, the son of a draper and the grandson of a magistrate, King joined the navy as a captain's servant on the *Swallow* at twelve years of age and spent five years in the West Indies and off the coast of America at the start of the War of Independence. In 1775 he was promoted to midshipman and in 1778 to lieutenant. It was in 1778, while serving on the *Ariadne*, that he met Captain Arthur Phillip, who later took him on the first fleet to establish the convict colony in New South Wales.

Only a week after reaching Sydney in January 1788, Phillip asked the then twenty-nine-year-old King to take a small party to establish a settlement on Norfolk Island, in the Pacific Ocean about 1500 kilometres to the northeast of Sydney. Phillip was in a hurry to stop the French claiming the island and instructed King 'to secure the island and prevent it being occupied by the subjects of any other European power'.[3] The British wanted the land, which had been noted by Captain Cook eighteen years earlier, because they thought it could produce superior hemp, or flax, which was used to make sails and canvas for the Royal Navy.

Less than three weeks after the arrival of the first fleet, King left Sydney in a tiny ship, the twenty-metre-long *Supply*, with perhaps the smallest party ever sent to establish a colony of the British Empire. The group included a surgeon, a carpenter, a weaver, two marines, eight male convicts and six female convicts.

For the next two years King supervised the tiny settlement, organising the clearing of land and struggling against grubs, rats, hurricanes and, occasionally, troublesome convicts. Thanks to the soil being more fertile than that in Sydney, he was able to report favourably on the island's harvests, but he was not successful in cultivating the flax plants.

In 1796, shortly after King had met Flinders for the first time, Flinders arrived at Norfolk Island on the *Reliance* with fresh supplies. Subsequently, King – who was plagued by illness, including severe gout – was given permission by Governor John Hunter to return to England. There he managed to manoeuvre himself into a position to replace his former boss Hunter as governor of New South Wales. After months of delays, carrying the letter of dismissal to deliver to his former friend, King sailed on the *Speedy*, which left England in November 1799. He reached Sydney the following April, but had to wait until September for Hunter to leave before he could formally take over.

When Flinders arrived in Sydney two years later on the *Investigator*, he gave Governor King an account of his explorations of the south coast and handed over a copy of his instructions, which included an order that the *Lady Nelson* – which was by then in Sydney Harbour – be made available to him. According to Flinders, King was eager to help in any way he could:

> His Excellency was pleased to assure me that every assistance in the power of the colony to render should be given to forward a service so interesting to his government, and to himself.[4]

When he reached Sydney, Flinders learned that while he had been preparing for his expedition in Portsmouth and later sailing from the west along the south coast of the great southern continent, two young Sydney-based English officers had been exploring much of the south coast of New South Wales using the *Lady Nelson*.

Twenty-eight-year-old Lieutenant James Grant had sailed the small sixty-ton *Lady Nelson* from Portsmouth to Sydney. He had left in March 1800, when Matthew Flinders was still on his way back to England on the *Reliance*, after five years in New South Wales. Grant – who reached Sydney nine months later, in December – was the first to sail west to east through Bass Strait.

On the way to Sydney through the strait, he named and made rough sketches of some of the prominent features along almost 600 kilometres of coastline stretching eastwards from near the current South Australia–Victoria border. These features included Mount Gambier, Cape Northumberland, Cape Bridgewater, Cape Nelson, Portland Bay, Cape Otway and Westernport, the last of which had previously been seen by George Bass on his whaleboat exploration in 1797.

In March the following year, when Matthew Flinders was still in England starting the preparations for his voyage on the *Investigator*, Governor Philip King sent Grant back to southern New South Wales to undertake a more comprehensive survey.

The *Lady Nelson* left Sydney on 8 March 1801 with Grant; Ensign Francis Louis Barrallier, who was the cartographer; George Caley, a botanist; the ship's mate, John Murray; and four soldiers from the New South Wales Corps. They also took two Aboriginal men to help them communicate with any locals they might meet.

Over the next two months Grant and his crew surveyed Westernport bay and further east along the coast to Wilsons Promontory; but, facing bad weather and the onset of winter, after some weeks they turned back to Sydney, arriving on 14 May. On their return, a disappointed King said that while he admired Grant as a seaman, he was less impressed with him as a surveyor.[5]

From all accounts, Grant was unhappy in New South Wales and was given permission to return to England in August 1801. Determined that the exploration continue, Governor King promoted the *Lady Nelson*'s mate, twenty-five-year-old Murray, to sublieutenant and sent him back to the south coast to complete the job that had been left unfinished by Grant.

Leaving Sydney on the *Lady Nelson* in September 1801, Murray surveyed the Kent Group of islands and the Furneaux Group of islands in Bass Strait, before crossing to map Westernport in December. At the time Murray was charting Westernport bay, Matthew Flinders was in King George Sound on the south-west of the continent, about to start his exploration of the south coast, and Nicolas Baudin was sailing from Timor for Van Diemen's Land.

In January 1802 Murray sailed into the bay where the city of Melbourne would later be established and took formal possession of the region in the name of King

George III, in a little ceremony that involved hoisting the flag on what he named Point Paterson. Murray named the bay King Bay, but on his return to Sydney in March 1802 Philip King renamed it Port Phillip Bay, in honour of his former boss and commander of the first fleet.

Matthew Flinders reached Port Phillip Bay ten weeks after John Murray, on his way to Sydney.

(Over the next twenty-five years the *Lady Nelson* would be involved in most of the important exploratory developments in the colony, including voyages that led to the later colonial establishment of Launceston, Hobart, Melbourne and Brisbane.)

Neither Flinders nor Baudin had any idea until they both reached Sydney in 1802 that when they had been charting the south coast of Australia, much of what is the current-day Victorian coast had already been explored by James Grant and then by John Murray. Between the two of them, Grant and Murray sketched or mapped more than 600 kilometres of coastline, though their achievements have attracted little recognition in the history of Australian exploration.

*

When Flinders had arrived in Sydney, the French ship *Le Naturaliste*, which had become separated from Baudin's *Le Géographe* two months before off the north-east coast of Van Diemen's Land, was already in the harbour. Also safely on board *Le Naturaliste* was Charles-Pierre Boullanger and the other eight French crewmen from the longboat that had been lost in the same area when surveying for *Le Géographe*. They had been picked up in Bass Strait by a small British brig, the *Harrington*, and brought to Port Jackson.

After losing *Le Géographe,* Captain Hamelin had continued on *Le Naturaliste* to survey both sides of Bass Strait, including Waterhouse Island, the Furneaux Group of islands, Port Dalrymple and Westernport. After several weeks, having given up any chance of finding Baudin's ship, Hamelin had headed for Sydney, where he'd arrived two weeks before Flinders.

Surprisingly, Hamelin left Sydney only a week after Flinders's arrival, even though Flinders had passed on the message that Baudin was heading for Port Jackson.[6] Hamelin said that he left early because, despite the cooperation of Governor King, there was a shortage of food in the colony and he wanted to find and warn Baudin:

> I have been able to procure here some wheat and brandy ... some potatoes and pumpkins. The Governor, Philip Gidley King, and Lieutenant Paterson have done all in their power to help us ... I leave tomorrow, to join if I can Commander Baudin, and to inform him of the scant resources offered by this colony, in which there is at present no salt meat, or rice or beans.[7]

Hamelin also said that if he did not find Baudin within six weeks, he would head for Mauritius and wait for him there. Five weeks after *Le Naturaliste* had left Sydney, Baudin arrived. According to Matthew Flinders, almost all of Baudin's crew was stricken with scurvy:

> It was grievous to see the miserable condition to which both officers and crew were reduced by scurvy; there being not more out of one hundred and seventy, according to the commander's account, than twelve men capable of doing their duty.[8]

As soon as *Le Géographe* anchored, Baudin sent his second-in-command, François-Michel Ronsard, to pay his respects to Governor King, who immediately invited the Frenchman to join him and his wife for dinner. Ronsard, who said that he was so hungry that he 'ate enough for four', was reassured by King, who spoke perfect French, that 'having gone around the world himself, he had more than once been in a similar position'.[9]

The sickest of the French sailors were taken into the colony's small hospital and, despite the shortage of fresh meat, some cattle were killed to help restore the health of the French:

> Before their arrival, the necessity of augmenting the number of cattle in the country had prevented the governor from allowing us any fresh meat; but some oxen belonging to the government were now killed for the distressed strangers.[10]

Baudin expressed his gratitude:

> [King provided] all that I could wish for, and from that moment he has not ceased to load us with kindness, furnishing us with provisions, all the things needed to cure our sick.[11]

Baudin also left a letter with the governor addressed to the French administration in Mauritius for the benefit of any English navigators who landed on the island and needed assistance. It is unfortunate that Flinders did not take a copy of the letter with him when he left Sydney, as it may have helped him considerably with the problems that awaited him on the island.

In Sydney, the French and the English got along well, helped by 'the intelligence of peace between the

two countries, which had just arrived'.[12] Baudin and
Governor King developed a genuinely warm friend-
ship. They were of similar age and rank, and both had
risen from relatively modest backgrounds to senior
positions in the navy. Also, King's fluent French helped
him converse with Baudin, who did not speak English
very well. When Baudin left Sydney, he donated fifty
pounds for a girl's orphanage in Sydney and promised
to write regularly, saying that he hoped he had been
able to inspire in King the same feelings that King had
inspired in him. King responded by saying it would be the
'greatest pleasure' to keep in touch.[13] Indeed, they would
continue to write to each other after the Frenchman had
left Sydney.

Flinders described a dinner he hosted on the *Investigator* for Governor King, Baudin and a number of French
officers, including the French zoologist François Péron
and King's deputy, William Paterson, who was an enthusiastic naturalist. During the evening, Flinders showed
Baudin some of his maps of the south coast. Baudin said
that he had not made maps, because he would take all his
'bearings and observations' to France, where 'the charts
were made at a future time'.[14]

Now they had landed, some of the French officers
made no secret of their resentment that the French expedition had thus far been more focused on natural history
than exploration, while the English were making important discoveries of hitherto unknown lands. According
to Flinders, the twenty-three-year-old French sublieutenant Henri Freycinet complained to him about Baudin's
leadership at a dinner hosted by Philip King at Sydney's
Government House: 'Captain, if we had not been kept
so long picking up shells and catching butterflies in Van
Diemen's Land, you would not have discovered the south
coast before us.'[15]

*

Baudin said he was astounded that Hamelin had sailed out of Sydney on *Le Naturaliste* before the arrival of *Le Géographe*. So undoubtedly he would have been equally surprised to see *Le Naturaliste* sail back into Port Jackson several weeks later.

After leaving Sydney, Hamelin had taken *Le Naturaliste* south, but when he was unable to find Baudin and *Le Géographe*, he decided to head for Mauritius. He first tried to sail through Bass Strait but was forced back by strong westerly winds and high seas. He then tried to navigate around the south of Van Diemen's Land, but it was too late in the season and he was again thwarted by strong headwinds. He also realised that he had used up valuable time and had to admit to his colleagues that they would not have enough provisions to reach Mauritius. So he decided to turn back to Sydney.

For the next six weeks the *Investigator*, *Le Géographe* and *Le Naturaliste* would all be in Port Jackson together. Realising Baudin and his men were on the same quest to complete the map of Terra Australis, Flinders was eager to resume his exploration, but he seemed to be the only one in a hurry to leave, noting that the French 'were in no forwardness for sailing'.[16] He stayed in Sydney for barely eleven weeks before heading out on the next leg of his expedition in July. By comparison, *Le Géographe* stayed five months and *Le Naturaliste*, omitting the temporary absence, five and a half. The two French ships eventually left four months after the *Investigator*, on 18 November 1802.

Baudin never gave an explanation as to why he was so slow in resuming his exploration. He was already more than a year behind schedule and appeared to have completely abandoned the timetabled instructions he had been issued before leaving France.

According to those, at the time he was still in Sydney in November 1802, he should have already completed his expedition and been more than halfway home to France:

> As soon as the last part of the expedition was finished, Citizen Baudin was to head towards Ile de France.
>
> This he will presumably reach before the end of Fructidor [mid-September]. After staying in the colony the length of time that he judges it necessary for giving his crew the rest that they may need, for repairing his ships and for supplying himself with food and refreshments, he will set sail again to return to Europe. If he is ready to do so in the first ten days of Brumaire, year 11 [end of October 1802], he could be back in a French port by the middle of Ventose [first days of March 1803].[17]

It was now more than eighteen months since Baudin had left Europe. For the first eighteen months some casualness may have been understandable, because he did not know that the British had sent out a rival expedition on a similar quest to his. However, now he had met Flinders and been made aware of the intentions of the British, his lack of haste is difficult to understand.

*

Preparing the *Investigator* for the next voyage was initially no easy task for Flinders, as the *Coromandel*, which had been sent by Evan Nepean with additional supplies from England, had not yet reached Sydney. The convict settlement of Sydney was still experiencing severe food shortages and high prices:

> The price of fresh meat at Port Jackson was so exorbitant, that it was impossible to think of purchasing it on the public account. I obtained one quarter of beef for the ship's company, in exchange for salt meat, and the Governor furnished us with some baskets of vegetables from his garden . . . Fish are usually plentiful at Port Jackson in the summer, but not in winter time . . . a few were, however, occasionally brought alongside, from boats which fished along the coast.[18]

Flinders managed to buy 30,000 pounds of biscuit, 8000 pounds of flour and 156 bushels of wheat; but he ordered that if anyone wanted more than the most basic food, they had to buy it for themselves.

Part of the ship's preparations involved erecting on the quarterdeck a greenhouse that had been designed at the behest of Joseph Banks. However, when they began to assemble the parts, which had been stored below, they discovered it was too big. Flinders said they feared that the structure, pots, soil and plants would make the ship top-heavy in rough seas, so the greenhouse was cut back in size.

Over the next two months Flinders supervised the work on his ship. The *Investigator's* hull was in fairly good shape considering it had been in the water without significant maintenance for more than a year. The ship had been leaking when they left England and had been caulked in Cape Town the previous October. This involved squeezing tar into the gaps between the planks, and after that Flinders said it was much improved.

Finally, in June, to Flinders's relief, the *Coromandel* arrived. His preparations were greatly helped by the arrival on it of more food and also replacement sails, cables, ropes, anchors, chains, tar, paint and varnish.

During the stay in Sydney after ten hard months at sea, he had disciplinary problems with some his crew, who were enjoying the benefits of being ashore. On five occasions he had to order the lash for a variety of offences, including absences from sentry posts, drunkenness and 'mutinous expression'.[19]

He also needed more crew – both for the *Lady Nelson*, which would accompany him on the next leg of his journey, and to replace the eight men he had lost off the south coast:

> Finding it impossible to fill up the complement with free people, I applied to the Governor for his permission to enter such convicts as should present themselves and could bring respectable recommendations.[20]

He was able to recruit nine convicts and was given the power by Governor King to grant conditional emancipation or absolute pardons if they conducted themselves well. To complete the crew he also took two local Aboriginal men, who it was hoped would allow 'friendly intercourse with the inhabitants of other parts of the coast'.[21] One was a 'good-natured lad' named Nanbaree, who would leave the expedition and return to Sydney within a month. The other was Bungaree (or Bongaree), whom Flinders described as a 'worthy and brave fellow'.[22]

Bungaree was born in Sydney; when he met Flinders his age was unknown. He had first been with Flinders on the exploration of the north coast of New South Wales on the *Norfolk* in 1797. And it was with Flinders that he would become the first Aboriginal to circumnavigate Australia. Wearing discarded English uniforms and a cocked hat, the tall Bungaree was a well-known figure in the colony from the time of Governor Hunter, in the 1790s, until that of Sir Thomas Brisbane, almost a quarter of a century later. He was married to several women, and in 1815 Governor Lachlan Macquarie gave him a farm on the outskirts of Sydney for his extended family. In 1817 he set off again on a major British exploration when he sailed with Phillip Parker King on an expedition around the north-west Australian coast. He died in 1830 and was buried in Rose Bay, on Sydney Harbour.

*

Before he left Sydney, Flinders wrote a number of letters home, including to his wife, Ann, to whom he said, 'Heaven knows with what sincerity and warmth of affection I love thee.'[23] He also wrote to Sir Joseph Banks:

> I placed in the hands of Governor King two copies of my chart of the south coast of Terra Australis, in six sheets; three with other sheets of particular parts, on a large scale. One copy I requested him to send with my letters to the secretary of the Admiralty, by the first good opportunity that was offered; the other was to remain in his hands until my return, or until he should hear of the loss of the Investigator, when it was also to be sent to the Admiralty.[24]

The *Investigator* sailed out of Sydney Harbour on 23 July 1802, heading north to continue surveying the coast in an anticlockwise direction. When Flinders was saying goodbye to Baudin:

He told me that we should probably meet in the Gulf of Carpentaria in December or January. I understood that he meant to return to the south coast, and after completing its examination, to proceed northward, and enter the Gulf with the north-west monsoon; but it appeared to me very probable, that the western winds on the south coast would detain him too long to admit of reaching the Gulf of Carpentaria at the time specified, or at any time before the south-east monsoon would set against him.[25]

Baudin was still slowly completing preparations to resume his exploration to the south in a clockwise direction. *Le Naturaliste* was particularly plagued by rats, which had eaten not only much of the food on board but also sails, cable and paper, as well as some of the crew's clothing.

Both ships were completely emptied and cleaned, and after more than five months they had been re-equipped with everything from 'jersey frocks to hair ribbons'. Seventy-two bottles of lime juice to combat scurvy had been bought at twelve shillings each, paid for with promissory notes to be later redeemed from the French government.[26]

With Governor King's permission, Baudin also now purchased a schooner, the *Casuarina*. At thirty tons and twenty-nine feet long, it was smaller and capable of surveying closer to shore than either *Le Naturaliste* or *Le Géographe*. Now he had this new ship, Baudin decided to send *Le Naturaliste* back to France with the bulk of what was already a large collection of plants, seeds, animals and minerals, and a 'number of useless men' he believed incapable of making a positive contribution to the next stage of the expedition. [27]

On 18 November 1802 the three French ships finally left Port Jackson. They planned to sail together through Bass Strait, before *Le Naturaliste* headed for France via Mauritius and *Le Géographe* and the *Casuarina* continued the exploration of the south coast.

CHAPTER 10

ENCIRCLING AUSTRALIA

*A*fter consulting Governor Philip King on the route he would take, Matthew Flinders left Sydney in July 1802 with the *Investigator* and the *Lady Nelson*, to begin what would become his circumnavigation of Australia.

As he was about to start out, Flinders appeared totally undaunted by a voyage of nearly 14,000 kilometres, around the entire coast of a continent that had no settlements or established ports in which to replenish supplies or seek refuge:

> My instructions directed me to consult with Governor King upon the best means of proceeding in the execution of the voyage . . . It was decided to proceed to the northward – examine Torres Strait and the east side of the Gulf of Carpentaria before the north-west monsoon should set in – proceed as I might be able during its continuance – and

afterwards explore the north and north-west coasts; returning to Port Jackson when, and by such route as might be found most advisable, and conducive to the general purpose of the voyage.[1]

As he proceeded north along the east coast of New South Wales, he kept a lookout for any wreckage of the ships of the lost French explorer La Pérouse, who had disappeared more than a decade before. Flinders speculated that *La Boussole* and *L'Astrolabe* could have been smashed on the island of New Caledonia, more than 1000 kilometres to the east, and that parts of the wrecks might have floated to the north coast of Australia:

> At every port or bay we entered . . . my first object of landing was to examine the refuse thrown up by the sea. The French navigator La Pérouse, whose unfortunate situation, if in existence, was always present to my mind, had been wrecked, as it was thought, somewhere in the neighbourhood of New Caledonia; and if so, the remains of the ships were likely to be brought along this coast by the trade winds, and might indicate the situation of the reef or island which had proved fatal to him . . . though the hope of restoring La Pérouse or any of his companions to their country and friends could not, after so many years, be rationally entertained, yet to gain some certain knowledge of their fate would do away the pain of suspense.[2]

Flinders's first objective was Breaksea Spit, at the end of Hervey Bay, some 1300 kilometres north of Sydney. He had first explored this area three years before, and had discovered Fraser Island there. He now realised that thirty years before, Captain Cook had misjudged the width of Hervey Bay and that all his calculations from there to Torres Strait were therefore inaccurate. As Flinders headed north, with the help of more accurate timekeepers, he correctly charted that the coast trended further to the west and that Torres Strait was nearly sixty kilometres further west than Cook had thought.

At the end of July, the English had their first threatening encounter with the locals, when Robert Brown, the ship's botanist, and Peter Good, its gardener, went ashore at Sandy Cape, on the northern point of Fraser Island, to collect samples as some of the other crew collected fresh water and firewood. Near the cape, the English were met by a group of local Aboriginal men, who were gesticulating to them to retreat. Bungaree, one of the two Aboriginal men from Sydney aboard the *Investigator*, came to the rescue and defused the situation:

> Several Indians . . . were waving at us to go back. Bongaree stripped off his clothes and laid aside his spear, as inducements for them to wait for him; but finding they did not understand his language, the poor fellow, in the simplicity of his heart, addressed them in broken English, hoping to succeed better. At length they suffered him to come up, and by degrees our whole party joined, and after receiving some presents, twenty of them returned to the boats, and we feasted on the blubber of two porpoises.[3]

Charting the north-east coast through the Great Barrier Reef proved to be difficult going, through constant shoals and mangrove swamps, which required a smaller boat that could reach up the shallow coastal streams, to get closer and accurately map the coastline. The *Lady Nelson* should have been invaluable in areas such as these, but to his disappointment Flinders found it was not up to the task. In his journal he recommended against trying to sail inside the reef:

> The commander who proposes to make the experiment, must not, however, be one who throws the ship's head round in a hurry, so soon as breakers are announced from aloft; if he does not feel his nerves strong enough to thread the needle, as it is called, amongst the reefs, while he directs the steerage from the mast head, I would strongly recommend him not to approach this part of New South Wales.[4]

In early October the *Lady Nelson* lost her anchor, and two of her three sliding keels were damaged. Flinders said her poor sailing and slowness made her more of a hindrance than a help, so he decided to send Murray and the ship back to Sydney and continue exploring alone with the *Investigator*:

> The *Lady Nelson* sailed so ill . . . that she not only caused us delay, but ran great risk of being lost; and instead of saving the crew of the *Investigator*, in case of accident, which was one of the principal objects of her attendance, it was too probable we might be called upon to render her that assistance . . . she was become, and would be more so every day, a burden rather than an assistant to me.[5]

Before the *Lady Nelson* left, three of its crew were brought aboard the *Investigator*, including midshipman Denis Lacy, who had been lent to the *Lady Nelson*'s captain, John Murray, at the start of the voyage. Nanbaree, the other of the two young Aboriginal men with Flinders, was homesick and was allowed to go home on the *Lady*

Nelson, leaving Bungaree to complete the expedition on the *Investigator*.

On 20 October, having logged 800 kilometres in fourteen days, the *Investigator* broke out of the Great Barrier Reef into the Pacific Ocean and headed for the Torres Strait, which it reached nine days later. For three days, Flinders nosed his way through the shallow passages of the strait. He had been there a decade before, when he sailed on Captain William Bligh's second expedition to fetch breadfruit plants from Tahiti.

He was eager to get through the strait and begin the survey of the Gulf of Carpentaria, as the November monsoons were soon approaching, but he suggested a more comprehensive survey of the strait be undertaken later by the British to ensure that the safest passage through its narrow shoals could be found for shipping.

As he passed into the Gulf of Carpentaria, Flinders acknowledged that nearly two centuries before, in 1606, the Dutchman Willem Janszoon had been here, though he had thought he was still following the New Guinea coast and was unaware that he had in fact discovered the coast of the great southern continent:

> The course of the *Duyfken*, from New Guinea, was southward, along the west side of the Torres Strait, to that part of Terra Australis, a little to the west and south of Cape York; but all these lands were thought to be connected, and to form the west coast of New Guinea. Thus, without being conscious of it, the commander of the *Duyfken* made the first authenticated discovery of any part of the Great South Land, about the month of March, 1606.[6]

From late October, Flinders began surveying the coastline. On Sunday, 15 November he reached the southernmost point of the gulf, where he was satisfied that the Old Dutch charts were correct and that no strait split Australia:

> In the afternoon our course along the shore was more westward; and this, with the increasing shallowness of the water, made me apprehend that the Gulf would be found to terminate nearly as represented in the old charts, and disappoint the hopes formed of a strait or a passage leading out at some other part of Terra Australis.[7]

While on the mainland to collect botany samples, the English met a group of Aboriginal men who fished in canoes built from branches of mangroves lashed together at each end. Flinders said they were the tallest 'Indians' he had ever seen but that otherwise 'their features did not much differ from those of their countrymen on the South and East coasts'.[8]

In late November, almost five months after leaving Sydney, Flinders found himself in the remote Top End of Australia near an island that he named after Lord William Bentinck, the governor of Madras. His ship was leaking badly – taking in twenty-five to thirty-five centimetres of water an hour – so, understandably concerned, he ordered a thorough assessment of the vessel:

> While the carpenters have been employed caulking the ship's bends, they have been bringing to me, almost every hour, report after report, of rotten parts found in the different parts of the ship, timbers, planking, bends, tree-nails, etc., until it is become quite alarming. Taking the matter into consideration I determined to have an accurate statement of the condition of the ship as could be obtained without impeding the progress of our voyage.[9]

The report provided by the ship's master, John Aken, and the carpenter, Russel Mart, was indeed alarming. Many of the timbers below the waterline were rotten and the ship could not be beached and put on its side for repairs for fear that it would not bear its own weight. Master Aken said that when ships such as the *Investigator* began to rot, 'they went very fast' and that even if the weather remained fine and the ship suffered no accidents, it might survive only another six months.[10] He even suggested:

> In a strong gale, with much sea running, the ship would hardly escape foundering; so that we think she is totally unfit to encounter much bad weather . . . We have no doubt that, if the ship should get on shore under any circumstance, she would immediately go to pieces.[11]

Flinders was angry that the poor condition of the ship had not been detected before:

> If the condition of the ship is as bad as above stated, it surprises one that something of it should not have been found out before, when the ship was in the dock at Sheerness, or when she was caulked at the Cape of Good Hope, or at least in Port Jackson . . . Two years back when the *Investigator* underwent repair in dock, she could not be a quarter part so bad as she now is.[12]

Flinders's claim that he was surprised at the news of the ship's poor condition is a little hard to understand. Having been given the *Investigator* in England, he'd spent more than six months on its preparation and surely would have had the opportunity to ensure its hull was shipshape. Not only that, but before he left England he declared that it

was the best ship for the voyage ahead.[13] Certainly, early
on in the voyage from England he complained that the
ship did leak very badly, but after being caulked in Cape
Town it took on little water for the rest of the voyage to
New Holland. Also, before the ship had left Sydney, only
three months before Aken and Mart's inspection, Flinders
had supervised several months of maintenance of the ship,
during which rotten timbers might have been detected.

At any rate, given the precarious state of his ship,
Flinders had to make a decision as to how to proceed.
They were 2000 kilometres from the nearest European
settlement, in Timor, and 6000 kilometres from Sydney:

> Laying aside the two great questions, our safety,
> and the completion of the voyage, for the present,
> I have decided to go on in the examination of the
> gulf, if the north-west monsoon does not prove too
> great a hindrance, and afterwards act as the rising
> circumstances shall most seem to require.[14]

Though he decided to continue with the expedition – he
had very little choice, because of their location – Flinders
admitted that the coast could not be 'minutely examined'
as he had to stay a fair distance from the shore to avoid
being hit by breaking waves.

In the gulf country, Flinders saw no more potential for
settlement than the Dutch had more than a hundred years
before; he said its soil was infertile and the trees small and
only fit for firewood.

At the end of November they encountered another
group of Aboriginal men and were surprised they were
not hostile:

> I had been taught by the Dutch accounts to expect
> that the inhabitants of Carpentaria were ferocious,

and armed with bows and arrows as well as spears. I found them to be timid; and so desirous to avoid intercourse with strangers, that . . . there was then nothing ferocious in their conduct.[15]

While the ship anchored for a few days near the Wellesley Islands in early December, the crew restored their stock of fresh food by catching seven tons of turtles and seven tiger sharks; the largest of the sharks was almost three metres long. They also cut out the turtles' and sharks' livers and boiled them down for oil, which was used to fuel the ship's lamps.

As Christmas approached, the *Investigator* began to sail up the western side of the gulf, landing on islands that Abel Tasman had thought were part of the mainland and had named Cape Vanderlin. Flinders renamed them the Sir Edward Pellew Group of islands; Pellew, who had by then served in the navy for thirty years, had become famous five years earlier, in 1797, for his victory in a sea battle against the French.

Flinders made no reference in his journal to Christmas Day, which the crew presumably spent sailing, in contrast to the previous year, when they held a party at King George Sound, on the south-west coast.

At the end of December Flinders said he found plenty of evidence of what he thought was a Chinese settlement on the islands:

> Indications of some foreign people having visited this group were almost as numerous, and as widely extended, as those left by the natives. Besides pieces of earthen jars and trees cut with axes, we found remnants of bamboo lattice work, [and] palm leaves sewn with cotton thread into the form of such hats as are worn by the Chinese.[16]

They also found the remains of blue cotton cloth – 'of the fashion called moorman's', which they believed were Chinese-style trousers – and 'a wooden anchor of one fluke', the triangular blade at the end of an anchor designed to catch in the ground.[17]

Flinders said they were puzzled by a stone wall and a structure that appeared to house a number of fireplaces; they guessed they were made by Chinese for processing nutmegs:

> What puzzled me most was a collection of stones piled together in a line, resembling a low wall, with short lines running perpendicularly at the back, dividing the space behind into compartments. In each of these were the remains of a charcoal fire, and all the wood near at hand, had been cut down. Mr. Brown saw on another island a similar construction, with not less than thirty-six partitions, over which was laid a rude piece of frame work; and the neighbouring mangroves, to the extent of an acre and a half, had been cut down. It was evident that these people were Asiatics, but of what particular nation, or what their business here, could not be ascertained; I suspected them, however, to be Chinese, and that the nutmegs might possibly be their object.[18]

It was now the height of the southern hemisphere summer and the English were plagued by flies, which were the curse of all European explorers to Australia. Flinders noted 'their extraordinary numbers, and impudence' and wrote: '[They] get into the mouth and the nose, and settle on the face or any other part of the body . . . [and are not] driven away easily.'[19]

As the new year of 1803 – which would be an awful one for Flinders – began, the *Investigator* reached Groote

Eylandt, which had been charted by Abel Tasman, and featured prominently on old Dutch maps. Near the island, one of the *Investigator*'s crew, seaman William Murray, was drowned when he fell out of the whaleboat in which he had been sent ahead to check the sea depth.

On the mainland opposite Groote Eylandt, they saw 'pieces of bamboo and other traces of the same foreign people' they had seen before, and an unusual cemetery:

> No natives were seen anywhere; but several skeletons were found, standing upright in the hollow stumps of trees; and the skull and bones being smeared or painted, partly red and partly white, made a very strange appearance.[20]

On a nearby island they were to name Chasm Island, botanist Brown found some new species of edible plants, including a *Eugenia*; it bore fruit that was about the size of an apple and quite tasty, and it showed 'the admirable power in nature to accommodate itself to local circumstances'.[21] And Flinders recorded that they made their first discovery of Aboriginal art:

> In the steep sides of the caverns ... upon the walls ...
> I found rude drawings, made of charcoal or something like red paint upon the white ground of the rock. These drawings represented porpoises, turtle, kangaroo, and a human hand.[22]

The artist on the *Investigator*, twenty-two-year-old William Westall, analysed the art. He counted thirty-two people in single file following a large kangaroo. The third person in line was twice the height of the others and carried in his hand a *whaddie*, or wooden sword, which Westall thought represented superior power in a group that was in the early stages of social organisation.[23]

On 21 January some crew who'd been sent ashore for wood and water were confronted by a group of Aboriginal men armed with spears. Bungaree was not with the *Investigator*'s men when the master's mate, John Whitewood, reached out for a spear he thought he was being offered and was pierced by it in the chest. A number of musket shots were fired and spears thrown, which resulted in one of the Aboriginals being killed. John Whitewood was carried back to the *Investigator* with four spear wounds. A marine – Thomas Morgan, who had been in the sun all day without a hat – was 'struck with a coup-de-soleil', or sunstroke, and was also carried on board but 'died in a state of frenzy, the same night'.[24]

As the exploration continued, Flinders named scores of places along the north-east coast and across the north of Australia as he had done along the southern coast the year before.[25] He named Melville Bay after the 2nd Viscount Melville, who would later become First Lord of the Admiralty; Port Curtis after Admiral Sir Roger Curtis; Port Bowen after the British naval commander at Madeira when the *Investigator* had been there two years before; Mount Grindhall after a vice admiral; Point Blane after Sir Gilbert Blane of the Naval Medical Board; and Caledon Bay after the 2nd Earl of Caledon, who was later the governor at the Cape of Good Hope.

Flinders even named some features of the coast after earlier Dutch explorers, including Duyfken Point, after the Dutch ship of Willem Janszoon; Pera Head, after a later Dutch ship to sail into the Gulf of Carpentaria; and the Wessel Islands, after the name on one of the Dutch charts used by Flinders. To the channel leading into the Torres Strait he gave the name Pandora Entrance, after the English ship the *Pandora*, which had sunk there when returning with some of the captured mutineers from the *Bounty*.

In mid-February, 105 days since passing through the Torres Strait, Flinders named a cape after William Wilberforce – 'the worthy representative of Yorkshire' – and said the Dutch navigators had done a pretty good job mapping the coastline:[26]

> And thus was the examination of the Gulf of Carpentaria finished, after employing one hundred and five days in coasting along its shores and Strait to Cape Wilberforce . . . It will be remarked that the form of it, given in the old charts, is not very errone-ous, which proves it to have been the result of a real examination.[27]

On Friday, 16 February, Flinders was surprised to see six small boats at anchor on the remote north-west of the Australian coast. At first he thought they might be pirates and sent his younger brother Samuel 'with a boat manned and armed to learn who the people were'.[28] He discovered they were Malays collecting trepang, or sea cucumber, which they dried and smoked and took back to the Tanimbar Islands, about 500 kilometres to the north-west, from where they were shipped to China for making soup.

Deducing these men meant no harm, Flinders invited the captains of each of the six ships aboard the *Investigator*:

> On looking into the launch, [they] expressed great horror to see hogs there; nevertheless they had no objection to port wine, and even requested a bottle to carry away with them at sunset.[29]

With his Malay cook, Abraham Williams, acting as inter-preter, Flinders learned that the six boats were part of a fleet of about sixty carrying roughly 1000 men, now spread out along the coast; they came each year from as far north as

Makassar, in Celebes (current-day Sulawesi). The fishermen explained that they expected other boats to arrive soon, and together they would go east, into the Gulf of Carpentaria.

Apparently fishermen had been working along the north Australian coast for centuries and formed part of the Aboriginal stories in this area.[30] Their boats weighed about twenty-five tons and each carried twenty-five men. Pobassoo's carried two small brass Dutch guns. The fishermen carried no charts, and their only nautical instrument was a 'very small pocket compass, apparently of Dutch manufacture'. In the dry season they carried about a month's supply of drinking water and several months' supply of rice, coconuts and dried fish.[31] Before leaving, Flinders asked Chief Pobassoo if he knew of any major rivers along the coast further to the west, and Pobassoo said no.

After this, Flinders spent several weeks charting a group of islands in north-east Arnhem Land. He named one Pobassoo Island, after the leader of the Malay fishermen, and others the English Company Islands, after the English East India Company.

He then abandoned further exploration. Saturday, 5 March 1803 was the last day of surveying Flinders, aged twenty-nine, ever did. On the remote north-west coast of Australia – more than 6000 kilometres from the only European settlement, in Sydney – he decided to cease his survey because of the deteriorating condition of the *Investigator* and the declining health of the crew:

> I judged it imprudent to continue the investigation longer. In addition to the rottenness of the ship, the state of my own health and that of the ship's company were urgent to terminate the examination here; for nearly all had become debilitated from the heat and moisture of the climate – from being a good deal fatigued – and from the want of nourishing food.[32]

Flinders was also in a hurry to replenish his supplies at Timor and hurry back to Sydney before the southern hemisphere winter:

> I calculate, that if we sail immediately for Port Jackson, our arrival will complete very nearly the six months specified in the survey [of the ship's poor condition] and that we shall pass along the south coast and through Bass Strait, where the worst weather is to be expected, before the hard winter winds have gained their strength . . . a heavy gale would probably founder her, and be the loss of almost the whole produce of our risks and labours, as well as the loss of our lives.[33]

Flinders was at a low ebb. On the way to Timor he penned a letter to his wife Ann in which reiterated his love for her:

> My dearest love . . . Our voyage has hitherto gone on prosperously upon the whole, but the poor ship is worn out, – she is decayed both in skin and bone. I am going to Coupang Bay [Kupang] to get refreshments for my noble fellows, that they may the better stand the fatigues of the remaining part of the voyage . . . Not knowing what opportunity may offer of sending home letters; I have begun to write already: but as the greater part of what I have to say must depend upon the occurring circum-stances at Coupang, my writing must cease till they are known . . . I am indeed, my only beloved, thine with all the fervour with which I loved thee after marriage; for before that time, I thought indeed I loved thee much, but knew not what much was till afterward. In evenings I oft take a book, reclining on my little couch, and running o'er some pleasant

tale or sentiment, perhaps of love, my mind retraces
with delight, our joys, our conversation, our looks,
our everything of love . . . Good bye, my love . . .
and rest assured of the sincere love of thy Matthew
Flinders.[34]

The sail to Timor took three weeks, during which time the
health of the crew further deteriorated due to the stifling
heat and insufficient food. During the voyage, the ship's
surgeon, Hugh Bell, reported that twenty-two of the crew
were stricken with scurvy and four were unable to do any
work. Flinders realised that more than one and a half
years away from England – most of it at sea – had taken
its toll on the men:

> It is now more than nineteen months since we sailed
> from England, and during this time there have been
> only two opportunities of receiving the usual port
> refreshments: four days at Madeira, and eight days
> at the Cape of Good Hope, and once on His Majes-
> ty's birth-day at Port Jackson . . . For the last eight
> months, we have had no refreshments but what
> chance threw in our way, and fruit and vegetables,
> the best antiscorbutics, formed no part of what was
> procured. During this period the crew has been
> exposed to almost incessant fatigue in the oppres-
> sively hot climate.[35]

The stricken ship entered the harbour of the small
Dutch outpost with its sick crew on 31 March 1803.
After anchoring, Flinders sent Samuel ashore to pay his
respects to the Dutch governor, Mynheer Giesl and to
arrange the proper salute, which involved firing the ship's
guns – as a sign of respect, and peace – and flying the
host's ensign.

The Dutch administration was obliging but explained that it was unable to provide much help. There was little surplus food in Kupang, as the locals imported many of their supplies from the larger Dutch provincial port of Batavia, almost 2000 kilometres further west, at the other end of the Indonesian archipelago.

It was too early in the season for many local fruits to be available, but the English were able to buy some coconuts, oranges, limes and bananas, and some vegetables, which were expensive and of poor quality. They also managed to purchase some rice and meat – including local buffalo, small pigs and goats – as well as tea and sugar from the little shops kept by the local Chinese-Malays.

Flinders was disappointed to learn that he could not send any of his charts and journals to England: a ship bound for the Cape of Good Hope had left only ten days before, and it was not known when the next would sail. Nor was there any other ship in the port available for sale that might replace the *Investigator* for the rest of the voyage.

He observed that, like Batavia and other Dutch outposts in the East Indies, Kupang was a decidedly unhealthy place for Europeans, and said that anyone who stayed any length of time there looked 'sickly'. He also recorded in his journal that Baudin, who had been there the year before, 'had lost twelve men from dysentery'.[36]

The *Investigator* stayed only a week at Kupang, during which time the botanists studied the local flora and Flinders busied himself with some astrological observations and wrote a number of letters, including to his wife and to Sir Joseph Banks. These would take a long time to reach England, because they first had to wait for a ship that would head for Batavia, then the Cape of Good Hope, then probably Amsterdam and finally London.

On 7 April, when the *Investigator* was ready to leave, it was discovered that two of the crew, seaman Mortlake and the Malaysian cook, Abraham Williams, had deserted. Desertions like these were unsurprising at such times. The seamen who feared the dangers of another long voyage would stay in hiding until the ship left, then would hope to secure passage on the next one arriving in the port on its way to Europe. Captains coming into port with depleted crews due to scurvy and other diseases and misadventures at sea would rarely ask questions of able-bodied crewmen who presented and declared themselves prepared to work for their passage home. Flinders sent Lieutenant Fowler to report the desertions to the governor, who was sympathetic but not encouraging. So Flinders weighed anchor, saluted the Dutch with thirteen guns and, with inadequate fresh food on board, was again on his way.

The 8000-kilometre return journey to Sydney by way of the western Australian coast would establish Flinders's reputation as the first man to circumnavigate Australia – even though the French explorer Bruni D'Entrecasteaux could have claimed to have done it a decade before, in 1792, when he had sailed from Van Diemen's Land and back.

The voyage back on the *Investigator* was a nightmare. Within two weeks of leaving Timor and heading south, Surgeon Bell reported that in addition to worsening scurvy there were ten cases of dysentery on the ship. The men began to die. On 13 May they reached Cape Leeuwin, on the tip of south-west Australia, and five days later landed on an island in the Archipelago of the Recherche to look for food and water.

For three days some of the men were sent to fish and hunt seals. Others searched for drinking water, but most of the wells were too salty. Before they left, William Hillier, who Flinders said was one of his best sailors, died and was buried on the island.

On 25 May, as they passed Spencer Gulf, the sergeant of marines, James Greenhalgh, died and eighteen of the crew were too sick to work and lay 'stretched in their hammocks almost without hope'.[37] Winter was approaching, and now, instead of the unbearably hot and humid tropics, the crew had to contend with rain and the cold air of the Southern Ocean. Finally, after sailing through Bass Strait, the *Investigator* headed north, but quartermaster John Draper and seaman Thomas Smith died, almost within sight of Port Jackson, and were buried at sea.

When Flinders left Timor to sail back to Sydney he would have again passed – but did not see – his rival Nicolas Baudin off the north-west coast of New Holland. By the time Flinders had reached Sydney, Baudin had reached Kupang, having completed his survey of the south coast, and much of the west.

Over the previous year both Nicholas Baudin and Matthew Flinders had faced many unforeseen difficulties, great hardship and even tragedy – but for both of them there was much worse to come.

Abel Tasman with his wife and daughter. Tasman was responsible for two great voyages of discovery. In 1642 he was the first to reach Van Diemen's Land, which he named and claimed for Holland before sailing on to discover the South Island of New Zealand. In 1644 he sailed along more than 5000 kilometres of the north Australian coast from the east of the Gulf of Carpentaria to North West Cape.

While on an eight-year adventure sailing around the world, in 1688 the pirate William Dampier became the first Englishman to land on Australia. A decade later, he made a second visit as commander of a British navy expedition.

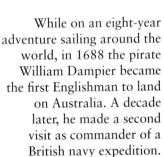

In 1769 James Cook was sent on the *Endeavour* to the South Pacific by the British government to observe the Transit of Venus, the first of three great voyages there. He then sailed west and in 1770 landed on the east coast of Australia, which he named New South Wales and claimed in the name of King George III.

Twenty-six-year-old Joseph Banks cemented his reputation as a botanist on Cook's *Endeavour*. Over the next fifty years Banks was a dominant influence on British expeditions to Australia and on the decision to establish a convict settlement at Botany Bay.

Jean François de Galaup La Pérouse was in the third year of his vast Pacific exploration when he sailed into Botany Bay in January 1788, only days after the arrival of the first fleet of British convicts. He left three weeks later and was never seen again.

Joseph-Antoine Raymond de Bruni D'Entrecasteaux was sent by King Louis XVI in 1791 to search for La Pérouse and to continue French exploration of Australia. He became the first to sail around the continent – a decade before Matthew Flinders.

CIGNE NOIR DU CAP DE DIEMEN.

On D'Entrecasteaux's expedition, botanist and artist Jacques-Julien Houtou de Labillardière made beautiful drawings of the flora and fauna the men came across.

After the mutiny on the *Bounty* in 1791, William Bligh returned to Australian waters, with eighteen-year-old midshipman Flinders on his crew, on another expedition to collect samples of the breadfruit from the Pacific.

WILLIAM BLIGH

John Hunter, Arthur Phillip's deputy on the first fleet of convicts in 1788, returned as the second governor of New South Wales in 1795. During his tenure he ordered Matthew Flinders on his first expeditions north and south of Sydney.

In 1795 Matthew Flinders and George Bass set off to explore the rivers and bays south of Sydney in the three-metre *Tom Thumb*, which was probably the smallest vessel ever used in European exploration history.

George Bass.

After confirming Van Diemen's Land was an island and charting the Bass Strait with his friend Flinders in 1798, George Bass resigned from the navy to become a trader. He left Sydney for South America on his ship *Venus* in 1803 and was never seen again.

Matthew Flinders by Toussaint Antoine de Chazal de Chamerel, painted in Mauritius in 1806–7. In July 1801 twenty-seven-year-old Matthew Flinders left England – seven months after his rival Nicolas Baudin had left France. Both men hoped to chart the 'unknown' south coast of Australia.

Government House in Sydney by William Westall. Westall produced over 1500 paintings and drawings of his visit to Australia on Matthew Flinders's *Investigator*. In 1802 Governor Philip King hosted a number of dinners in Government House for officers of the rival English and French expeditions, who were in Sydney at the same time.

The ill-fated Nicolas Baudin was a popular choice to lead the French exploration of the Australian coast, but he became isolated from fellow officers and scientists on the expedition because of his autocratic manner and a series of injudicious decisions.

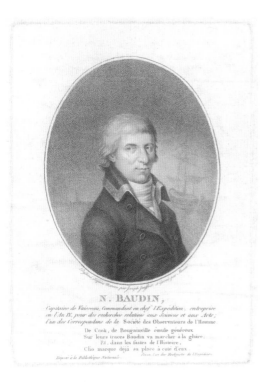

Botanist François Péron was given the task of writing the official account of Baudin's expedition, after his commander died on the way back to France. However, Péron himself died before finishing his narrative.

In Sydney, Lieutenant Henri Freycinet complained to Flinders about his leader, Baudin, saying that the French would have beaten the English in mapping the south coast had they not been 'kept so long picking up shells and catching butterflies' in Van Diemen's Land.

As governor of the French-controlled island of Mauritius, Charles Mathieu Isidore Decaen held Flinders prisoner even after Napoleon had agreed to his release. Flinders called in at the island for fresh water and supplies on his way back to England and was held captive there for more than six years.

CHAPTER 11

THE FRENCH
HEAD FOR HOME

Le Géographe, *Le Naturaliste* and *Casuarina* had left
Sydney together on 18 November 1802 and headed
south down the New South Wales coast to complete the
French mapping of the Australian coastline.

As he left Sydney, Baudin recorded an interesting story
of how, with the connivance of his friend Governor Philip
King, he helped the young daughter of a convict woman
escape on *Le Naturaliste*. The seventeen-year-old came
aboard as the assistant to an English surgeon named
Thompson and his wife, whom Baudin had agreed to take
back to Europe as passengers. As a result of meeting this
young girl, Baudin described in his journal some of the
more extreme consequences of convict transportation:

> At about eleven at night an English girl name Mary
> Bickaith appeared aboard in men's clothing. I had

known her during my stay at Port Jackson and she had more than once asked me to obtain Governor King's permission for her to return to England as Mr. Thompson's assistant. I had promised her to interest myself in her case and indeed spoke to the Governor. He would not have refused me this request had it not been contrary to the general instructions concerning deported persons, but he told me that if she wanted to leave, no inquiry would be made about her. She was therefore taken aboard the *Naturaliste*, on the day before departure, but she was unable to re-enter England without authentic permission from the Governor. I have embarked her to set her down somewhere in the Moluccas [Maluku Islands].[1] Her youth will soon be noticed there and will find her some happy fate. The young lady comes from a good family in England. She voyaged out to accompany her mother, who had been condemned to end her days at Port Jackson for having taken a length of muslin from a shop where she had made some other purchases. The girl preferred to accompany her mother in to exile rather than be put in a convent – the only consolation offered her for the loss of her mother.[2]

Baudin added that he found her more interesting 'on account of her behaviour than for her prettiness', though it may be that her looks didn't harm her cause.

Once through Bass Strait, the French ships split up after Captain Emmanuel Hamelin hosted a farewell dinner on *Le Naturaliste*, anchored off King Island, for Baudin and his officers. Baudin said he was deeply emotional and saddened by the departure of Captain Hamelin, little knowing that he would never see him again:

We wished each other safe journey and good health, and she bore away. This moment of separation was extremely painful for me and I felt a pang that obliged me to seek my cabin. I was truly fond of Captain Hamelin for his personal qualities, and when one shares the same dangers for two years it was natural to feel as I did at his departure.[3]

Four days after the farewell, Baudin was surprised by a visit from Captain Charles Robbins, on the English ship the *Cumberland*, which had hurried from Sydney with a letter from Governor King. In the letter, King said that immediately after the French had left Sydney, he had been alarmed to hear from his deputy, William Paterson, a rumour that the French planned to establish their own colony on Van Diemen's Land:

> You will be surprised to see a vessel so soon after you . . . but this has been hastened by a report communicated to me soon after your departure, 'that the French intended to settle in Storm Bay Passage, somewhere about what is now called Frederick Hendricks Bay, and that it was recommended to you by the Republic' . . . You will easily imagine that if any information of that kind had reached me before your departure I should have requested an explanation.[4]

Baudin wrote two letters – one official and the other private – to reassure the governor that the French had no plans to establish a settlement, and Robbins took them back to King. In the official letter, Baudin said the rumour King had heard was baseless and that if he had been instructed by the French government to settle somewhere in Van Diemen's Land, he would still be there and not hundreds of kilometres further west. In the private letter to his friend, he gave further assurances, even questioning European colonisation of new lands:

> I now write to you as Mr. King my friend, for whom I shall always have a particular regard . . . To my way of thinking, I have never been able to conceive that there was justice or even fairness on the part of Europeans in seizing, in the name of their governments, a land seen for the first time, when it is inhabited by men who have not always deserved the title of savages or cannibals that has freely been given them; whereas they were still only children of nature and just as civilised as your Scotch Highlanders or our Breton peasants, etc., who, if they do not eat their fellow-men, are just as objectionable. From this it appears to me that it would be infinitely more glorious for your nation, as for mine, to mould for society the inhabitants of its own country over whom it has rights, rather than wishing to occupy itself with the improvement of those who are very far removed from it by beginning with seizing the soil which belongs to them and which saw their birth.[5]

Baudin went on to describe how British settlement was devastating the local culture and how attempts at assimilation were failing:

> If you will reflect on the conduct of the natives since the beginning of your establishment upon their territory, you will see that their aversion for you, and for your customs, has been occasioned by the idea which they have formed of those who wished to live among them. In spite of your precautions and the punishments undergone by those of your people

who have ill-treated them, they have been able to discern your projects for the future, but being too weak to resist you, the fear of your arms has made them emigrate, so that the hope of seeing them mix with you is lost, and you will soon remain the peaceful possessors of their heritage, as the few who now surround you will no longer exist.[6]

Baudin's letter is unusual for its insight into the injustice of European annexation of territory, and enlightened for its time. It is also remarkable for its accurate prediction that white occupation would devastate Aboriginal civilisation.

King may have been assured that his friend was not about to establish a settlement to Sydney's south, but he was nevertheless suspicious of the French government's intentions. Later the same year, he sent a group to settle on the Derwent River, near what is now Hobart, and dispatched David Collins, the colony's first judge, to found a settlement on Port Phillip Bay, near current-day Melbourne. The following year, another party was sent to settle at Port Dalrymple, near the future site of Launceston.

In early January 1803 *Le Géographe* and the *Casuarina* circumnavigated Kangaroo Island, which had earlier been charted by Flinders, before sailing across to conduct a more detailed study of Spencer Gulf and Gulf St Vincent. The French would stir up considerable controversy in 1811 when they renamed the two gulfs Golfe Bonaparte and Golfe Josephine.

At Kangaroo Island and along the south coast, Baudin's party collected a number of kangaroos, some of which were believed to have been new species. Initially the animals were kept in a gangway of *Le Géographe* and covered by a tarpaulin. Two died and the others were suffering from exposure and the wet weather, so the naturalist

Louis Leschenault and Sublieutenant Joseph Ransonnet were ordered to vacate their cabin in order that the surviving animals could be housed more comfortably. Baudin acknowledged in his journal that forcing the two men out of their accommodation added them to the list of 'malcontents' among his fellow officers and the scientists.[7]

In early February, the French ships reached the islands of St Francis and St Peter in the Nuyts Archipelago. Here *Le Géographe* and the *Casuarina* became separated. Louis-Claude Freycinet, who had been appointed by Baudin to command the *Casuarina*, headed for King George Sound, some 1500 kilometres to the west, where the ships met again in Princess Royal Harbour on 17 February.

Two days after reaching King George Sound, the French had a chance encounter with an American sealing ship, the *Union*. The ship's captain explained that they had left New York five months before but after visiting several places had 'only' collected 'three to four hundred skins'. They needed to get about 20,000 before heading to China to sell the catch.[8] They said they had come to King George Sound because the English explorer George Vancouver had reported the seals were plentiful there, but they had found fewer than they expected. Baudin invited the captain aboard for dinner and gave him a number of maps of the south coast and Bass Strait, where the Americans hoped to have more luck with their fishing.

The French stayed in King George Sound for eleven days to collect water and firewood and catch fish, and there they recorded the first encounter by Europeans with the Aboriginal people of the area. Sublieutenant Ransonnet was sent with some men to survey further along the coast and encountered a group of eight Aboriginals. The three women hurriedly left, but the five men accepted gifts of the Frenchmen's coat buttons and happily consumed the coffee, salt pork and biscuits offered to them, though they would not eat the bacon.[9] The locals responded by giving Ransonnet a stone axe. According to Ransonnet, the men were tall, thin and very agile, with long black hair, flat noses and fine white teeth. They were naked except for thick belts woven from kangaroo skins, and they talked a great deal and sang in a monotone. They were relaxed with the Europeans and took them to a well, which had excellent water, but would not let the French move in the direction where their women were hiding.

Freycinet and his commander had a number of arguments while they were in King George Sound. Freycinet listed in his journal several complaints against Baudin, including his restrictions on lending the *Casuarina* small boats from *Le Géographe* with which to collect fresh water and firewood from the mainland.[10]

The French left King George Sound at the beginning of March 1803 and sailed back around Cape Leeuwin to conduct a more detailed survey of Geographe Bay, where Baudin had started his Australian expedition the year before.

Much of the west coast of New Holland had been sighted by Europeans during the previous 200 years – mostly by the Dutch – but swathes had not been charted, and Baudin planned to fill in the gaps. On the way to Geographe Bay, he ordered a search for the equipment lost when the longboat had capsized the year before, when Thomas Vasse was believed drowned.

By now Baudin was issuing instructions to Louis-Claude Freycinet in writing, including a threat of disciplinary action if the *Casuarina* again lost contact with *Le Géographe*. 'From now on, then, it rests with you to accompany me or not,' he wrote.

> [The] separations that we have already experienced . . . you could have easily prevented, either by manoeuvring or by carrying out the orders given to

you. [In the event of another separation], you will have to be personally answerable to the authorities in France.[11]

After Geographe Bay, Baudin continued to survey until he reached Shark Bay in mid-March. By now Freycinet had lost any respect for his commander, and relations between the two men were so strained that other than Baudin's written instructions there was practically no communication between them. Baudin recorded that he gave Freycinet 'a scolding I hope he will never forget for the good of the service as for himself'.[12]

On Faure Island on the entrance to Shark Bay, French sailors found the remains of a creature Baudin believed to be a hippopotamus. The English explorer Dampier had made a similar claim more than a hundred years before, but it is widely believed that it was, in fact, a dugong:

> I had always regarded as most extraordinary, and I would say improbable, Dampier's report of having found part of a head of a hippopotamus in a shark's stomach. But to go by the dead animal that the men found in the Isle aux Tortues [Turtle Island] when they went turtle hunting, there seems hardly any doubt that the teeth that they brought back and handed me belonged to a similar species . . . The animal was possibly six foot long . . . By means of reasoning, its head could have been a third of the size of its body and its tail roughly two foot long . . . However imperfect the description given me of this animal might be, I thought I recognised in it a perfect resemblance to the hippopotamus, which I am well acquainted with, having killed several in the [Congo].[13]

After six days at Shark Bay, the ships left and began to survey 1500 kilometres of coast from North West Cape to the Bonaparte Archipelago, which had been seen by a number of explorers since Abel Tasman but had not been comprehensively charted. Features along this part of the coastline included Exmouth Gulf, Thevenard Island, Barrow Island, Delambre Island, the Muiron Islands, the Rosily Islands, and the Geographe Shoals.

In March 1803 they sailed through the Dampier Archipelago, which they named after the Englishman who had been there a little more than one hundred years before. Further north, they named Roebuck Bay after Dampier's ship. Then they took bearings from thirteen capes, including Cape Gantheaume (current-day Gantheaume Point), named after a French admiral; and Cape Boileau, after the French poet Nicolas Boileau-Despréaux.

It was while Baudin was exploring this coastline that the *Investigator*, on its return journey to Sydney, would have passed the French ships. The English would have sailed within about a hundred kilometres of the French, who were charting closer to shore, on about 18 April.

Off the north-west tip of New Holland, the French then had what Baudin said was an extraordinary encounter with Malay fishermen, as Flinders had had off the coast of Arnhem Land several months before. Baudin described seeing four canoes carrying men who were similar in appearance to some he had seen when he was previously in Timor. The fishermen were hunting turtles and told Lieutenant Freycinet that they came to the area only at certain times of the year and did not establish any settlements on the shore.

At the end of April, having reached the same point he had the year before, Baudin again quit the coastal survey and headed to Timor to replenish, before returning to explore the north and the Gulf of Carpentaria. Baudin and one or two of his men were ill, but the rest of the crew was in reasonable condition. While they were in the tropics everyone had been given a daily drink of lime juice, which had been taken on board at Port Jackson. The object of the lime juice was not only to stave off scurvy, but also to combat the heat.

The ships reached the port of Kupang in the middle of May, only days before Matthew Flinders and the *Investigator* arrived back in Sydney.

During their four-week stay on Timor, the French restocked food and water, and the naturalists continued to collect botanical and zoological samples. The animal they had the most difficulty catching was a crocodile. The local Malays were superstitious and frightened of the crocodile and would only guide the French to its haunts about forty kilometres from Kupang, where the giant beast was shot by the French. The zoologist François Péron skinned it, and the skeleton and skin were carried on a cart pulled by a horse that was led by a local Malay holding a very long rope. On board the ship, the skin began to putrefy and was thrown overboard, but the skeleton was eventually exhibited in a museum in Paris.

On 3 June *Le Géographe* and the *Casuarina* left Timor, heading to survey the Gulf of Carpentaria. Six of Baudin's crew had deserted in Kupang, but four had been found and dragged back to the ship. Many others on board were sick with venereal disease, and shortly after leaving the port, Timor's 'malevolent legacy' of dysentery spread among the crew. Only two days out of Kupang, the twenty-three-year-old astronomer Pierre François Bernier died.[14] Baudin, who was still sick himself, was deeply saddened by the loss, saying that Bernier 'worked the hardest' of all the scientists on the expedition:

> The loss of Citizen Bernier is an unhappy event, not only for us, but also for the Government, for there

is no doubt that he would have become a learned astronomer.[15]

Baudin headed to the north-west coast of Australia and charted more than 1000 kilometres from the region of Cambridge Gulf, Cape Dussejour (named after the mathematician Achille Pierre Dionis du Séjour) and Lacrosse Island (after the French navyman Jean Baptiste Raymond de Lacrosse), over to what he named Joseph Bonaparte Gulf (after Emperor Napoleon's oldest brother). On the way, he named Lesueur Island, after the artist on *Le Géographe* Charles-Alexandre Lesueur; Cape Rulhiers, after a poet; Cape Bernier, after the late astronomer on the expedition; and Cape St Lambert, after another poet.

Just as Flinders had failed to find major rivers on the east and south coasts, Baudin failed to find the major rivers that entered the north-west coast, including the Ord, the Fitzroy and the Victoria, which were all named decades later.[16] The mouths of all three rivers are behind islands and enter the sea in bays deep inland. To confirm the sources of the rivers would have required searching the shorelines of the bays and inlets for up to hundreds of kilometres.

Baudin left the coast and sailed across to Bathurst and Melville islands. The winds were now against him as he sailed directly east to his destination, the Gulf of Carpentaria; and on 7 July 1803, after a quest of nearly three years, he finally abandoned the remainder of his expedition and turned for home. The final stages of the voyage had been dogged by bad winds, lack of food and water, sickness and the poor sailing of the *Casuarina*, which was not as good a boat as the *Geographe*. Baudin was also becoming increasingly ill, and complained of 'a worse bout of blood spitting' than he'd had previously:

> It is not without regret that I decided upon this step.
> A thousand reasons should have made me take it

even earlier; but without listing them all, I shall limit
myself to saying that we no longer had anything
more than a month's supply of biscuit, at the rate
of six ounces per man, and two months of water,
as a result of the amount consumed by the birds
and the quadrupeds. Twenty men were ill, several
with dysentery, the others unfit for duty because of
the serious venereal disease contracted at Timor.
Nobody to replace me. The *Casuarina*, which I have
never been able to make good headway, no matter
what I have tried, and which is the sole reason for
my not having reached the gulf a long time ago, etc.,
etc., etc.[17]

Rather than experiencing disappointment, the exhausted
French crew was delighted at the decision, said a mid-
shipman on *Le Géographe*, Charles Baudin (no relation to
Nicolas):

One night, at nine o'clock [the captain] came on
deck and ordered the officer of the watch to steer
a course for the Ile de France [Mauritius] . . . In an
instant the news spread throughout the ship. The
half of the crew asleep below sprang up in a transport of joy, congratulating and hugging each other,
and everyone spent the night on deck dancing and
singing.[18]

Indeed, Baudin said that a number of the crew regularly
checked the ship's compass to make sure they had turned
for home, and that during the night there were more men
on deck than ever before.

It was also the case that by now the French had almost
enough information from their own charts and those
of earlier explorers to complete a map of the continent

of Australia. They had not completed a detailed survey of the Gulf of Carpentaria, as Flinders had done. However, they had extensive charts from their exploration of the west and north-west coasts, where Flinders had not undertaken any mapping.

Le Géographe reached Mauritius a month later. The Casuarina – separated from the bigger ship in a storm, during which a member of its crew fell overboard and drowned – arrived twelve days later.

After anchoring in Port Louis, the French heard news of Le Naturaliste, which they had last seen at King Island, off the south coast of Australia, eight months before. Le Naturaliste's Captain Hamelin had not intended stopping on his voyage back to France but had been forced to call in to the French port for ten days for fresh water and to caulk the leaking ship. Hamelin had left a letter for Baudin, in which he reported that he had taken on board more animals on Mauritius and that most of the live animals they were taking back to France were in good health for the voyage home.

Many of the crew of Le Géographe and the Casuarina were sick with scurvy on arrival in Port Louis and were taken immediately to the local hospital. Baudin at least had been lucky enough to have survived this latest outbreak. In a letter sent a week later on a passing American ship to his old friend Philip King, he said that his health had been a concern but that he was getting better. However, the disease in his lungs, now believed to have been tuberculosis, continued to worsen, and a month later Baudin died.

François Péron, who later wrote a description of the funeral, said his captain had been ill for a long time and his death inevitable:

> Since our arrival in the colony, his condition has become much worse; for a long time all hope of

a cure has been lost, and the doctors' efforts were intended only to defer for a few days the end determined by the nature of his illness. At last the moment arrived, and on 16 September 1803, around noon, Mr. Baudin ceased to exist. On the 17th he was interred with the honours due to the rank he held in the navy. All the officers, all the scientists of the expedition assisted in the procession, which was attended also by the principal authorities of the colony.[19]

Midshipman Charles Baudin was far more candid. He had joined *Le Géographe* as an eighteen-year-old in 1800 and went on to serve for almost fifty years in the French navy, eventually reaching the rank of admiral. In his memoirs he described the death and funeral of his chief:

His funeral was nothing less than dismal; he was universally detested. He had shown great strength of spirit in his last days. He had collected in a jar of spirits of wine the lungs he had brought up in his untold suffering, and he showed them to everyone who came to visit him. 'Are the lungs indispensable to life?' he would say. 'You see, I no longer have any, yet I still exist.'[20]

A note of sympathy for Nicolas Baudin came from Lieutenant Pierre Milius of *Le Naturaliste*. Milius had fallen sick after the French had been at Timor the first time, in 1802, and had left the expedition in Sydney and later reached Mauritius by sailing via China. He said that Baudin was prepared to sacrifice 'even his life to fulfil entirely the objects of his mission'.[21]

The command of *Le Géographe* passed to the thirty-one-year-old Milius, who took the ship back to France, along with Louis-Claude Freycinet and the crew of the *Casuarina*. The *Casuarina* was left behind in Port Louis.

Le Géographe left Mauritius in December 1803 and arrived back in France on 24 March 1804 after an expedition of nearly three and a half years. Unfortunately, many of the animals collected on the voyage had died on the journey home, including six kangaroos, two emus, two wombats and forty-five birds. The survivors included two kangaroos, two emus and five parrots, and a number of animals from the East Indies they had loaded aboard at Timor. When they reached the Cape of Good Hope they loaded more animals, including an ostrich, a cassowary, two lions, two panthers, a civet, two mongooses, a jackal, a hyena, a gnu, a zebra, two deer, five lemurs, two monkeys, two porcupines and thirty-two tortoises.[22]

The *Géographe* was now extremely overcrowded. In addition to the large number of birds and animals loaded in Australia, Timor, Mauritius and the Cape, Milius also had to accommodate the crew of the *Casuarina* and twenty passengers who boarded at Mauritius. As more of the cabins were needed for the extra animals, all the officers were now forced out of their quarters to lodge together in the great cabin.

On arrival at Le Havre, the surviving animals were loaded into nine carriages and escorted by a troop of gendarmes and Joséphine Bonaparte's bird keeper in a procession to Paris, which attracted large crowds. Separately, thousands of seeds and nearly 300 plants were carried to the city in special tubs.

With Baudin dead and unable to write the customary account of the expedition, twenty-nine-year-old François Péron lobbied the French government to be permitted to write it. Only a month after *Le Géographe* arrived back in France in 1804, he wrote to the Minister of Marine pointing out that he was the last of the naturalists who had left France in 1800 with Baudin. All the others had either died or left the expedition.[23]

Baudin's reputation and legacy suffered as a result of his dying before he could write up an account of his expedition. It was no secret that Péron had despised his commander, and in his official account – of which the first volume was published in 1808 – he made a series of highly critical comments about Baudin's decisions. He could not bring himself to mention Baudin by name except when he wrote 'Mr. Baudin ceased to exist'; in all other cases he referred to him only as 'our leader' or 'the commandant'.

Among Péron's criticisms of Baudin was that he did not take sufficient measures to prevent scurvy, which resulted in unnecessary deaths.[24] It was claimed that the death rates on Le Géographe and Le Naturaliste were too high compared with other long voyages.[25]

In fact, the number of deaths on Baudin's expedition was no higher, and probably lower, than on comparable voyages.[26] According to Lieutenant Pierre Milius, thirty-two died on Le Naturaliste and Le Géographe out of a total of 238 who left France. By comparison, Matthew Flinders lost twenty out of seventy-eight who sailed on the Investigator, and Cook forty-one out of ninety-four on the Endeavour. On the other French voyages, the D'Entrecasteaux expedition lost eighty-nine out of 219 on his ships, La Recherche and L'Espérance; and La Pérouse lost thirty-five out of 220 on L'Astrolabe and La Boussole before both ships disappeared. Also, relatively few of Baudin's crew died of scurvy. The greatest cause of death was dysentery, which attacked the crew after they had visited Dutch East Indies ports. The rest of the deaths were the result of tuberculosis, drowning and other accidents.

François Péron helped shape an overwhelmingly negative view of Baudin and his achievements in France.

After reading Péron's account, Conrad Malte-Brun, the eminent Danish-French geographer, condemned the choice of Baudin as the expedition's leader:

> If one is to believe the authors of this narrative, the impressive travellers who at the call of glory threw themselves into a dangerous career, saw themselves delivered over to the ineptitude of a leader who neglected all of his instructions, ran headlong into all the obstacles that he had been warned to avoid, knew nothing of how to use the winds or currents, hindered even the investigation he was required to promote, and, to crown it all, sacrificed to a solid avarice or to a culpable negligence, the health and life of all his colleagues.[27]

Disfavour of Baudin reached all levels of the French government, even Napoleon Bonaparte, who is said to have commented, 'Baudin did well to die; on his return I would have had him hanged.'[28]

Certainly Baudin made many mistakes and some strange decisions. He did not complete the mapping of much of the coast he had been instructed to survey. Also, by not keeping to his timetabled instructions and arriving in Australia months after he was due to, he squandered the start he had had over his rival, Matthew Flinders, and lost the opportunity to be the first to chart the south coast.

But there can be no doubt Baudin's expedition achieved a number of things, notably in geography, zoology, botany, anthropology and art. His ships brought back to Europe some 200,000 botanical and zoological species, many of them previously entirely unknown to the Old World. The specimens of plants and animals – some dead and some alive – included shells, plants, seeds, kangaroos, wombats and emus. Many of the botanical and zoological samples were recorded in 1500 magnificent paintings and drawings by Charles-Alexandre Lesueur, and the Aboriginal people were portrayed in the work of artist Nicolas-Martin Petit. The French also advanced Europe's anthropological knowledge of Australia and could point to overwhelmingly peaceful encounters with the Aboriginal people they met.

Baudin's problem was that none of the survivors of the expedition was prepared to promote his achievements or defend his reputation after they returned to France. With his autocratic manner and bizarre decisions, he had become increasingly isolated as the voyage progressed. He had begun to lose the support of many of his colleagues from the start of the voyage, in 1801, and by the time of his death many of his fellow officers and most of the scientists had come to detest him.

CHAPTER 12

SHIPWRECK

*W*hen Flinders arrived back in Sydney in June 1803, after his circumnavigation of Terra Australis, he had enough information from his own exploration and previous navigators' charts to set to work compiling the first complete map of Australia, and was therefore keen to return home to England.

But the crew of the *Investigator* was, of course, in a terrible state, including Flinders, who had by now broken out in sores from scurvy. Eleven of his men were too ill to walk ashore and needed to be carried to the small hospital in Sydney. There, four days later, the *Investigator*'s popular gardener Peter Good died. The remainder of the crew was put on a diet of fresh vegetables and fresh meat, which Flinders said were now more plentiful in Sydney than previously:

> Such was the favourable change in the state of the colony in one year, that the meat, pork one day and

mutton the other, was obtained at the average price of 10 pence per pound, which before, if it could have been obtained, would have cost double the sum.[1]

Waiting for the explorer in Sydney were letters from home, including one in which his mother broke the news that Flinders's father had died. In a letter sent back to his mother, he expressed great sorrow:

> My dearest mother,
>   . . . The death of so kind a father and who was so excellent a man, is a heavy blow and strikes deep into my heart . . . I laid such a plan of comfort for him as would have tended to make his latter days the most delightful of his life . . . how I valued my father. One of my fondest hopes is now destroyed. O, my dearest, kindest father, how much I loved and revered you, you cannot know how.[2]

Flinders also responded to the six letters that were waiting for him from Ann, and learned that his good friend George Bass – who three years before had left the navy to become a trader – had been back in Sydney while Flinders had been away. Bass had arrived in Sydney with a cargo of goods but had left again on the *Venus* four months before Flinders's return. Before leaving Sydney, Bass had negotiated a contract with Governor Philip King to import pork to the colony from the Pacific Islands and to bring in other food from New Zealand and South America. He left Sydney on 5 February 1803 for South America and was never heard of again.

In his journal, Flinders noted how much the now fifteen-year-old convict colony had advanced in the eight years since he had first arrived there with Captain John Hunter:

In 1803, it was progressively advancing towards a state of independence on the mother country for food and clothing; both the wild and tame cattle had augmented in a proportion to make it probable that they would, before many years, be very abundant; and manufactures of woollen, linen, cordage, and leather, with breweries and a pottery, were commenced. The number of inhabitants was increasing rapidly; and that energetic spirit of enterprise which characterises Britain's children seemed to be throwing out vigorous shoots in this new world . . . All this, with the commerce carried on from Sydney to Parramatta and the villages at the head of the port . . . made the fine harbour of Port Jackson a lively scene of business, highly interesting to the contemplator of the rise of nations.[3]

He also wrote that in Sydney and Parramatta, brick and stone houses were replacing those made of timber and bark; roads, bridges and wharves were being constructed; and agriculture was expanding to the west of Sydney:

Increasingly on the west of Sydney and Parramatta where the soil is more fertile, wheat, barley, oats, maize and the vegetables and fruits of southern Europe were being grown.[4]

The population of the colony had more than doubled, to 7000 people (with another 1500 on Norfolk Island); 125,000 acres (42,000 hectares) of land had been granted to individuals for farming; and there were now 2500 cattle, 11,000 sheep, 8000 pigs and 350 horses.

Quite apart from the poor health of his crew, stymying Flinders's eagerness to return home was the bad condition of the *Investigator*. An inspection ordered by Governor

King reported that the ship was unlikely to be able to complete the voyage back to England. The inspection – conducted by the colony's master boatbuilder, Thomas Moore, a naval officer and two other sea captains in Sydney at the time – found that more than ninety per cent of the timbers below the waterline were rotted through:

> The above being the state of the *Investigator* thus far, we think it altogether unnecessary to make any further investigation, being unanimously of the opinion that she is not worth repairing in any country, and that it is impossible in this country to put her in a state fit for going to sea.[5]

Flinders immediately began a search in Sydney for a replacement vessel. His first choice was the *Buffalo*, which at 462 tons was much larger than the *Investigator*, but it was on a voyage to Penang and Calcutta to purchase horses and cattle for the colony and was not expected back until the following year. Flinders therefore had to settle for the 300-ton *Porpoise*, which had been captured by the English from the Spanish three years before. He had to wait until July for the *Porpoise*, which was taking settlers to Van Diemen's Land. However, it encountered very bad weather and returned to Sydney before completing the mission. (Despite the report that condemned the *Investigator*, it was repaired and sailed back to England two years later and continued in navy service until 1810. It was later completely rebuilt and given its original name of the *Xenophon*, then sailed extensively around the globe. Nearly half a century later, during the Australian gold rushes, it brought a cargo of timber and other goods from Liverpool, England, to Melbourne in 1853. It is recorded as having been broken up in 1872.)

So in July, the *Porpoise* was brought alongside the *Investigator*, and men, provisions and equipment were transferred to the new ship. The greenhouse that had been designed by Sir Joseph Banks and modified and installed on the *Investigator* was taken across to the deck of the *Porpoise* with the live plants in pots. The seeds and dry specimens were loaded into the hold.

Flinders was the senior officer on the *Porpoise* but was travelling as a passenger, so the ship was commanded by Robert Fowler, who had been the first lieutenant on the *Investigator*. Also sailing with Flinders was his younger brother Samuel; the *Investigator*'s master, John Aken; Flinders's servant, John Elder; and Trim the cat.

On 10 August – accompanied by two merchant ships, the *Bridgewater* and the *Cato* – the *Porpoise* left Sydney bound for England. The three ships were farewelled by a flotilla of little boats that followed them down the harbour, and Governor King travelled on the deck of the *Porpoise* as far as the Port Jackson heads. The *Bridgewater* and the *Cato* were both bound for Batavia and had been persuaded to follow Flinders, who wanted to prove his claim to have found a better and quicker route through the Torres Strait:

> The company of these ships gave me pleasure; for if we should be able to make a safe and expeditious passage through the Strait with them, of which I have but little doubt, it would be manifest proof of the advantage of the route discovered in the *Investigator* and tend to bring it into general use.[6]

To begin with, they had light breezes, which gave way to stronger winds; and in the first week they covered well over 1000 kilometres, sailing several hundred kilometres out to sea to ensure they were to the east of the

Great Barrier Reef. However, on the night of Wednesday, 17 August they sailed too close to a reef:

> In half an hour, and almost at the same instant by the *Investigator*'s carpenter on the forecastle, and the master who had charge of the watch on the quarter deck – breakers were seen ahead. The helm was immediately put down, with the intention of tacking from them; but the *Porpoise* . . . scarcely came up to [took] the wind.[7]

Flinders said that they smashed onto the reef very quickly and were unable to fire a cannon to warn the other two ships:

> In about a minute, the ship was carried against the breakers; and striking upon the coral reef, took a fearful heel over on her larboard [port] beam ends . . . A gun was attempted to be fired, to warn the other vessels of the danger, but owing to the violent motion and the heavy surf, this could not be done.[8]

As the *Porpoise* was pushed repeatedly by the waves onto the reef, the foremast broke, the hull broke open and the hold filled with water. At first they thought the *Cato* had managed to avoid the reef, but it soon crashed, close to the *Porpoise*:

> The exaltation we felt at seeing this most imminent danger passed was great, but of short duration; the *Cato* struck upon the reef about two cable lengths from the *Porpoise*; we saw her fall over on her broad side, and the masts almost immediately disappeared.[9]

With their ships pinned on the rocks, the crews of the *Cato* and the *Porpoise* could see the *Bridgewater* had safely cleared the reef, and they expected to be rescued the next morning:

> Turning our eyes toward the *Bridgewater*, a light was perceived at her masthead, by which we knew she had cleared the reef, and our first sensations were, that the commander would certainly tack, and send boats to our assistance; but . . . it became evident that he would not choose to come so near the reef in the night, blowing fresh as it did; and still less send his boats and his people into the breakers, to their certain destruction.[10]

During the night, the survivors clung to the wreckage of the two ships. Flinders and some of his crew tried to row over to help those on the more seriously damaged *Cato* but were unsuccessful; they were forced by the high seas to spend the night soaked in small boats.

Samuel Smith, a sailor on the *Porpoise*, said they tried to stabilise the ship but were terrified that they would not survive the night:

> We cut the foremast away to ease the ship. It was likewise proposed to take the hatches off to get a boat out we had stored between decks, but this was countermanded by reason that it would weaken the ship so that it would go to pieces directly . . . we then cut down our . . . main rigging and the mast, which then fell over the side. In this miserable situation we spent the night, every breast filled with horror, continual seas dashing over us with great violence.[11]

On the *Cato*, survivors tied themselves to the boat to avoid being washed away by the waves:

In a short time the decks and the holds were torn up, and everything was washed away; and the sole place left, where the unfortunate people could hope to avoid the fury of the sea, was in the larboard fore channel [the front, left section of the ship below deck], where they all crowded together. Every time the sea struck the *Cato*, it twisted her upon the rock with such violent jerks, that they must have expected the stern, which was down in the water, would part every moment. In this situation, some lashing themselves to the timber heads, others clinging themselves to the metal plates and the dead eyes, and to each other, Captain Park and his crew passed the night; their hope being, that the forecastle of the ship might hold upon the rock till morning, and that the *Bridgewater* would then send her boats to save them.[12]

At daybreak, the survivors saw they were 'not more than half a mile distant' from a dry sandbank, and they began to unload water and provisions to be rowed to shore. They also sighted the *Bridgewater* but were surprised to see it tack, and 'soon afterwards . . . no more was seen' of it.[13]

The men on the *Cato* began trying to reach the *Porpoise* or the shore:

Captain Park and his men, throwing themselves into the water with any pieces of spar or plank they could find, swam through the breakers . . . to the *Porpoise*, where they received food and some clothing. Several men were bruised against the coral rocks, and three young lads were drowned.[14]

Throughout the day, the survivors, who included Samuel Flinders and the *Porpoise*'s Captain Fowler, were carried on the ship's small boat to the sandbar; and before dusk they had managed to land 'five half hogsheads' (about 1300 litres) of drinking water, some flour, salt meat, rice and spirits, and some pigs and sheep that had escaped drowning.[15]

While they waited to be rescued, Flinders took command, considering himself authorised 'as the senior officer', and the castaways began building a camp:

> A top-sail yard was set up and secured as a flag staff on the highest part of the bank, and a large blue ensign hoisted to it with the union downward, as a signal to the *Bridgewater* . . . We expected, if no accident had happened, that she would come to release us from our critical situation.[16]

Little did they know that their companion ship had instead sailed towards Batavia, leaving them to their fate. Flinders later wrote critically of Captain Palmer, saying that he could easily have launched a rescue attempt after the *Bridgewater* had escaped the reef and was out of danger:

> He bore away around all; and while the two hapless vessels were still visible from the masthead, passed to the leeward extremity of the reef, and hove to for the night. The apprehension of danger to himself must then have ceased; but he neither attempted to work up in smooth water, nor send any of his boats to see whether some unfortunate individuals were not clinging to wrecks, whom he might snatch from the sharks or save from a more lingering death.[17]

Palmer said that he had not attempted a rescue because he thought all of the crew of the *Cato* and the *Porpoise* had drowned. Five months later, when he reached Calcutta, he was quoted in a local newspaper as saying that the

Bridgewater had been only a ship's length away when the *Porpoise* hit the reef, and he had seen early next morning that there were no survivors:

> On the 18th, when the day was broke, we had the mortification to see the *Cato* had shared the fate of the *Porpoise* . . . the [*Cato*] lay with her bottom exposed to the sea, which broke with tremendous fury over her; not a mast standing. Finding we could not weather the reef, and that it was too late had it been in our power to give any assistance; and still fearing that we might be embayed or entangled . . . we therefore determined, while we had the day before us, to run for the westward of the northern reef.[18]

But Palmer's claim that there was nothing he could have done was contradicted by one of his crew, Mr Williams, who at the time was the third mate on the *Bridgewater*. Williams said that the following morning the weather had improved, and the crew was happy at the prospect of mounting a rescue of survivors:

> At half past seven a.m. we saw the reef . . . the weather abated much, we set our sails, and every man rejoiced that they should have it in their power to assist their unfortunate companions . . . The ships were very distinctly seen from aloft, and also from the deck; but instead of rendering them any succour, the captain ordered the ship to be put on the other tack, and said it was impossible to render them any relief.[19]

Palmer was never punished or officially admonished for abandoning the men on the *Cato* and the *Porpoise*. Eventually he left Bombay for London, after which there is no record of him.[20]

By the third day after the *Porpoise* and *Cato* had been wrecked, almost all of the salvaged provisions had been landed and stored in a large tent made from one of the ship's sails. Flinders said that many of his papers had been damaged but that the charts and 'log, bearing books and astronomical observations' were all saved, though some of them were in a 'wet and shattered state'.[21] Many of the plants, seeds and dried specimens bound for the Royal Botanic Gardens, at Kew, had been ruined by the sea water, but much that had been collected by the *Investigator* over the preceding two years was still safely in Sydney.

The men were now organised to make tent cabins using sails recovered from the wrecked ships. To maintain discipline and ensure the crew's 'manner of living and working had assumed to same regularity as before the shipwreck', Flinders ordered one of the men, who was 'guilty of disorderly conduct', to be flogged. 'The articles of war were publicly read, and the man punished at the flag staff,' he wrote.[22]

The sandbar on which almost a hundred men were forced to make their home was less than 300 metres long, one hundred metres wide and barely a metre above the high-water mark. There were no trees on it, and for firewood the men relied on scraps of timber from the stricken *Porpoise* and *Cato* and on occasional pieces of driftwood. On the first night, they found on the shore a piece of 'worm-eaten and almost rotten' timber, which the master of the *Porpoise* calculated might have come from the sternpost of a ship of about 400 tons.[23] The discovery led Flinders to speculate that it might have come from one La Pérouse's ships, which might have crashed on the same reefs:

I have thought it might, not improbably, have belonged to *La Boussole* or *Astrolabe*. Monsieur

La Pérouse, on quitting Botany Bay, intended to visit the south west coast of New Caledonia, and he might have encountered in the night, as we did, some one of the several reefs which lie scattered in this sea. Less fortunate than we were, he probably had no friendly sand bank near him, upon which his people might be collected together and the means of existence saved out of the ships; or perhaps his two vessels both took the unlucky direction of the *Cato* after striking, and the seas which broke into them carried away all his boats and provisions; nor would La Pérouse, his vessels, or crews be able, in such a case, to resist the impetuosity of the waves more than twenty-four hours.[24]

When it became obvious that the *Bridgewater* was not coming to the rescue, a meeting of officers decided to send a group on a six-oared cutter from the *Porpoise* to seek help from Sydney, more than 1000 kilometres to the south.

It was calculated that they had managed to salvage enough food and water for the ninety-four survivors left on the sandbank to survive for three months – and even longer if they could collect rainwater and fish off the reef. It was also decided that the ships' carpenters stranded on the reef should immediately start to build two new boats from the timbers of the wrecked ships, which could be used for a second rescue attempt if the first failed.

On 26 August, a little more than a week after the shipwreck, Matthew Flinders, with Captain Park of the *Cato* as his deputy, left the sandbar to seek help in the cutter, which had been named *Hope*. They took with them twelve seaman, which would allow two groups of six to alternate at the oars.

After only one day, the little boat was sitting hazardously low in the water. They were forced to lighten their load by throwing overboard one of their two water casks and most of the stones that had been laid on the bottom of the boat to contain a fire for cooking.

It had been decided that they would first head west towards the coast then follow the shore south to Sydney. Taking advantage of favourable winds and rowing alternate shifts, they made good time in the little boat, and after four days Flinders calculated they had already reached the halfway point of their journey. On the fifth day, running short of water, they landed to replenish their cask and were surrounded by 'about 20 Indians . . . who seemed peaceably disposed, amusing us with dances in imitation of the kangaroo'.[25] On the following days, they passed coastal features named by Captain Cook when he first sailed north along this coast more than thirty years before, in 1770, including Mount Warning and Byron Bay. (Cook had named Byron Bay after Lord Byron of the Admiralty and not, as is popularly believed, after the poet, who was not born until eighteen years after Cook's voyage.)

On 6 September they passed the islands at the entrance of another of Cook's landmarks – Port Stephens – and reached the mouth of the Hunter River. Two days later they saw the north head of Broken Bay, and on Friday, 9 September entered Sydney Heads.

As soon as he reached Sydney Cove, the bedraggled and unshaven Flinders reported immediately to Governor King, who was at the time sitting down to lunch with his family at Government House. Flinders said that after King's initial surprise, he moved quickly to organise the relief of the nearly one hundred men stranded on the sandbar.[26] The merchant ship *Rolla* was in Sydney, ready to sail for China. King arranged with its captain to stop at Wreck Reef, as it would become known, and take on all those who wanted to go as far as Canton (current-day

Guangzhou), where they would be able to connect with other English ships to reach home.

King also ordered the small colonial schooner *Francis* to go with the *Rolla* to salvage whatever stores and equipment it could from the wrecked ships and bring back to Port Jackson those who chose to return to Sydney rather than go to China.

At the same time, King was eager to help Flinders get back to England with his charts and journals, as several valuable months had already been lost. The only available vessel in Sydney was a tiny ship, the twenty-nine-ton *Cumberland*, which could accommodate a crew of only ten. It was slow and too small to afford Flinders enough room to work on his maps while he sailed, but in the absence of any other option, King stipulated:

> It being essential to the furthering of His Majesty's service that you should reach England by the most prompt conveyance with your charts and journals, I have directed the commissary to make that vessel over to you . . . with a proportion of provisions for six months, for ten officers and men.[27]

Flinders left Sydney on the *Cumberland* on 21 September, with the *Rolla* and the *Francis*, and after only nine days' sailing reached the reefs near where the ships had sunk. But it took another week of searching before they sighted the ensign on the sandbar where the castaways were waiting. It had been six weeks since Flinders and Park had gone for help. Samuel Smith, a seaman from the *Porpoise* who had been left on the sandbank, described the happiness of the castaways when they were rescued:

> About 2 o'clock p.m. we espied a sail, afterwards two more . . . Every heart was overjoyed at the unexpected delivery; accordingly they came close and brought

up leeward to our bank. We fired a salute of thirteen guns and upon Captain Flinders stepping on shore we cheered him.[28]

While marooned on the sandbar, the survivors had fared well. They had also completed the construction of a new vessel, the *Resource*, which they had intended to use to seek help if Flinders failed to return.

Within three days, the men were loaded onto the three rescue ships. Most, including Robert Fowler and Samuel Flinders, went on the *Rolla* to China, where they transferred to other ships and eventually reached England. The others boarded the *Francis* to return to Sydney. Flinders took only a crew of eleven on the tiny *Cumberland* for the voyage to England, including John Aken, the master of the *Investigator*; boatswain Edward Carrington; Flinders's servant, John Elder; and seven seamen. And Trim the cat.

No doubt he thought he would be back in England considerably sooner than the men who left on the *Rolla* and the *Francis*. In fact, Flinders did not reach his homeland for another seven years.

Chapter 13

Imprisoned on Mauritius

*A*fter rescuing his stranded crew, Flinders left Wreck Reef on 11 October 1803 – two months after Baudin and *Le Géographe* had reached Mauritius. Sailing north to Cape York Peninsula and through the Torres Strait, he took only four more days to navigate across the top of the Gulf of Carpentaria from east to west. The previous year on the *Investigator* he had taken a total of 105 days to conduct a detailed survey of its coastline.

By the end of October the *Cumberland* had reached the top of Arnhem Land, and on 6 November the crew sighted Timor, where they learned from the local Dutch governor that Baudin had been on *Le Géographe* several months before.

Flinders left Timor on 14 November 1803. He wrote in his journal that he planned to stop regularly on the way to England:

The small size of the *Cumberland* made it neces-
sary to stop at every convenient place on the way to
England, for water and refreshment; and I proposed
Coepang Bay [Kupang], Mauritius, the Cape of Good
Hope, St Helena, and some of the Western Isles.[1]

However, before Flinders left Sydney, King had urged
him not to stop at the French-controlled island of Mauritius because he was suspicious of France's intentions and
did not want to 'encourage any communication between
the French colonies and Port Jackson'.[2] Flinders said
he rejected King's advice because the *Cumberland* was
leaking badly and needed repairs before trying to round
the Cape of Good Hope into the Atlantic Ocean:

> This state of things made it necessary to take into
> serious consideration the propriety of attempting
> the passage around the Cape of Good Hope, without
> first having the vessel caulked and the pumps fresh
> bored . . . After turning these circumstances over in
> my mind for a day or two and considering what else
> might be urged both for and against the measure,
> I determined to put in to Mauritius.[3]

Flinders reached the island ten days before Christmas
1803, intending to stay only a few days to repair his boat
and collect fresh water. While skirting its southern shore,
the English ship encountered a French schooner and
followed it into Baie du Cap (Cape Bay), on the south-
west of the island. Once in the port, the crew saw the men
of the French ship hurriedly talk to several others with
muskets, and Flinders said he was suddenly apprehensive:

> They were met by a person who, from the plume
> in his hat, appeared to be an officer, and presently

we saw several men with muskets on top of the hill; this gave another view of the schooner's movements, and caused me to apprehend that England and France were either at war or very near it.[4]

The master of the *Cumberland*, John Aken, went ashore with the French passport issued to Flinders four years before in England and reported to the senior French military officers, Major Dunienville and Etienne Bolger. With the assistance of an interpreter, the French pointed out that the passport had been issued for the *Investigator* and not the *Cumberland* and sent an urgent report about the arrival of the English to the military governor in the island capital of Port Louis, some fifty kilometres to the north. Later the same evening, orders arrived from Governor Decaen that the *Cumberland* was to sail immediately to Port Louis under the control of a French pilot.

Governor Charles Mathieu Isidore Decaen, who had arrived on the island to take up the role of governor only four months earlier, was to play an important part in the next years of Flinders's life. At thirty-four years of age, Decaen was only five years older than Flinders, but he was vastly more senior in rank. Orphaned at the age of twelve, he had studied law under the guidance of one of his father's friends, and his devotion to the law was said to have heavily influenced his officious manner later in life.[5] Shortly after the start of the Revolution, when France was at war with most of its neighbours, Decaen signed up and served on the Rhine under Jean Baptiste Kléber, one of Napoleon's prominent generals.

He rose rapidly in the army and experienced his baptism of fire during an assault on a Prussian post in April 1793. Despite earning a reputation for courage and tenacity, he readily admitted being afraid on that occasion:

I believe that there are few men, however coura-
geous that they may be, who have not experienced
a chill, and even a feeling of fear, when for the first
time they hear around them the whistling of a shot,
and above all when they first see the field strewn
with killed and wounded comrades.[6]

Later in 1793, Decaen fought at the Vendée, in western
France, against royalists opposed to the Revolution, and
was subsequently promoted to adjutant general. In 1795,
at twenty-six, he transferred back to the Rhine, under Jean
Victor Moreau, another of Napoleon's great generals.
Following the successful retreat of his forces through the
Black Forest, Decaen was awarded the Sword of Honour
for his bravery. In 1800, as the general of a division during
the successful Battle of Hohenlinden against the Austrians,
he came to the attention of Napoleon, whom he greatly
admired.

During discussions with Napoleon on one occasion,
Decaen suggested France should take greater control of
India from the British. He was then offered the chance to
govern the former French possessions there. The French
East India Company had first established a trading base
at Pondicherry – about 150 kilometres to the south of
Chennai, on the Indian east coast – in 1674.

Decaen left for India in February 1803, during the
uneasy Peace of Amiens between France and England – but
before he could reach India, war was again declared. As
his ship sailed up Pondicherry Harbour, British flags were
flying over government buildings and British warships
were protecting the port. When it became obvious that the
French would have difficulty claiming the town, Decaen
was directed instead to Ile de France (Mauritius) to take
up the post of governor.

When Flinders sailed into Port Louis on the afternoon
of 17 December, he said he was 'determined to go immediately' with his 'passport and commission' to meet the
governor. [7] Dressed in his frock uniform, he was rowed
ashore and taken to Decaen's residence, where he was
told the governor was at dinner. He was then forced to sit
outside, under the shade of a tree, for two hours. When
he was finally granted an audience, Flinders was kept
waiting another half-hour at the door before being shown
into Decaen's office for the first of a number of unpleasant
encounters:

> At length the interpreter desired me to follow him,
> and I was shown into a room where two officers
> were standing at a table, the one a shortish thick man
> in a laced round jacket . . . which was the captain
> general De Caen, [who] fixed his eyes sternly upon
> me, and without salutation or preface demanded
> my passport, my commission! Having glanced over
> them, he asked in an impetuous manner, the reason
> for coming to Isle of France in a small schooner
> with a passport for the Investigator.[8]

Flinders attempted to explain his changed circumstances:
that the *Investigator* had become rotten, that King had
given him the schooner *Cumberland* in which to return to
England, and that he needed to call in to Ile de France
to repair his boat and take on board fresh water and
provisions.

> At this answer, the general lost the small share of
> patience of which he seemed to be possessed, and
> said with much gesture and an elevated voice –
> 'you are imposing on me, sir! (Vous m'en imposez,
> monsieur!).'[9]

Decaen then returned Flinders's passport to him, and Flinders was ushered back by the interpreter to the *Cumberland*. There he was forced to hand over his books, papers, charts and journals, which were put into a trunk and taken away by the French.

It was nearly one in the morning when Flinders and Aken were asked to accompany the French aide-de-camp, Colonel Louis Monistrol, into town, leaving the rest of the *Cumberland*'s crew on board. They were taken to a large guesthouse named Café Marengo and up some stairs Flinders described as dirty to a small room, which contained two small beds and two chairs and had one window. Flinders complained that they spent the night pestered by 'mosquitoes above' and 'bugs below', with an armed guard outside the door.[10]

The next day, after a hearty breakfast and lunch, he was taken by Colonel Monistrol for another interview with Decaen. Flinders said a battery of questions was asked in the presence of a German secretary, who spoke English:

> How it was that I appeared at the Isle de France in so small a vessel, when my passport was for the Investigator? What was become of the officers and men of science who made part of the expedition? Whether I had any knowledge of the war before arriving? . . . What were my objects in putting into Port . . . and by what authority [did I do so]?[11]

In the course of the afternoon, Flinders received an invitation to dine that evening with the governor and his wife – but, indignant at his incarceration, he refused to go, saying he would accept only when he 'should be set at liberty'.[12] By declining, Flinders perhaps lost the opportunity to find an amicable resolution to his problems:

when told of Flinders's rejection, Decaen tartly replied that the Englishman would be invited again only when he was at liberty.

During further questioning in the afternoon, Flinders referred the French to his journals, which, he said, would demonstrate that he was in Mauritius legitimately. But on going through the journals, his interrogators found evidence that strengthened their fear he was spying: they saw strategically important references to Mauritius, including information about the local prevailing winds.

Also among the papers taken from the *Cumberland* were a number of letters from Governor Philip King, which Flinders was taking to England. One of them was addressed to Lord Hobart, the Secretary of State for War and the Colonies, and discussed the possibility of establishing a new British colony 'to the northward of New South Wales'. Carrying such documents was a serious blow to Flinders's claim that he was carrying out strictly neutral scientific explorations. He was also in breach of the explicit instructions he had received from the British Admiralty before leaving England not to take on board 'letters or packets other than such as you receive from this office, or the office of His Majesty's Secretary of State'.[13]

By now the French evidence against the Englishman was growing stronger. He was not travelling on the vessel for which the French had issued a passport; he carried no instructions saying he should call in at Mauritius; he had written in his journal information about Mauritius that could be strategically important to enemies of France; and he was carrying military information, in contravention of his instructions to conduct a scientific mission.

Flinders nevertheless persisted in claiming his innocence in a series of indignant letters to Decaen. In one he questioned the honour and the ethics of the French:

Now, Sir, I would beg to ask you whether it becomes
the French nation, independently of all passport, to
stop the progress of such a voyage, and of which the
whole maritime world are to receive the benefit? . . .
I sought protection and assistance in your port, and
I found a prison . . . Sir, judge, for me as a British
Officer employed in a neutral occupation – judge
for me as a zealous philanthropist, what I must feel
at being thus treated.[14]

Far from helping the situation, Flinders's letters only
antagonised the governor, as Decaen later complained in a
letter to the Minister of Marine in Paris:

Captain Flinders imagined that he would obtain
his release by arguing, by arrogance, and especially
by impertinence; my silence with regard to his first
letter led him to repeat the offence.[15]

When Flinders arrived at Port Louis, he learned that
Nicolas Baudin had been there on Le Géographe and the
Casuarina four months before and that Le Géographe had
left to return to France the day before Flinders reached
Mauritius on the Cumberland. He also noted simply in his
journal that 'Captain Baudin died soon after his arrival'
and was buried on the island.[16]

The other French ship from the Baudin expedition, Le
Naturaliste, which had gone ahead to France earlier in the
year, had got home six months before Flinders reached
Mauritius. When Le Naturaliste sailed into the English
Channel, it was detained by a patrolling English frigate
but was released ten days later on orders of the Admiralty,
following representations by Sir Joseph Banks, to whom
Captain Hamelin had appealed.

Meanwhile, as Christmas was approaching, Port Louis
had become unbearably hot, with 'unrelieved humidity

lying like a cloak over the town', and both Flinders and Aken broke out in sores.[17] On Christmas Eve, Flinders was given permission to write letters but was told he had to submit them, unsealed, to be read by the French authorities. After sending another petulant letter to Decaen, his permission was revoked, for 'overstepping the bounds of civility'.[18] This would have been a blow to Flinders, since no one in England – neither the authorities nor his wife – had any idea of the fate that had befallen him.

Flinders started 1804 by beginning to work on an account of his expedition. He was handicapped by the confiscation of the third and final volume of his journal but helped by his roommate, John Aken, who had kept his own journal a secret from the French. Their living conditions improved a little with the allocation of an additional room at the Café Marengo and with the issuing of mosquito nets for their beds.

Because Flinders and Aken were restricted in their movements, Flinders's servant, John Elder, who was permitted to visit the market regularly, became their contact with the outside world. He would take messages to the *Cumberland*, where the crew was still living – in accommodation even worse than their captain and ship's master.

Flinders and Aken had their food and lodging provided for them, but they soon ran out of money for other expenses, including laundry, wine, fruit and clothing. With the help of a French interpreter, Flinders was able to get a visiting Danish ship's captain to cash a promissory note equal to several weeks of his back pay and redeemable from the British Admiralty.

Flinders's repeated attempts to meet again with Decaen to discuss his release were ignored, and the only dealings he now had with the French were with his interrogator, Colonel Louis Monistrol, and interpreter, Joseph Bonnefoy.

In February 1804 Flinders met a French navy captain, Jacques Bergeret, who would become a close friend and help improve the explorer's living conditions. Bergeret had joined the French navy as a twelve-year-old and by the age of twenty had experienced fighting against the British and been promoted to the rank of lieutenant. In 1795 he was captured by the British and while in captivity became friends with Rear Admiral Sir Edward Pellew, who had been a supporter of Flinders. Two years after his capture, Bergeret was sent by the British to Paris to negotiate a swap: his freedom for the release of Admiral Sidney Smith, who had been taken by the French during a naval battle in April 1796 off Le Havre. Bergeret was unable to persuade his side to agree to the exchange and was obliged to return to England to continue his imprisonment.

In May 1798 Smith was rescued by French royalists, who smuggled him out in a boat to the British ship *Argo* in the English Channel, which returned him safely to London. Grateful to Bergeret for his efforts to have Smith released, the British released him anyway. He returned to France, bought the ship *Psyche* and began trading in the Indian Ocean. With the renewal of war between France and England, he rejoined the French navy and began raiding English ships out of Port Louis, successfully capturing three English vessels and their crews in 1803. It was while visiting his captured English navy officers and their wives, who were prisoners in Port Louis, that Bergeret met Flinders.

In March 1804 – and probably at Bergeret's urging – the crew of the *Cumberland*, who had been detained on the ship for four months now, was allowed to move to a prison about thirty kilometres from Port Louis. Also with the help of Bergeret, Flinders and Aken were permitted to leave their cramped rooms in the Café Marengo and move to a spacious house known as the Garden Prison. The grand plantation house with several acres of gardens lay on the edge of Port Louis and had been built by a French doctor, who then rented it to the French government as an open prison to hold captured English officers.

At the Garden Prison, Flinders enjoyed the fresh air, which made him 'think it was paradise' in comparison to Café Marengo.[19] Flinders was extremely grateful to Bergeret for getting him out of the cramped accommodation, where his health was beginning to fail him, and he wrote to Governor King:

> I became very ill in this confinement, the scurvy breaking out in my legs and feet. A surgeon was sent to attend me, but altho' he represented the necessity of taking exercise, yet was I not permitted to take a walk outside in the air for near four months, nor was any person allowed to speak to me without the general's permission. Through the intercession of the excellent Captain Bergeret, of the French navy, I was removed to the house where the English officers, prisoners of war, were confined. This house is situated a little without the town, enjoys a pure air, and is surrounded by a wall enclosing about two acres of ground. In this place Mr. Aken and me [sic] soon recovered our health.[20]

Trim the cat, who had shared all the adventures and misfortunes of his master, including life at Café Marengo, also moved to the Garden Prison. However, Flinders feared Trim might be maltreated by the prison guards and arranged for him to be cared for by a local Frenchwoman as a companion for her little daughter. Only a fortnight later the cat disappeared; Flinders, who later wrote a detailed account of Trim's life, believed he had been caught and stewed by local slaves.

In March 1804, after Flinders had been captive for four months, *Le Géographe* finally reached France, after an expedition of nearly three and a half years. At the same time, the British government now became aware of Flinders's incarceration via one of his letters, which had been smuggled out of Port Louis on a ship via America. When it finally reached London, its contents were immediately reported in the *London Chronicle*.

Both the Colonial Office and the Admiralty acted quickly and were soon urging the French Ministry of Marine to release Flinders. In pressing his case, they reminded the French of the assistance the British had given to Nicolas Baudin while *Le Géographe* and *Le Naturaliste* had been in Port Jackson. However, as the war between Britain and France had intensified and official channels of communications between the governments in Paris and London were effectively closed, it was difficult for the British to make representations on Flinders's behalf, and those they did make came to nothing.

Sir Joseph Banks also received a letter from Flinders in 1804, and he too tried to have him released. On 22 August Banks wrote, as the president of the Royal Society, to his French counterpart at the Institute of France, of which he was also a member, claiming Flinders had wrongly been branded a spy by Governor Decaen.[21] Banks also wrote to Governor King in Sydney to say that he was reminding the French of the good treatment Baudin had received in Sydney:

> Poor Flinders, you know, I suppose, put into Isle de France for water, and was detained as a prisoner and treated as a spy. Our Government have no communication with the French; but I have some with their literary men and have written . . . and have sent in my letter a copy of the very handsome one Mr. Baudin left with you.[22]

But Banks was lobbying on Flinders's behalf unaware that the explorer's passport for the *Investigator* was invalid for the *Cumberland*, that the French had found incriminating material in Flinders's journal and that he was carrying dispatches containing military material from Governor Philip King in Port Jackson to England.

In October 1804 the explorer was able to send back to England 'a general chart of Terra Australis, comprehending the whole' of his 'discoveries and examinations in abridgement, and a paper on the magnetism of ships addressed to the President of the Royal Society'.[23] The documents were taken via America by English officers who were part of a prisoner exchange; such exchanges regularly occurred after sea battles in which one side had captured enemy ships and crew. The map arrived in London in 1805 and was eventually published in January 1814, almost four years after the return of Flinders.

Flinders first used the name Australia, as well as Terra Australis, in a letter to his brother on 25 August 1804, when he said, 'I call the whole island Australia or Terra Australis. New Holland is properly that portion of it from 135 degrees of longitude westward; and eastwards New South Wales.' The name Australia, meaning 'southern' – as well as Australische, Australes and Austrialia – had been previously used, but not specifically in relation to the country that, after Flinders's maps were published, would bear this name.[24]

While incarcerated on Mauritius, Flinders used the name Australia regularly in letters he wrote later in 1804, and in 1806, 1809 and 1810, but it would be years before Terra Australis was dropped and only Australia used.[25]

By 1805 most of the *Cumberland*'s crew had already been able to leave the island; and in May, Flinders's colleague and master on the *Cumberland*, John Aken, was allowed to go. He sailed on an American ship, *James*, which left Mauritius bound for New York.

The next month, June 1805, the English ship *Thetis*
arrived at Mauritius flying a flag of truce and offering an
exchange of prisoners. But the French would not agree to
include Flinders, whom they thought now knew far too
much about the island to be handed over to their enemy.
As a result, Flinders now remained the only naval officer
of his rank held captive on the island.

In August 1805 an article appeared in the London *Times*
about Flinders, contrasting his fate to Baudin's treatment
by the English in Sydney two years before. The story had
appeared the previous April in the *Sydney Gazette* and was
based on a letter Flinders had managed to send Governor
Philip King in Sydney:

> Captain Flinders put in at the Isle de France, where
> he arrived on 16th of December last; he waited on
> the Governor who is a General named De Caen
> and after being kept two hours waiting in the street
> had an audience – but it was to be told he was an
> imposter, and the impossibility of Captain Flinders
> coming in so small a vessel being thought too great
> a discredit to his passport and his commission.
> Finally [he and Aken] were carried ashore prisoners
> at 2 o'clock in the morning; all his books and his
> papers were carried away, and a sentinel with fixed
> bayonet placed in the room where they were lodged
> . . . Captain Flinders could obtain no other satisfac-
> tion for this harsh and uncommon treatment . . . he
> was considered a spy, and given to understand that
> his letters gave great offence.[26]

In August, after sixteen months in the Garden Prison,
Flinders was told that he would be permitted to live on
the interior of the island. After looking at a number of
options, he chose a large house of the widow Madame

D'Arifat, on a plantation at Wilhelm's Plains, some thirty kilometres to the south of Port Louis. A condition of his release was that he sign parole papers promising he would not attempt escape and that he would not travel more than three leagues (about fourteen kilometres) from the homestead without the governor's permission.

On moving to his new home, Flinders was embraced by the island's society.[27] Great social changes may have occurred in revolutionary France, but here in the Indian Ocean outpost the good life had survived, and Flinders was invited to a variety of parties, concerts, card games and shooting parties, and taught to play chess by the family and friends of his hostess.

At Wilhelm's Plains he took possession of two small pavilions, one for himself and one for his two servants. In addition to the long-serving John Elder, he had acquired a black servant who had worked for another English officer recently freed as part of a prisoner exchange.

Flinders's normal daily routine began with a bath in the bathhouse behind his pavilion and a shave, before a breakfast at eight of coffee or tea, bread and butter and eggs and sometimes a salad. During the morning he studied French phrases and grammar, and in the afternoon he would go on long walks. After dinner he would read or play the flute till suppertime, around 8 pm. His food included puddings, vegetables, milk, chicken and a wide range of fruit and vegetables.

Now he had access to his charts and papers – except his third and final logbook, which contained details of the voyage of the *Cumberland* and was still held by the French – Flinders worked on writing up his journal. By July 1806 he had drafted an account of his adventures up to the point of his departure from the Garden Prison.[28]

Throughout 1805 many in England continued to agitate for his release. The governor-general of India,

Lord Wellesley, urged that Flinders be allowed passage to
India in any neutral ship, and Rear Admiral Sir Edward
Pellew proposed the exchange of Flinders with any French
prisoner of similar rank held by the English. But nothing
came of the initiatives.

In March 1806 news reached Mauritius of more spectacular French victories in Austria, which were republished
in the local gazette. Also in the news, but not mentioned in
the local paper, was the Battle of Trafalgar, which had been
fought the previous October. The naval battle – between
more than thirty British warships and support vessels and
an even greater number of French and Spanish ships off
the coast of Spain, between Cape Trafalgar and Cádiz
– resulted in the defeat of the French and thwarted Napoleon's planned invasion of England. During the fighting,
more than twenty French and Spanish ships were sunk,
crippled or captured, while none of the English ships was
lost. An estimated 18,000 men were killed in the encounter. Some drowned, while others – including the admiral
of the British fleet, Horatio Nelson – died from injuries
sustained during the battle. Trafalgar was one of the most
decisive events of the Napoleonic Wars.

In April 1806 Flinders's faithful servant, John Elder, and
a seaman, William Smith, who had missed leaving with
the other crew of the Cumberland as he was recovering
from a broken leg, were allowed to go back to England.
They went via America on the Martha, leaving Flinders
the ship's sole remaining prisoner on Mauritius.

By September he had returned to work in earnest on his
charts, and in October finished his map of the west side of
the Gulf of Carpentaria.[29] By the end of the year, after three
years on Mauritius, he was able to converse fairly fluently
in French. On Christmas Day he first sat for his portrait, to
be painted by Toussaint Antoine de Chazal de Chamerel.
(The portrait, which was finished a few weeks later, has a

fascinating history. It stayed with the artist's family in Mauritius and was taken with them when they later migrated to Madeira, north of the Canary Islands. In 1987 it was bought by the Australian businessman Alan Bond for more than a million dollars. Shortly before Bond's business empire collapsed and he went to jail, the painting vanished. Its whereabouts were unknown until it was discovered several years later in a packing crate in a London warehouse. It had been flown out of Australia to Switzerland wrapped in a blanket and strapped to the floor of one of Bond's private jets. The painting now hangs in the Art Gallery of South Australia, having been bought in 2000 by the gallery from the liquidators of Bond's companies.)

In March 1807 Flinders turned thirty-three, and was granted permission to occasionally visit Port Louis. He hoped for – but was denied – permission for an audience with Governor Decaen to further plead for his release. In July he was shown a letter written by the French Minister of Marine, dated March 1806, which indicated that he could be freed and that the decision had been approved by Napoleon himself. Copies of the authorisation for Flinders's release were sent on four French ships because the increased British control of the seas meant that a single ship might not make it to the island. The first letter reached Mauritius sixteen months after it had been sent – on an English ship, the *Greyhound*, flying a flag of truce. The British had intercepted the letter after capturing one of the French ships and, under the instructions of Rear Admiral Sir Edward Pellew, delivered it in the hope of securing Flinders's release.[30]

Notwithstanding the approval of Napoleon himself, Decaen deferred the release, saying that it was still too dangerous to let Flinders go:

> The circumstances having become still more difficult, and the officer appearing to me to be always

> dangerous, I want a more propitious time for putting
> into execution the intentions of His Majesty.[31]

Decaen may have been vindictive towards Flinders – as
the English and Flinders alleged – but it is also highly
likely that the governor genuinely believed Flinders was a
spy whose knowledge of Mauritius would be valuable to
enemies considering invading the island.

In August, Flinders received a letter from the man who
had first interrogated him, Colonel Monistrol, telling him
that he could go and collect the remainder of his journals
and papers still held by the French, which he found had
been significantly damaged by the gnawing of rats.

Over the next year, Flinders busied himself working on
his charts and journals, and practising his French, while
continuing to take long walks and enjoy an active social
life with the established French families on the island.

By now Flinders had been on Mauritius for more than
four years, and one might expect him to have suffered
some mental deterioration after such a long time in captivity. However, in his journal (which, of course, he had the
opportunity to edit after his release), apart from railing
against what he saw as the injustice of his incarceration
and the vindictiveness of his gaoler, Decaen, he consis-
tently demonstrated the ordered and disciplined mind that
had been characteristic of his career thus far.

In early 1809 he was shocked to read in the French
newspapers François Péron's account of Baudin's expedition. Péron's A Voyage of Discovery to the Southern
Hemisphere had been published in Paris in 1807, and in
July 1808 a summary of the book appeared in Le Moniteur
Universel, which Flinders saw in March 1809, once a copy
of it had reached Mauritius.

Flinders was livid that Péron made extensive references to a number of places the French had visited and

named on the Australian coast that he had, in fact, surveyed first:

> The publication of the French voyage of discovery, written by M. Péron, was in great forwardness; and the Emperor Napoleon considering it to be a national work, had granted a considerable sum to render the publication complete. From the *Moniteur* of July 1808, it appears that French names were given to all my discoveries and those of Captain Grant on the south coast of Terra Australis; it was kept out of sight that I had ever been upon the coast; and in speaking of M. Péron's first volume the newspapers asserted, that no voyage ever made by the English nation could be compared with that of the *Geographe* and *Naturaliste*.[32]

Flinders also complained that the French had learned much about the coast they were exploring from him:

> It may be remembered, that after exploring the south coast up to Kangaroo Island, with the two gulfs, I met Captain Baudin, and gave him the first information of the places and the advantages they offered him; and it was but ill return to seek to deprive me the little honour attending the discovery. No means were spared by the French Government to enhance the merit of this voyage, and all the officers employed in it had received promotion; but the *Investigator's* voyage seemed to obtain as little public notice in England as in France.[33]

The French must have had some idea that Flinders's discoveries on this coastline predated theirs. At the chance encounter between the *Investigator* and *Le Géographe*

off the south coast in April 1802, Flinders had told Baudin
that he had already surveyed the south coast from the west.
Also, when they met again in Sydney several months later,
he said he showed the French his charts and the French
had 'made no objection' to those parts of the south coast
he had marked as having been discovered by the British.[34]

In January 1809 news began filtering through to Mauritius of growing British superiority at sea, and Flinders
began to pack papers, journals and charts in trunks so
that he would be able to leave at short notice in the event
that he was freed. By now the hostilities on the seas had
reduced the number of ships that could safely reach Mauritius from Europe, and the cost of living on the island had
increased dramatically. Flinders said that he was forced to
pay twenty dollars for a hat that would have cost less than
a pound (eighteen shillings) in England, and sixteen dollars
for a pair of boots that usually cost a guinea (one pound
and one shilling).[35] However, he was able to continue to
eat well and inexpensively by purchasing locally grown
products, including maize, chicken, pork, coffee and bread,
which cost only three pence for a pound (450 grams) loaf.

On 4 June he entered in his diary that he toasted the
birthday of King George III, who, having become king in
1760, had now been on the throne for almost fifty years.
Flinders would have had no idea that King George III's
health was failing. Within a year he would be replaced as
monarch by his son the Prince Regent.

In mid-1809 there were rumours of an impending
British attack on Mauritius, and all remaining British prisoners on the island were 'taken from their paroles and
closely shut up', except Flinders, who was allowed to stay
in the countryside.[36] In the middle of July the British ships
offshore 'quitted the island unexpectedly', and a fortnight
later news reached the island that they had successfully
attacked and taken the smaller French-controlled island of

Bourbon [current-day Réunion], about fifty kilometres to the south-west of Mauritius.[37]

On 23 September, after nearly six years in captivity, Flinders made an unauthorised visit to Port Louis, where he met with an English sea captain who had sailed into the port under the flag of truce to try to negotiate a further prisoner exchange. The French again excluded Flinders from the negotiated prisoner swap, and he was reprimanded for breaching his parole conditions by coming to town without the prior approval of the governor.

By now the British control of the sea around Mauritius had become so tight that Decaen ordered that one in twenty privately owned black slaves on the island be conscripted to bolster by 600 soldiers the French defences of the island. In October, the British blockade of Mauritius resumed and Flinders was denied further permission to come to Port Louis. In December, another prisoner exchange was negotiated, but yet again Flinders was excluded.

In January 1810, when Flinders was left the sole British prisoner on the island, he heard rumours that he might finally be released. Then on 13 March he received a letter from an English captain sent to negotiate a prisoner exchange solely for Flinders, which said his release had been approved by Decaen. However, he refused to believe it:

> On March 13th, a letter came from Mr. Hope, the commissary of prisoners, to inform me that he obtained from the captain-general a promise for my liberty, and departure from the island with him on the *Harriet*. This unhoped for intelligence would have produced excessive joy, had not experience taught me to distrust even the promises of the general; and especially when, as in the present case, there was no cause assigned for this change in his conduct.[38]

But a fortnight later he was advised by Colonel Monistrol that Decaen had indeed capitulated:

> His Excellency the captain-general charges me to have the honour of informing you, that he authorises you to return to your country in the cartel *Harriet*, on condition of not serving in a hostile manner against France or its allies during the course of the present war. Receive, I pray you, Sir, the assurance of the pleasure I have in making you this communication.[39]

Why, after such intransigence over so many years, did Decaen have this sudden change of heart? Flinders later speculated that the governor had decided to free him to the very group of ships that was poised to attack Mauritius:

> He suffered me to depart in a cartel bound to the place where the attack was publicly said to be in mediation. This is the sole motive which, upon review of the general's conduct, I can assign for being set at liberty so unexpectedly, and without any restriction on my communications; and if such a result to an attack upon Mauritius were foreseen by the present count De Caen, captain general of Catalonia, events have proved that he was no mean calculator.[40]

It is more likely that Decaen knew the British were about to attack and that at best the French could hold out for only a short time before they would be overrun by superior forces. (The British took the island in December of the same year.) Decaen would also have known that there was little purpose holding on to a prisoner who was feared to be dangerous because he knew too much about the island and its defences, when it was going to be overrun anyway.

Over the next two months, while waiting to go, Flinders said his goodbyes to his many French friends at a host of parties in both the countryside and Port Louis. As part of his preparation for departure, he sent his black servant with a letter of recommendation to Madame D'Arifat, while taking a new servant, a seaman named Herman, for the voyage home.

Flinders left Mauritius on 13 June 1810, after six years, five months and twenty-seven days. He boarded the *Harriet* bound for India, which meant it might take him another year to get back to England. However, when the *Harriet* joined the other blockading ships, Flinders managed to cross to the *Otter*, which was going to Cape Town.

On the *Otter*, he reached False Bay within the month, to discover that another British ship was due to leave nearby Table Bay the following day for England. With an escort of dragoons and relays of fresh horses, he raced nearly forty kilometres in less than four hours, only to see the ship sailing out of the bay. He had to wait six weeks for the next ship, the *Olympia*, which finally landed in Portsmouth on 24 October 1810. Flinders had been away from England for nine years and three months.

CHAPTER 14

COMPLETING
THE MISSION

*N*ews of Flinders's release from captivity on Mauritius had already reached Cape Town and was taken on to England on the ship Flinders had only narrowly missed catching. When Sir Joseph Banks heard the news, he immediately wrote to Flinders's wife, Ann:

> Madam,
>
> I have infinite satisfaction in informing you that Captain Flinders has at last obtained his release and is expected in England in a few weeks, and that on his arrival he will immediately be made a Post Captain.
>
> I am Madam your most faithful servant,
> Jos. Banks[1]

Ann's sister Isabelle said that even before they received Banks's letter, the family already knew of Flinders's release, having read about it in the newspapers:

> One evening we were preparing to go to church – the post came – it was only a newspaper, it would keep till we returned. I was first ready, and while I waited I took up the despised newspaper, – I read in the ship news from the Cape that a ship had arrived there, having on board Captain Flinders as a passenger . . . we read it again and again, could it be true?[2]

On the day he arrived in Portsmouth, Flinders called on Admiral Roger Curtis, who had been in Cape Town when the explorer had arrived there on the *Investigator* at the beginning of his expedition almost a decade before. That evening Flinders caught the overnight mail coach to London; he arrived early the following morning and took rooms at the Norfolk Hotel. At noon he met with Ann, who had hastily travelled to the city. She had not seen her husband for almost ten years and had had no news from him for the past four. John Franklin, Flinders's cousin, who was in the room during what must have been a very tender moment, later wrote to Flinders explaining why he had quickly left:

> Some apology would be necessary for the abrupt manner I left you,– I felt so sensibly the affecting scene of your meeting Mrs. Flinders that I could not have remained any longer in the room under any consideration.[3]

Over the next few days Flinders saw many former colleagues. On his first evening in London he met with the *Investigator*'s botanist, Robert Brown, with whom he had had an at-times frosty relationship during the expedition. Brown was to become Sir Joseph Banks's librarian, and later in 1810 he published *Prodromus Florae Novae Hollandiae*, which was based on specimens he collected during the *Investigator's* expedition.

Flinders also saw one of the artists on the *Investigator*, Ferdinand Bauer, who had been back in England for five years. Bauer had brought back more than 2000 drawings and paintings with which he was preparing his book *Illustrationes Florae Novae Hollandiae*, which was published three years later.

Over the next month Flinders attended to a number of official navy matters, including submitting a report to the Admiralty explaining his loss of His Majesty's ship the *Cumberland*, which had been impounded by the French at Mauritius. At the Colonial Office he met up with his old commander William Bligh, who had returned to England only a day after Flinders, having been deposed as governor of New South Wales by an uprising of colonists.

Among the many old friends with whom he was reunited was Henry Waterhouse, who had commanded the *Reliance* when Flinders had first gone to Port Jackson on the same voyage as John Hunter, fifteen years before. Waterhouse had been trying to trace his brother-in-law and Flinders's friend, George Bass, who was still missing after having left Sydney in 1803. There was considerable speculation about what had happened to Bass when he headed across the Pacific to trade in Chile, but no evidence has ever surfaced about the fate of the *Venus* and its crew of twenty-five men. Waterhouse was in poor health and drinking heavily, and he died eighteen months later, aged forty-two.

Flinders and his story attracted a great deal of interest, and he and Ann were invited to dine at the best tables, including as guests of the First Lord of the Admiralty, Lord Charles Yorke. In November 1810, the couple moved into a house in King Street in London's Soho, close to the townhouse of Sir Joseph Banks, where Flinders intended to complete his maps and account of the expedition.

His younger brother Samuel was also back in England. After returning from Wreck Reef via China, he and Robert Fowler and other officers of the *Porpoise* had undergone an obligatory court martial, during which they were exonerated for the wreck of the ship. Samuel returned to the navy but was demoted for disobeying orders while he served on the *Bloodhound*. When his older brother eventually came home to England, he helped for a while in the preparation of Matthew's Australian charts, but he was never reinstated to his former rank in the navy.

After a Christmas break of six weeks, during which Flinders and Ann visited their families in Lincolnshire, they returned to London in early 1811. The following month news reached the capital that Mauritius had fallen to a British invasion force. In Europe, France continued to fight Portugal and Spain, and Napoleon began preparations for the massive invasion of Russia the following year that would have calamitous consequences. In Britain, King George III, who had been on the throne for more than fifty years, was lapsing into apparent mental illness, and the Regency Act was passed for his son to become Prince Regent.

Flinders received wide acclaim in London and at the Admiralty for his achievements. Sir Joseph Banks took him to the Royal Society and gave a dinner in his honour. The Duke of Clarence, who later became King William IV, was fascinated with sailing and met Flinders, to whom he talked about his charts.

In 1811, with the support of the navy, Flinders finally began to write up the account of his expedition. The Admiralty agreed to pay for the engraving of the maps and the reproduction of the illustrations, and appointed Sir Joseph

Banks and Sir John Barrow to oversee the project. (Sir John Barrow was the Second Secretary to the Admiralty for an amazing forty years, from 1804 till 1844.) It was agreed that while writing the book Flinders would receive half-pay and that profits from the sales of the book would pay for the costs associated with its production, including fees for the artists and the costs of printing, paper and bookbinding.

The maps were to be engraved by the celebrated London cartographers Arrowsmith's. On Flinders's original charts, many of the principal locations on the Australian coast had been identified by numbers, and now he had to supply Arrowsmith's with placenames.

Flinders began writing his account in May 1811 and continued working on the project for more than two years. During the writing, he complained that he was struggling:

> It does by no means advance according to my wishes, morning, noon and night I sit close at writing, and my charts, and can hardly find time for anything else.[4]

Throughout the drafting of the book, Flinders referred to Terra Australis, even though there was some opposition to the new name. The chart makers, Arrowsmith's, wanted to stick to the name New Holland, which had always been used on their maps; and, according to Flinders, Sir Joseph Banks still disapproved of the name Terra Australis as late as August 1813.[5]

Eventually Flinders was able to write in the introduction to his book that a consensus had been reached on the name of the continent:

> I have, with the concurrence of opinions entitled to deference, ventured on the adoption of the original Terra Australis; and of this term I shall hereafter

make use when speaking of New Holland and New South Wales, in a collective sense.[6]

However, in a footnote, he made it clear that he favoured Australia as the name, as he thought it sounded better and fitted phonetically with the names of Africa, Asia and America:

> Had I permitted myself any innovation upon the original term, it would have been to convert it into AUSTRALIA; as being more agreeable to the ear, and assimilation to the names of the other great portions of the earth.[7]

Flinders had not devised the name Australia, but after the publication of his book, it increasingly came into common use, though it would take many more years before it became the country's official name.[8]

While he was still writing the account of his expedition and preparing his maps for publication, a French map of the entire coastline of Australia was published in Paris in late 1811 – three years before Flinders's would be. The French map was produced by thirty-two-year-old Louis-Claude de Saulces de Freycinet, who had charted much of the Baudin expedition. He had taken over the task of completing the map after François Péron – who had published the first volume of the account of the expedition in 1807 – died of tuberculosis in 1810, aged thirty-five. The publication of the French map had been delayed when the Paris engraver stopped work for two years because he had not been paid.[9]

Despite the delay, Freycinet had considered the race with the British to produce the first complete map of Australia far from over. In a letter to the French Minister of Marine in August 1811, he warned the French government that time was of the essence if the French were to beat the English, as Flinders was back in England and the British government was supporting him in the earliest publication of his map. Reminding the minister of the rivalry between the French and British to complete the first map of Australia – and the glory it would entail – he urged the completion of his map even before the written account of the Baudin expedition:

> Very powerful reasons, Monsieur, appear to demand that the atlas should be published with very little delay, and even before the text which is to accompany it. Independently of the advantages to me personally as author, of which I shall not speak, the reputation of the expedition ordered by his Majesty appears to me strongly involved. I have the honour to remind your Excellency that Captain Flinders was sent to discover Terra Australis a short time after the French Government had dispatched an expedition having the same object. The rival expeditions carried out their work in the same field, but the French had the good fortune to be first to return to Europe. Now that Flinders is again in England, and is occupied with the publication of numerous results of the voyage, the English Government, jealous on account of the rivalry between the two expeditions, will do all it can for its own . . . If the English publish before the French the records of the discoveries made in New Holland, they will, by fact of that priority of publication, take from us the glory which we have the right to claim.[10]

Freycinet managed to portray an outline of the continent by combining the charts of earlier explorers with French maps from Baudin's voyage. These included the maps

from the Baudin exploration of Bass Strait, the Tasmanian coast, Port Phillip Bay, Spencer Gulf, Gulf St Vincent,
Kangaroo Island, King Island, the south coast as far west
as Nuyts Archipelago, the coast from King George Sound
to Cape Leeuwin, and the west and north-west coasts as
far as Melville Island.

Freycinet is widely acknowledged as having done a
good job in the circumstances. He admitted the task was
difficult because he had to compile a single map from
thousands of pages of information sketched by many
different hands:

> I was bound to find at times some gaps, but more
> often a superabundance of observations of the same
> points; which helped to slow my work while multi-
> plying the difficulties.[11]

More than 300 French names dotted the Freycinet
map, including those of members of Napoleon's family;
generals and admirals who had fought in Napoleon's
campaigns and the revolutionary wars; and statesmen,
writers, scientists and historical figures of all kinds. Many
of the names were added by Péron and Freycinet in Paris
during preparations for the publication of the map,
although some of the places had been given names by
Baudin during the expedition.

Just as Flinders had been furious at Péron's account of
the Baudin voyage of 1807, the British were now incensed
that Freycinet's chart made no reference to Flinders's
discoveries in this area and that the entire south coast
as far west as the Nuyts Archipelago had been named
Terre Napoleon. Particularly galling was the naming of
the Golfe Bonaparte and Golfe Josephine. Flinders and the
British believed that during Flinders's meeting with Baudin
at Encounter Bay in 1802, the French became well aware

that the Englishman had charted these gulfs first and had named them Spencer Gulf and Gulf St Vincent. However, at the time Freycinet was preparing his map, Flinders had not produced his, so it would not have been so clear to the French at the time exactly which places Flinders had visited first and given names to.

The British were nonetheless highly critical of the French and alleged their rivals had copied some of Flinders's maps while they were held by Governor Decaen. However, no one has ever been able to specify which parts of the Frenchman's map might have been plagiarised from Flinders's charts.[12]

Meanwhile, Flinders continued with the preparation of his own publication. On 1 April 1812, he became a father, when Ann gave birth to a baby daughter, who, following the custom of the time, was whisked away to be raised by a nanny for the first eighteen months of her life, thus enabling Flinders to continue his work uninterrupted.

In March 1812, he gave evidence to a House of Commons committee inquiring into convict transportation to Australia. The inquiry had been set up to look at how transportation to New South Wales was working after twenty years. Flinders told the committee that he had been to the colony the first time for around five years between 1795 and 1800, when he had confirmed the existence of Bass Strait, and twice more for periods of about three months during his expedition on the *Investigator* in 1802 and 1803. The committee was particularly interested to know if more fertile soil could be found in the vicinity of the colony to support further settlement. In answer to a parliamentarian's question, Flinders told them that the amount of fertile land around Sydney was limited and that it would be difficult to expand beyond the coast, because of the mountains:

[Parliamentarian]: Did the difficulty of penetrating the country exist only in one direction?

Captain Flinders: I believe it exists in every direction from Port Jackson, the country cannot be penetrated from Port Jackson, as I know from experiments that have been made, which have all proved fruitless.[13]

But he advised the committee that there was fertile land in both the north and south of Van Diemen's Land that would support settlement.

Flinders was not alone in believing the mountains to the west of Sydney were impenetrable. Several years before, Governor Philip King had said he believed the mountains could never be crossed. In fact, less than a year later, three explorers – William Charles Wentworth, Gregory Blaxland and William Lawson – did cross them, and thus opened up vast grazing country.

By the end of 1812 Flinders had finished drafting his first volume and begun work on the second. By the end of 1813 he had almost finished the narrative, and the maps were being engraved and printed by Arrowsmith's. In March 1814, following a particularly savage winter in England, the now forty-year-old Flinders became ill with what was believed to be a recurrence of renal colic, a painful condition often associated with kidney stones.[14] He spent April correcting the proofs of his work but was sick for most of May.[15] His worried wife complained to a friend that 'he looked full 70 years of age and was worn to a skeleton'.[16] On Sunday, 10 July Flinders wrote in his diary that he could not get out of bed before 2 pm and felt 'weaker than before'. It is said that the final proofs of his book were brought to him while he lay on his sickbed. He died nine days later, the day after his book and map of Australia were published.

The English names of Flinders's discoveries began to replace the French ones on maps published after his. On modern maps, more than 400 places first surveyed by Flinders now carry his nomenclature. The French names remain on those parts of the coast first surveyed by Baudin, particularly from Port Phillip Bay (in current-day Victoria) to Cape Northumberland (on the current South Australian coast), and on many parts of the west coast that Flinders never saw.

So why did Flinders take so long to publish his map and the account of his discoveries? Even allowing for his long imprisonment on Mauritius, he could still have beaten the French; instead, he took almost four years to complete his book, even after his return to England. (The second volume of the French account of Baudin's expedition was not published till 1816. The first volume had appeared in 1807, and Freycinet's map in 1811.)

Part of the reason he gave was the disappearance of the third volume of his journal, which had been taken by the French. Flinders hoped that when the British took Mauritius, his papers would be returned. However, they were not handed over to the British when France surrendered the island, and a later search ordered by Britain's Admiral Bertie failed to find them. It was later discovered that Decaen had taken Flinders's journal back to France and had ignored requests for its return for three years. The journal was then stored in the French Hydrographic Office for another eleven years before being handed over to the British ambassador in Paris in 1825. It was passed on to the Admiralty, which finally lodged it in the Public Records Office.

The full title of Flinders's book is *A Voyage to Terra Australis: Undertaken for the Purpose of Completing the Discovery of That Vast Country, and Prosecuted in the Years 1801, 1802, and 1803 in His Majesty's ship the Investigator, and Subsequently in the Armed Vessel*

Porpoise and Cumberland Schooner. With an Account of the Shipwreck of the Porpoise, Arrival of the Cumberland at Mauritius, and Imprisonment of the Commander During Six Years and a Half in That Island.

The book contains sixteen maps of different parts of the coast, landscape paintings and drawings by artist William Westall, and ten botanical paintings by Ferdinand Bauer. It starts with an introduction that covers the earlier European explorations of Australia, beginning with Janszoon and Torres. It then canvasses the expeditions over the next 200 years, up to Flinders's explorations with George Bass that led to the discovery of Bass Strait and the separate island of Van Diemen's Land.

Most of the book deals with the expedition of the *Investigator*, including the encounter with Baudin off the south coast and the later aborted exploration of the north coast. Flinders then tells the stories of the wreck of the *Porpoise*, the journey of the *Cumberland* and his years of imprisonment on Mauritius.

Flinders's *A Voyage to Terra Australis* is comprehensive and offers plausible accounts of his misfortunes, including his failure to complete the survey of the north and western Australian coasts and his foolhardy decision to sail into the French-occupied island of Mauritius. Perhaps Nicolas Baudin's reputation would have suffered less if he, too, had lived long enough to write an account of his own expedition.

As well as being a successful voyage of discovery, the *Investigator*'s expedition was important on a number of other counts. Many decades after Flinders's death and some years after Darwin's voyages on the *Beagle*, Sir Joseph Dalton Hooker, the great biologist and later director of the Royal Botanic Gardens at Kew, said the Flinders expedition was 'as far as botany is concerned, the most important in its results ever undertaken'.[17]

Flinders was also eulogised by a number of biographers for his exceptional navigation and mapping skills, patience, intellect and courage. On Flinders's death, the great Danish-French geographer Malte-Brun said that 'the geographic and natural sciences have lost in the person of Flinders one of their most beautiful ornaments'.[18]

Flinders may have been beaten in the quest to publish the first complete map of Australia, but his contribution to its exploration is unsurpassed. He was the first to explore the world's last remaining extensive unknown coastline, and in doing so confirmed that New Holland and New South Wales were not separated by sea but were part of the same large continental landmass. And he gave the country its name: Australia.

NOTES

CHAPTER 1: FIRST EXPLORATIONS

1. Flinders, M., 'Introduction', *A Voyage to Terra Australis*, vol. 1, G. and W. Nicol, London, 1814, facsimile edition, 1966, p. 18. Also online: www. gutenberg.net.au/ebooks/e00049.html

2. McClymont, J. R., *The Theory of an Antipodal Southern Continent During the Sixteenth Century*, Government Printer, Hobart, 1892, pp. 442–44

3. Richardson W. A. R., *Was Australia Charted Before 1606?: The Jave la Grande Inscriptions*, National Library of Australia, Canberra, 2006, p. 94

4. Flinders, *Voyage*, vol. 1, p. 109

5. Fitzgerald, Shirley, 'Chinese', Dictionary of Sydney, 2008, www.dictionaryofsydney.org/entry/chinese

6. Juxian, Wei, *The Chinese Discovery of Australia*, Hong Kong, 1960, quoted in *Who Got to Australia First?*, National Library of Australia Gateways:

www.pandora.nla.gov.au/pan/11779/20070524-0000/
www.nla.gov.au/pub/gateways/issues/83/story01.html

7. Estensen, M., *Discovery: the Quest for the Great South Land*, Allen & Unwin, Sydney, 1998, p. 119

8. McHugh, E., *1606: An Epic Adventure*, UNSW Press, Sydney, 2006, p. 4

9. Estensen, *Discovery*, p. 120

10. McHugh, *1606*, p. 12

11. McHugh, *1606*, pp. 9–12

12. Torres, Luis Váez de, letter to King Philip III of Spain, republished in English in Stevens, H. (ed.), *New Light on the Discovery of Australia as Revealed by the Journal of Captain Diego de Prado y Tovar*, George F. Barwick (trans.), Hakluyt Society, Liechtenstein, 1930, p. 221

13. Brooke, J., quoted in Ida Lee, 'The First Sighting of Australia by the English', *The Geographical Journal*, Royal Geographical Society, London, April 1934, www.gutenberg.net.au/ebooks06/0609031h.html

14. Bright, T., quoted in Lee, 'First Sighting of Australia'

15. Lee, 'First Sighting of Australia'

16. Brooke, quoted in Lee, 'First Sighting of Australia'

17. Pelsaert, F., *The Batavia Journal of Francisco Pelsaert*, Marit van Huystee (ed. and trans.), 9 June 1629, Algemeen Rijksarchief, The Hague, Netherlands, 1998, report of the Western Australian Maritime Museum, Department of Maritime Archaeology, no. 136, 1994, p. 4

18. Pelsaert, *Journal*, 16 June 1629, p. 5

19. Pelsaert, *Journal*, 16 June 1629, p. 6

20. Heeres, J. E. (ed.), *Abel Janszoon Tasman's Journal: His Life and Labours*, Frederick Muller, Amsterdam, 1898, p. 7

21. Heeres, *Abel Janszoon Tasman*, chapter II

22. Heemskerk is a town in North Holland.

23. Heeres, *Abel Janszoon Tasman*, chapter XIII
24. Tasman, A., *The Journal of Abel Jansz Tasman, 1642: with documents relating to his exploration of Australia in 1644,* Australian Heritage Press, Adelaide, 1964, appendix E. Also online: www.gutenberg.net.au/ebooks06/0600571h.html. Pympetien is the old Dutch name for a liqueur glass.
25. Tasman, *Journal*, 10 September 1642
26. Tasman, *Journal*, 24 October 1642
27. Tasman, *Journal*, 6 November 1642
28. Tasman, *Journal*, 25 November 1642
29. Tasman, *Journal*, 2 December 1642
30. Tasman, *Journal*, 3 December 1642
31. Tasman, *Journal*, 2 December 1642
32. Tasman, *Journal*, 3 December 1642
33. Heeres, *Abel Janszoon Tasman*, p. 114
34. Heeres, *Abel Janszoon Tasman*, p. 115
35. Heeres, *Abel Janszoon Tasman*, appendix J

Chapter 2: The First Englishman

1. Dampier, W., *A Supplement to the Voyage Round the World*, James Knapton, London, 1700, vol. 1, p. 194
2. Ibid.
3. Dampier, *Supplement*, vol. 1, p. 196
4. Dampier, *Supplement*, vol. 1, p. 202
5. Dampier, *Supplement*, vol. 1, p. 201
6. Dampier, W., *A New Voyage Round the World*, James Knapton, London, 1697, vol. 2, p. 128
7. Gray, Sir Albert, Introduction to Dampier, *A New Voyage*
8. Dampier, *Supplement*, vol. 1, p. 102
9. Dampier, *Supplement*, vol. 1, p. 113
10. Dampier, *Supplement*, vol. 1, p. 209
11. Dampier, *A New Voyage*, p. 276
12. Dampier, *A New Voyage*, p. 279

13. Dampier, *A New Voyage*, p. 280
14. Dampier, *A New Voyage*, p. 283
15. Dampier, *A New Voyage*, p. 297
16. Dampier, *A New Voyage*, p. 305
17. Dampier, *A New Voyage*, p. 365
18. Dampier, *A New Voyage*, p. 382
19. Dampier, *A New Voyage*, p. 409
20. Dampier, *A New Voyage*, p. 408
21. Dampier, *A New Voyage*, p. 395
22. Dampier, *A New Voyage*, p. 415
23. Dampier, *A New Voyage*, p. 461
24. The cove was named Cygnet Bay by the explorer Captain P. P. King in 1818, after Read's ship, but was given its current name of King Sound by Lieutenant John Stokes – who also named the Fitzroy River – in 1838.
25. Dampier, *A New Voyage*, p. 463
26. Ibid.
27. Dampier, *A New Voyage*, p. 464
28. The so-called Cossack skull found in north-west Australia with a missing front tooth is believed to be up to 6500 years old.
29. Dampier, *A New Voyage*, p. 464
30. Dampier, *A New Voyage*, p. 470. (Probably Christmas Island.)
31. Dampier, *A New Voyage*, p. 481
32. Abbott, J.H.M., *The Story of William Dampier*, Angus & Robertson, Sydney, 1911, p. 66
33. Dampier, *A New Voyage*, p. 519
34. Evelyn, J., *Diary*, 16 August 1698, quoted in George, A. S., *William Dampier in New Holland*, Bloomings Books, Melbourne, 1999, pp. 135–6
35. Dampier, W., *A Voyage to New Holland in the Year 1699*, James Knapton, London, 1703, p. 40
36. Dampier, *A Voyage to New Holland*, p. 114

37. Ibid.

38. Dampier, *A Voyage to New Holland*, p. 121

39. Hughes, UK Public Records Office, PRO ADM 52/94

40. Dampier, *A Voyage to New Holland*, p. 136

41. Dampier, *A Voyage to New Holland*, p. 219

42. Dampier, *A Voyage to New Holland*, p. 252

43. Preston, D. and M., *A Pirate of Exquisite Mind*, Random House, Sydney, 2004, p. 292

44. Coleridge, S. T., *The Table Talk and Omniana*, Oxford University Press, Oxford, 1917, p. 168

CHAPTER 3: THE BRITISH SETTLEMENT

1. Colville, Lord, letter to Secretary of the Admiralty, Admiralty 1/482, Public Records Office, Kew, UK

2. Hough, R., *Captain James Cook*, Hodder & Stoughton, London, 1995, p. 40

3. The eclipses occur at intervals of 8, 121.5, 8 and 105.5 years, then the cycle starts again. The latest eclipses are 1874 and 1882, 2004 and 2012. The next will be in 2117 and 2125.

4. Hough, *Cook*, p. 68

5. Cook, J., *Captain Cook's Journal during his First Voyage Around the World in HM Bark Endeavour 1768–71*, Elliot Stock, London, 1893, p. 163

6. Cook, *Journals*, 14 May 1769

7. Banks, J., *Journal of Joseph Banks in the Endeavour*, State Library of New South Wales manuscript, Mitchell Library safe 1/12-13. Transcription: http://gutenberg.net.au/ebooks05/0501141h.html#may1769, 14 April 1769

8. Cook, *Journals*, 6 June 1769

9. Banks, *Journal*, 30 April 1770

10. Banks, *Journal*, 4 May 1770

11. Cook, *Journals*, 22 August 1770

12. Ibid.

13. Cook, *Journals*, 9 November 1770
14. Cook, *Journals*, 26 December 1770
15. UK Public Records Office, PRO Admiralty 3/78
16. Journal of the House of Commons, UK Public Records Office, RB F342 4206/1
17. Ibid.
18. Ibid.
19. Letter from Lord Sydney to Treasury, 18 August 1786, HRNSW, vol. 2, pt 1, pp. 14–16
20. McIntyre, K. G., *Governor Phillip's Portuguese Prelude*, Sovereign Press, London 1984, p. 80
21. *London Observer*, 15 December 1793
22. McIntyre, *Governor Phillip's Portuguese Prelude*, p. 101
23. Hughes, R., *The Fatal Shore*, Random House, London, 1987, p. 73
24. Bowes Smyth, A., *A Journal of a Voyage from Portsmouth to New South Wales and China on the Lady Penrhyn*, P. G. Fidlon and R.J. Ryan (eds.), Australian Documents Library, Sydney, 1979, 1 December 1787
25. Clark, R., *The Journal and Letters of Ralph Clark, 1787–1792*, P. G. Fidlon and R. J. Ryan (eds), Australian Documents Library in association with the Library of Australian History, Sydney, 1981, p. 9
26. Phillip, A., in Tench, W., *A Narrative of an Expedition to Botany Bay*, Debrett, London, 1789, chapter VIII
27. Cook, *Journals*, 6 May 1770
28. Letter from Phillip, A. to Sydney, 15 May 1788, HRNSW, vol. 1, pt 2, p. 124
29. King, P. G., *The Journal of Philip Gidley King: Lieutenant, RN 1797–1790*, Australian Documents Library, Sydney, 1980, p. 37

30. Collins, D., *An Account of the English Colony in New South Wales*, vols 1 and 2, Stratham, London, 1802, p. 4

31. Tench, W., *A Complete Account of the Settlement at Port Jackson, in New South Wales*, G. Nicol and J. Sewell, London, 1793, chapter XVII

32. Instructions to Phillip, A., 25 April 1787, HRNSW, vol. 1, pt 2, p. 53

33. Phillip, A., letter to Lord Sydney, 15 May 1788, HRNSW, vol. 1, pt 2, p. 122

34. Phillip, A., letter to Lord Sydney, 28 September 1788, HRNSW, vol. 1, pt 2, p. 188

35. Phillip, A., letter to Nepean, E., 9 July 1788, HRNSW, vol. 1, pt 2, p. 155

36. Ross, R., letter to Stephens, 19 July 1788, HRNSW, vol. 1, pt 2, p. 173

37. Phillip, A., letter to Nepean, E., 13 July 1790, HRNSW, vol. 1, pt 2, p. 354

CHAPTER 4: ANOTHER FRENCH EXPLORATION

1. Labillardière, J. J. H., *Voyage in Search of La Pérouse*, John Stockdale, London, 1800, vol. 1, p. xi

2. Horner, F., *The French Reconnaissance: Baudin in Australia 1801–1803*, Melbourne University Press, Melbourne, 1987, p. 51

3. Horner, F., *Looking for La Pérouse: D'Entrecasteaux in Australia and the South Pacific, 1792–1793*, Melbourne University Press, Melbourne, 1995, p. 3

4. Horner, *Reconnaissance*, p. 35

5. Labillardière, *Voyage*, vol. 1, p. 71

6. Labillardière, *Voyage*, vol. 1, p. 73

7. Hunter, J., *Historic Journal of the transactions at Port Jackson and Norfolk Island*, John Stockdale, London, 1793, p. 240

8. Labillardière, *Voyage*, vol. 1, p. 112

9. D'Entrecasteaux, quoted in E. P. E. Rossel de, *Voyage de D'Entrecasteaux*, L'Imprimerie Imperiale, Paris, 1808, republished in Horner, *Looking for La Pérouse*, p. 54

10. Labillardière, *Voyage*, vol. 1, p. 205

11. Horner, *Looking for La Pérouse*, p. 94

12. Labillardière, *Voyage*, vol. 1, p. 282

13. Labillardière, *Voyage*, vol. 1, p. 307

14. Horner, *Looking for La Pérouse*, p. 108

15. Horner, *Looking for La Pérouse*, p. 101

16. Labillardière, *Voyage*, vol. 1, p. 406

17. D'Entrecasteaux, quoted in E. P. E. Rossel, *Voyage de D'Entrecasteaux*, republished in Horner, *Looking for La Pérouse*, p. 121

18. Labillardière, *Voyage*, vol. 2, p. 77

19. Horner, *Looking for La Pérouse*, p. 144

20. Labillardière, *Voyage*, vol. 2, p. 247

21. Ibid.

22. Labillardière, *Voyage*, vol. 2, p. 242

23. Labillardière, *Voyage*, vol. 2, p. 283

24. Horner, *Looking for La Pérouse*, p. 189

25. Labillardière, *Voyage*, vol. 2, p. 300

26. Horner, *Looking for La Pérouse*, p. 221

CHAPTER 5: MATTHEW FLINDERS

1. Estensen, M., *The Life of Matthew Flinders*, Allen & Unwin, Sydney, 2002, p. 4

2. *Naval Chronicle*, 'Biographical Memoir of Captain Matthew Flinders R.N, Naval Chronicle', London, vol. 32, 1814, p. 178

3. Scott, E., *The Life of Captain Matthew Flinders, R.N.*, Angus & Robertson, Sydney, 1914, p. 24

4. Scott, *Life of Flinders*, p. 26

5. Pasley, T., letter to M. Flinders, Flinders's Papers, National Maritime Museum: www.flinders.rmg. co.uk/DisplayDocument.cfm?ID=24&CurrentPage=1 &CurrentXMLPage=1&Search=pasley

6. Bligh, W., letter to Sir J. Banks, 17 December 1791, ML Microfilm CY3004/274, Mitchell Library, State Library of New South Wales, Sydney

7. Bligh, W., *A Narrative of the Mutiny, on Board His Majesty's Ship the Bounty, etc.*, George Nicol, London, 1790, p. 9

8. Estensen, *Flinders*, p. 19

9. Idsøe, O. and Guthe, T., 'The Frequency of Venereal Disease among Seafarers', www.whqlibdoc.who.int/bulletin/1963/Vol29/Vol29-No6/bulletin_1963_29(6)_773-780.pdf, p. 1

10. Rawson, G. *Bligh of the Bounty*, Philip Allan, London, 1932, p. 96

11. 'Matthew Flinders' Journeys', State Library of New South Wales, www.sl.nsw.gov.au/discover_collections/history_nation/terra_australis/index.html

12. Flinders, *Voyage*, vol. 1, p. 26

13. Smyth, W. H., 'Memoir of the Official Services of Captain Matthew Flinders', 1789–1814, compiled by Admiral William Henry Smyth, State Library of New South Wales, Sydney, May 1843, p. 2

14. Scott, *Life of Flinders*, p. 33

15. Estensen, *Flinders*, p. 27

16. Ibid.

17. Estensen, *Flinders*, p. 26

18. Flinders, letter to Sir J. Banks, 8 December 1806, Papers of Sir Joseph Banks, State Library of New South Wales, www2.sl.nsw.gov.au/banks/series_65/65_41.cfm

19. Estensen, *Flinders*, p. 33

20. Hunter, J., letter to Nepean, E., 3 September 1798, HRA, vol. 2, p. 220

21. Bass, G., letter to Sir J. Banks, 27 May 1799, Papers of Sir Joseph Banks, State Library of New South Wales, www2.sl.nsw.gov.au/banks/series_72/72_005.cfm

22. Flinders, *Voyage*, vol. 1, p. xcvi

23. This conflict is often referred to as the French Revolutionary Wars, which took place from 1792 until 1802.
24. Estensen, *Flinders*, p. 134
25. Estensen, *Flinders*, p. 135
26. Tench, W., *Settlement*, chapter IV
27. *Lloyd's Evening Post*, 29 May 1793
28. UK Public Records Office, TBP PRO T 1/733
29. Hunter, J. letter to King, P., 25 January 1795, HRNSW, vol. 2, p. 281
30. Flinders, *Journal on HMS Providence (1791–93)* Flinders's Papers, National Maritime Museum: www.flinders.rmg.co.uk/DisplayDocument.cfm? Author=41&CurrentPage=1&ID=88
31. Flinders, M., letter to Ann Chappell, Isabella Tyler and Mary Franklin, Flinders's Papers, National Maritime Museum: www.flinders.rmg.co.uk/ DisplayDocument.cfm?Search=little%20samuel& CurrentPage=1&ID=61&CurrentXMLPage=1
32. Mack, J. D., *Matthew Flinders, 1774–1814*, Nelson, Melbourne, 1966, p. 16

CHAPTER 6: GEORGE BASS AND MATTHEW FLINDERS

1. Colonial Secretary the Duke of Portland to Hunter, 11 September 1795, HRA, vol. 1, p. 528
2. Flinders, *Voyage*, vol. 1, p. 59
3. Ibid.
4. War broke out between England and France in 1793, and they were involved in what was known as the Revolutionary War until the Peace of Amiens in 1802. After the failure of the peace, the Napoleonic Wars began, continuing until 1815.
5. Banks, J., letter to J. Hunter, 1 February 1799, British Museum, N.H. DTC 11.187
6. Government and General Orders, 9 October 1797, HRA, vol. 2, pp. 203–4

7. Flinders, *Voyage*, vol. 1, p. 60
8. Arrowsmith, A., *A Topographical Plan of the Settlement of New South Wales. Including Port Jackson, Botany Bay and Broken Bay*, Arrowsmith, London, 1815
9. Lee, I., *The Coming of the British to Australia*, Longmans, Green and Co., London, 1906, Chapter V: www.gutenberg.net.au/ebooks09/0900091h.html
10. Flinders, evidence to Select Committee on Transportation, 25 March 1812, House of Commons. Online: www.nla.gov.au/nla.aus-vn4980067
11. Flinders, *A Biographical Tribute to the Memory of Trim*, Angus & Robertson, Sydney, 1997: www.flinders.rmg.co.uk/DisplayDocument.cfm?Search=trim&CurrentPage=1&ID=92&CurrentXMLPage=1
12. Collins, D., *An Account of the English Colony in New South Wales*, Stratham, London, 1802, vol. 2, chapter V
13. Ibid.
14. Mack, J. D., *Matthew Flinders, 1774–1814*, Nelson, Melbourne, 1966, p. 27
15. Flinders, *Voyage*, vol. 1, p. 66
16. Flinders, *Voyage*, vol. 1, p. 67
17. Flinders, *Voyage*, vol. 1, p. 69
18. From *Journey of a Whaleboat Voyage*, quoted in Flinders, *Voyage*, vol. 1, p. 69
19. Hunter, *Historic Journal*, p. 125
20. Hunter, J., letter to E. Nepean, 3 September 1798, HRA, vol. 2, p. 221
21. Flinders, *Voyage*, vol. 1, p. 82
22. Estensen, *Discovery*, p. 89
23. Flinders, *Voyage*, vol. 1, p. 88
24. Flinders, *Voyage*, vol. 1, p. 90
25. Flinders, *Voyage*, vol. 1, p. 91
26. Flinders, *Voyage*, vol. 1, p. 93
27. Flinders, *Voyage*, vol. 1, p. cxciii

28. Flinders, 'Observations on the Coast of Van Diemen's Land, etc.', HRNSW, vol. III, Appendix B, p. 786
29. Scott, *Life of Flinders*, p. 87
30. Flinders, *Voyage*, vol. 1, p. 108
31. Flinders, letter to C. Smith, 14 February 1800, Flinders's Papers, National Maritime Museum: www.flinders.rmg.co.uk/DisplayDocument.cfm?ID=62&CurrentPage=1&CurrentXMLPage=3

CHAPTER 7: EXPLORING THE UNKNOWN COAST

1. Estensen, *Discovery*, p. 111
2. Flinders, letter to J. Banks, 12 July 1804, HRNSW, vol. 5, pp. 397–98
3. Flinders, letter to A. Chappell, 25 September 1800, Flinders's Papers, National Maritime Museum: www.flinders.rmg.co.uk/DisplayDocument.cfm?Year=1800&CurrentPage=1&ID=94
4. Flinders, letter to J. Banks, 6 September 1800, Joseph Banks's Papers, State Library of New South Wales, series 65.01
5. Banks, J., letter to M. Flinders, 16 November 1800, Flinders's Papers, National Maritime Museum: www.flinders.rmg.co.uk/DisplayDocument.cfm?Year=1800&CurrentPage=1&ID=1
6. Mack, *Matthew Flinders*, p. 45
7. Scott, *Life of Flinders*, p. 99
8. Flinders, 'Observations on the Coast of Van Diemen's Land, etc.' HRNSW, vol. 3, Appendix B, p. 786
9. Ibid.
10. Flinders, *Voyage*, vol. 1, p. 109
11. Ibid.
12. Flinders, *Voyage*, vol. 1, p. 111
13. Flinders, M., letter to H. Flinders, 10 May 1801, Flinders's Papers, National Maritime Museum: www.flinders.rmg.co.uk/DisplayDocument.cfm?ID=63&CurrentPage=1&CurrentXMLPage=2&Search=spilsby

14. Flinders Snr, Diary and Account Book, UK National Archives: www.nationalarchives.gov.uk/a2a/records.aspx?cat=057-flinders&cid=1#

15. Letter from Ann to Betsy, 17 April 1801, Retter, C. and Sinclair, S., *Letters to Ann*, Angus & Robertson, Sydney, 1999, p. 26

16. Flinders, M., letter to A. Chappell, 6 April 1801, Flinders's Papers, National Maritime Museum: www.flinders.rmg.co.uk/DisplayDocument.cfm?ID=99&CurrentPage=2&CurrentXMLPage=2

17. Scott, *Life of Flinders*, p. 105

18. Banks, J., letter to Flinders, 21 May 1801, HRNSW, vol. 6, p. 372

19. Flinders, M., letter to J. Banks, 24 May 1801, Scott, *Life of Flinders*, p.106

20. Flinders, M., letter to Flinders, Snr, 10 July 1801, UK National Archives: www.nationalarchives.gov.uk/a2a/records.aspx?cat=057-flinders&cid=3-8#3-8

21. Flinders, M., letter to E. Nepean, 15 May 1802, HRNSW, vol. 4, p. 755

22. Nepean, E., letter to J. Banks, 28 April 1801, HRNSW, vol. 4, p. 348

23. Band, Stuart R., 'John Allen, miner: on board H.M.S. "Investigator" 1801–1804', *Bulletin of the Peak District Mines Historical Society*, 1987, vol. 10, no. 1, pp. 67–78

24. Flinders, *Voyage*, vol. 1, p. 115

25. Admiralty to Navy Board, 15 April 1801, UK Public Records Office, Admiralty, 2/296 172/5

26. Ibid.

27. Flinders, *Voyage*, vol. 1, pp. 112–13

28. Ibid.

29. Ibid.

30. Ibid.

31. Ibid.

32. Ibid.
33. Scott, *Life of Flinders*, p. 105
34. Ibid.
35. Flinders, *Voyage*, vol. 1, p. 114
36. Banks, J., letter to M. Flinders, 5 June 1801, HRNSW, vol. 4, p. 383
37. Flinders, M., letter to A. Flinders, 5 July 1801, Flinders's Papers, National Maritime Museum: www.flinders.rmg.co.uk/DisplayDocument.cfm?Receiver=25&CurrentPage=2&ID=102
38. Flinders, *Voyage*, vol. 1, p. 119
39. Flinders, *Voyage*, vol. 1, p. 129
40. Flinders, *Voyage*, vol. 1, p. 133
41. Flinders, *Voyage*, vol. 1, p. 139
42. Flinders, *Voyage*, vol. 1, p. 134
43. Ibid.
44. Flinders, *Voyage*, vol. 1, p. 135
45. Ibid.
46. Flinders, *Voyage*, vol. 1, p. 140
47. Ibid.
48. Good, P., *The Journal of Peter Good: Gardener on Matthew Flinders' Voyage to Terra Australis 1801–3*, Phyllis I. Edwards (ed.), British Museum, London, 1981, p. 51
49. Flinders, *Voyage*, vol. 1, pp. 150, 158
50. Flinders, *Voyage*, vol. 1, p. 155
51. Flinders, *Voyage*, vol. 1, p. 164
52. Flinders, *Voyage*, vol. 1, p. 163
53. Flinders, *Voyage*, vol. 1, p. 168
54. Flinders, *Voyage*, vol. 1, p. 171
55. Flinders, *Voyage*, vol. 1, p. 174
56. Flinders, *Voyage*, vol. 1, p. 173
57. Ibid.
58. Flinders, *Voyage*, vol. 1, p. 172
59. Flinders, *Voyage*, vol. 1, p. 175

60. Flinders, *Voyage*, vol. 1, p. 178
61. Flinders, *Voyage*, vol. 1, p. 177
62. Flinders, *Voyage*, vol. 1, p. 181
63. Flinders, *Voyage*, vol. 1, p. 182
64. Ibid.
65. Flinders, *Voyage*, vol. 1, p. 188
66. Flinders, *Voyage*, vol. 1, p. 193
67. Flinders, *Voyage*, vol. 1, p. 194
68. Flinders, *Voyage*, vol. 1, p. 196

CHAPTER 8: NICOLAS BAUDIN
 1. The Dutchman Frederik de Houtman is believed to
    be the first European to visit the river, in 1619, but it
    was not given its name until 1697, by another Dutch
    explorer, Willem de Vlamingh.
 2. 'Plan of Itinerary for Citizen Baudin', Horner,
    Reconnaissance, appendix II, p. 377
 3. Horner, *Reconnaissance*, p. 25
 4. Horner, *Reconnaissance*, p. 29
 5. Jussieu, Antoine-Laurent de, letter to French
    Minister of Marine, 20 July 1798, quoted in Horner,
    Reconnaissance, p. 36
 6. Horner, *Reconnaissance*, p. 41
 7. Baudin, N., *The Journal of Post Captain Nicolas
    Baudin, Commander-in-Chief of the corvettes
    Géographe and Naturaliste, assigned by order of
    the Government to a voyage of discovery*, Christine
    Cornell (trans.) and Jean-Paul Faivre (foreword),
    State Library of South Australia, Adelaide, 1974,
    p. 576
 8. 'Plan of Itinerary for Citizen Baudin', Horner,
    Reconnaissance, appendix II, p. 377
 9. Ibid.
10. Baudin, *Journal*, 19 October 1800
11. Baudin, *Journal*, 21 October 1800
12. Baudin, *Journal*, 22 October 1800

13. Baudin, *Journal*, 7 November 1800
14. Horner, *Reconnaissance*, p. 115
15. Horner, *Reconnaissance*, p. 116
16. Baudin, *Journal*, 19 April 1801
17. Baudin, *Journal*, 23 April 1801
18. Horner, *Reconnaissance*, p. 117
19. Baudin, *Journal*, 26 March 1801
20. Horner, *Reconnaissance*, p. 119
21. Horner, *Reconnaissance*, p. 114
22. Horner, *Reconnaissance*, p. 118
23. Horner, *Reconnaissance*, p. 139
24. Péron, F., quoted in Horner, *Reconnaissance*, p. 142
25. Freycinet, H., 'Report of Citizen Freycinet, commander of the boat at our first landing on the western coast of New Holland' quoted in Baudin, *Journal*, 31 May 1801
26. Baudin, *Journal*, 4 June 1801
27. Horner, *Reconnaissance*, p. 142
28. Moore, G. F., *Diary of an Early Settler in Western Australia 1830–1841*, Selwyn & Co., Sydney, 1884, p. 87
29. Baudin, *Journal*, 18 June 1801
30. Freycinet, L. C., quoted in Horner, *Reconnaissance*, p. 156
31. Ronsard, F.-M., quoted in Horner, *Reconnaissance*, p. 155
32. Baudin, *Journal*, 23 June 1801
33. Baudin, N., letter to Minister of Marine, 5 October 1801, quoted in Horner, *Reconnaissance*, p. 161
34. Baudin, *Journal*, 19 August 1801
35. Baudin, *Journal*, 30 August 1801
36. Baudin, N., quoted in Horner, *Reconnaissance*, pp. 181–82
37. Horner, *Reconnaissance*, p. 185
38. Péron, F., quoted in Horner, *Reconnaissance*, p. 189
39. Baudin, *Journal*, 14 January 1802

40. Baudin, N., letter to Minister of Marine, quoted in Horner, *Reconnaissance*, p. 210
41. Flinders, *Voyage,* vol. 1, p. 197
42. Baudin, *Journal*, 4 April 1802
43. Baudin, *Journal*, 8–9 April 1802
44. Flinders, *Voyage*, vol. 1, p. 197
45. Baudin, *Journal*, 8 April 1802
46. Flinders, *Voyage*, vol. 1, p. 197
47. Flinders, *Voyage*, vol. 1, p. 198
48. Ibid.
49. Baudin, *Journal*, 9 April 1802
50. Horner, *Reconnaissance*, p. 220
51. Baudin, *Journal*, 8 April 1802
52. Ibid.
53. Flinders, *Voyage*, vol. 1, p. 198
54. Mack, *Matthew Flinders*, p. 110
55. Péron, F., quoted in Horner, *Reconnaissance*, p. 223
56. Baudin, *Journal*, 17 April 1802
57. Baudin, *Journal*, 8 May 1802
58. Baudin, *Journal*, 31 May 1802
59. Baudin, *Journal*, 23 May 1802
60. Ibid.

CHAPTER 9: THE FRENCH AND ENGLISH RIVALS IN SYDNEY

1. Flinders, M., *Voyage*, vol. 1, p. 215
2. Portland, Lord, letter to J. Hunter, HRNSW, vol. 3, p. 738
3. Phillip, A., letter to P. King, 12 February 1788, 'Government of Norfolk Island', HRNSW, vol. 1, part 2, p. 137
4. Flinders, *Voyage*, vol. 1, p. 216
5. Scott, *Life of Flinders*, p. 127
6. Flinders, *Voyage*, vol. 1, p. 216
7. Horner, F., *The French Reconnaissance*, p. 246

8. Flinders, *Voyage*, vol. 1, p. 217

9. Horner, *Reconnaissance*, p. 415

10. Flinders, *Voyage*, vol. 1, p. 217

11. Baudin, *Journal*, June 1802

12. Flinders, *Voyage*, vol. 1, p. 218

13. Baudin, *Journal*, July 1802

14. Flinders, *Voyage*, vol. 1, p. 218

15. Flinders, *Voyage*, vol. 1, p. 199

16. Flinders, *Voyage*, vol. 1, p. 220

17. 'Plan of Itinerary for Citizen Baudin', Horner, *Reconnaissance*, appendix II, p. 377. Revolutionary France had its own calendar, which was used from 1793 till 1805. The new calendar aimed to remove all religious and royalist influences in the old one and was part of a broader program of decimalisation.

18. Flinders, *Voyage*, vol. 1, p. 219

19. Mack, *Matthew Flinders*, p. 114

20. Flinders, *Voyage*, vol. 1, p. 219

21. Flinders, *Voyage*, vol. 1, p. 220

22. Ibid.

23. Flinders, M., letter to A. Flinders, 20 July 1802, Flinders Papers, National Maritime Museum: www.flinders.rmg.co.uk/DisplayDocument.cfm?ID=107&CurrentPage=1&CurrentXMLPage=2

24. Flinders, *Voyage*, vol. 1, p. 220

25. Ibid.

26. Horner, *Reconnaissance*, p. 261

27. Letter from Baudin in Port Jackson to French Minister of Marine, quoted in Horner, *Reconnaissance*, p. 252

CHAPTER 10: ENCIRCLING AUSTRALIA

1. Flinders, *Voyage*, vol. 1, p. 220

2. Flinders, *Voyage*, vol. 2, p. 32

3. Flinders, *Voyage*, vol. 2, p. 14

4. Flinders, *Voyage*, vol. 2, p. 57

5. Flinders, *Voyage*, vol. 2, p. 54
6. Flinders, *Voyage*, vol. 2, p. 69
7. Flinders, *Voyage*, vol. 2, p. 72
8. Ibid.
9. Flinders, *Voyage*, vol. 2, p. 75
10. Ibid.
11. Ibid.
12. Flinders, *Voyage*, vol. 1, p. 109
13. Mack, *Matthew Flinders*, p. 136
14. Flinders, *Voyage*, vol. 2, p. 76
15. Flinders, *Voyage*, vol. 2, p. 77
16. Flinders, *Voyage*, vol. 2, p. 90
17. Ibid.
18. Ibid.
19. Ibid.
20. Flinders, *Voyage*, vol. 2, p. 95
21. Flinders, *Voyage*, vol. 2, p. 97
22. Flinders, *Voyage*, vol. 2, p. 98
23. Ibid.
24. Flinders, *Voyage*, vol. 2, p. 102
25. For a list of places named by Flinders on the Australian coast see *Scott, Life of Flinders*, Appendix C, p. 235
26. Flinders, *Voyage*, vol. 2, p. 113
27. Flinders, *Voyage*, vol. 2, p. 116
28. Ibid.
29. Ibid.
30. Mountford, C., *Records of the American Australian Scientific Expedition to Arnhem Land*, vol.1, Melbourne University Press, Melbourne, 1956, p. 95
31. Flinders, *Voyage*, vol. 2, p. 117
32. Flinders, *Voyage*, vol. 2, p. 125
33. Flinders, *Voyage*, vol. 1, p. 126
34. Flinders, letter to A. Finders, from Kupang, 28 April 1803, Flinders's Papers, National Maritime Museum: www.flinders.rmg.co.uk/DisplayDocument.cfm? Year=1803&CurrentPage=1&ID=108

35. Flinders, *Voyage*, vol. 2, p. 127
36. Flinders, *Voyage*, vol. 2, p. 130
37. Flinders, *Voyage*, vol. 2, p. 136

CHAPTER 11: THE FRENCH HEAD FOR HOME

1. The ultimate fate of Mary Bickaith is unknown. It is possible that Baudin left her in Timor, and possible that he transferred her to the merchant ship *Fanny*, which left Sydney at the same time, heading for Batavia. See Horner, *Reconnaissance*, p. 262
2. Baudin, *Journal*, 17 November 1802
3. Baudin, *Journal*, 5 December 1802
4. King, P., letter to N. Baudin, 23 December 1802, HRNSW, vol. 4, p. 1008
5. Baudin, N., letter to P. King, 23 December 1802, HRNSW, vol. 5, p. 826
6. Ibid.
7. Baudin, *Journal*, 3 February 1803
8. Baudin, *Journal*, 23 February 1803
9. Horner, *Reconnaissance*, p. 290
10. Freycinet, L., *Journal*, 19–28 February 1803, quoted in Horner, *Reconnaissance*, p. 291
11. Baudin, *Journal*, 28 February 1803
12. Baudin, *Journal*, 17 March 1803
13. Baudin, *Journal*, 23 March 1803
14. Baudin, *Journal*, 16 June 1803
15. Baudin, *Journal*, 26 June 1803
16. The Fitzroy was named after Robert FitzRoy, the captain of the *Beagle*, in 1837. The Ord was named after Sir Harry St George Ord, governor of Western Australia, by the overland explorer Alexander Forrest in 1879. And the Victoria was named after Queen Victoria in 1839 by Lieutenant J. C. Wickham, second-in-command of the *Beagle*.

17. Baudin, *Journal*, 7 July 1803
18. Horner, *Reconnaissance*, p. 314
19. Horner, *Reconnaissance*, p. 317
20. Ibid.
21. Ibid.
22. Horner, *Reconnaissance*, p. 328
23. Péron, F., 'Report from François Péron to General Decaen on the Colonization of New Holland', 12 December 1803, Scott, *Life of Flinders*, appendix B, p. 222
24. Péron, F., *A Voyage of Discovery to the Southern Hemisphere, performed by the order of the Emperor Napoleon, during the years 1801, 1802, 1803 and 1804*, Marsh Walsh Publishing, Melbourne, 1975, pp. 9, 343
25. Thévenard, report to Minister of Marine, 30 March 1804, quoted in Horner, *Reconnaissance*, p. 347
26. Horner, *Reconnaissance*, pp. 347–48
27. Horner, *Reconnaissance*, p. 3
28. Bonaparte, N., quoted in Horner, *Reconnaissance*, p. 338

CHAPTER 12: SHIPWRECK

1. Flinders, *Voyage*, vol. 2, p. 138
2. Flinders, letter to Elizabeth Flinders, Mitchell Library, MSS 1/55, State Library of New South Wales
3. Flinders, *Voyage*, vol. 2, p. 247
4. Flinders, *Voyage*, vol. 2, p. 248
5. Flinders, *Voyage*, vol. 2, p. 138
6. Flinders, *Voyage*, vol. 2, p. 148
7. Flinders, *Voyage*, vol. 2, p. 149
8. Ibid.
9. Ibid.
10. Ibid.

11. Smith, S., *Sailing with Flinders: the Journal of Seaman Samuel Smith*, Peter Monteath (ed. and introduction), Corkwood Press, Adelaide, 2002, p. 66
12. Flinders, *Voyage*, vol. 2, p. 151
13. Ibid.
14. Ibid.
15. Ibid.
16. Flinders, *Voyage*, vol. 2, p. 152
17. Ibid.
18. *Calcutta Orphan*, 3 February 1804, article republished in Flinders, *Voyage*, vol. 2, p. 153
19. Williams, quoted in Flinders, *Voyage*, vol. 2, p. 152
20. Scott, *Life of Flinders*, p. 159
21. Flinders, *Voyage*, vol. 2, p. 154
22. Ibid.
23. Ibid.
24. Flinders, *Voyage*, vol. 2, p. 156
25. Flinders, *Voyage*, vol. 2, p. 158
26. Flinders, *Voyage*, vol. 2, p. 160
27. Flinders, *Voyage*, vol. 2, p. 161
28. Smith, *Sailing with Flinders*, p. 69

Chapter 13: Imprisoned on Mauritius

1. Flinders, *Voyage*, vol. 2, p. 161
2. Ibid.
3. Ibid.
4. Flinders, *Voyage*, vol. 2, p. 175
5. Scott, *Life of Flinders*, p. 162
6. Decaen, C. M. I., *Memoirs*, quoted ibid.
7. Flinders, *Voyage*, vol. 2, p. 177
8. Ibid.
9. Ibid.
10. Flinders, *Voyage*, vol. 2, p. 178
11. Ibid.
12. Ibid.

13. Flinders, *Voyage*, vol. 1, p. 114
14. Flinders, M., letter to C. M. I. Decaen, quoted in Flinders, *Voyage*, vol. 2, p. 181
15. Decaen, C. M. I., letter to Minister of Marine, quoted in Scott, *Life of Flinders*, p. 237
16. Flinders, *Voyage*, vol. 2, p. 176
17. Flinders, *Voyage*, vol. 2, p. 182
18. Estensen, *Discovery*, p. 331
19. Flinders, *Voyage*, vol. 2, p. 189
20. Flinders, M., letter to P. King, Flinders, *Voyage*, p. 193
21. Banks, J., letter to President of Institute of France (undated), HRNSW, vol. 3, p. 445
22. Banks, J., letter to P. King, 29 August 1804, HRNSW, vol. 5, p. 458
23. Flinders, *Voyage*, vol. 2, p. 247
24. For the history of the name Australia, see Scott, *Life of Flinders*, 'Chapter 30: The Naming of Australia'
25. Scott, *Life of Flinders*, p. 216
26. *Sydney Gazette*, 7 April 1805
27. Hitchcock, W., *Flinders in Mauritius, 1803–10*, special collections, Flinders University Library, Adelaide, p. 3
28. Scott, *Life of Flinders*, p. 189
29. Hitchcock, *Flinders in Mauritius*, p. 10
30. Scott, *Life of Flinders*, pp. 191–92
31. Scott, *Life of Flinders*, p. 191
32. Flinders, *Voyage*, vol. 2, p. 225
33. Flinders, *Voyage*, vol. 2, p. 225
34. Flinders, *Voyage*, vol. 1, p. 218
35. Hitchcock, *Flinders in Mauritius*, p. 23
36. Flinders, *Voyage*, vol. 2, p. 226
37. Ibid.
38. Flinders, *Voyage*, vol. 2, p. 229
39. Flinders, *Voyage*, vol. 2, p. 228
40. Flinders, *Voyage*, vol. 2, p. 234

CHAPTER 14: COMPLETING THE MISSION

1. Banks, J., letter to A. Flinders, 25 September 1810, Flinders's Papers, National Maritime Museum: www.flinders.rmg.co.uk/DisplayDocument.cfm? Year=1810&CurrentPage=2&ID=148
2. Estensen, *Flinders*, p. 422
3. Franklin, J., letter to M. Flinders, 1 November 1810, Flinders's Papers, National Maritime Museum, Greenwich, UK
4. Scott, *Life of Flinders*, p. 393
5. Scott, *Life of Flinders*, p. 218
6. Flinders, *Voyage*, vol. 1, p. 17
7. Ibid.
8. Scott, *Life of Flinders*, p. 220
9. Horner, *Reconnaissance*, p. 10
10. Freycinet, L. C., letter to Minister of Marine, quoted in Scott, *Life of Flinders*, p. 200
11. Freycinet, L. C., quoted in Horner, *Reconnaissance*, p. 355
12. Horner, *Reconnaissance*, p. 11
13. 'Report from the Select Committee on Transportation', 10 July 1812, House of Commons. Online: www.nla. gov.au/nla.aus-vn4980067
14. Mack, *Matthew Flinders*, p. 233
15. Mack speculates that Flinders could also have had a malignant tumor of the bladder, a urinary tract infection and eventually 'renal destruction'. Mack, *Matthew Flinders*, p. 234
16. Flinders, A. letter to T. Pitot, 19 September 1814, 1/57 Mitchell Library, CY 1090, State Library of New South Wales
17. Hooker, J. D., *The Botany of the Antarctic Voyage of H.M. Discovery Ships Erebus and Terror*, Reeve Brothers, London, 1860, vol. 1, p. cxiv
18. Mack, *Matthew Flinders*, p. 238

BIBLIOGRAPHY

Abbott, J. H. M., *The Story of William Dampier*, Angus
& Robertson, Sydney, 1911

Anderson, Bern, *Surveyor of the Sea: the Life and Voyage
of Captain George Vancouver*, University of Toronto
Press, Toronto, 1960

Band, Stuart R., 'John Allen, miner: on board HMS
Investigator 1801–1804', *Bulletin*, Peak District
Mines Historical Society, 10(1): 67–78, 1987

Banks, Joseph, *The Endeavour Journal of Joseph Banks
1768–71*, vols 1 and 2, J. C. Beaglehole (ed.), Angus
& Robertson, Sydney, 1962

Banks, Joseph, *Journal of Joseph Banks in the
Endeavour*, State Library of New South Wales
manuscript, Mitchell Library, safe 1/12–13.
Also online: www.southseas.nla.gov.au/index_
voyaging.html

Banks, Joseph, papers and letters online:
State Library of New South Wales: www.nsw.gov.au/
banks

National Library of Australia, collection number MS 9: www.nla.gov.au/nla.ms-ms9

Joseph Banks Society (UK): www.joseph-banks.org.uk

The National Archive (UK): www.nationalarchives. gov.uk/catalogue/displaycataloguedetails.asp?CA TID=62340&CATLN=3&accessmethod=5&j=1

Bass, George, *Bass's Journal of the Whaleboat Voyage*, republished in Matthew Flinders, *A Voyage to Terra Australis*, vol. 1

Bateson, Charles, *The Convict Ships, 1787–1868*, Brown, Son & Ferguson, Glasgow, 1959

Baudin, Nicolas, *The Journal of Post Captain Nicolas Baudin, Commander-in-Chief of the corvettes Géographe and Naturaliste, assigned by order of the Government to a voyage of discovery*, Christine Cornell (trans.) and Jean-Paul Faivre (foreword), State Library of South Australia, Adelaide, 1974

Bligh, William, *A Log of the Proceedings of His Majesty's Ship Providence and the Second Voyage to the South Seas*, Genesis Publications, Guildford, England, 1976

Bligh, William, *A Narrative of the Mutiny, on Board His Majesty's Ship Bounty; and the subsequent voyage of part of the crew, in the ship's boat, from Tofoa, one of the Friendly Islands, to Timor, a Dutch settlement in the East Indies*, George Nicol, London, 1790

Bligh, William, *A Voyage to the South Sea . . . for the purpose of conveying the bread-fruit tree to the West Indies, in his majesty's ship the Bounty, commanded by Lieutenant William Bligh*, George Nicol, London, 1792

Bowes Smyth, Arthur, *A Journal of a Voyage from Portsmouth to New South Wales and China on the Lady Penrhyn*, P. G. Fidlon and R. J. Ryan (eds), Australian Documents Library, Sydney, 1979

Brasch, Nicolas, *Charting the Coast*, Macmillan Education, Melbourne, 2003

Brown, Anthony, *Ill-starred Captains: Flinders and Baudin*, Crawford House, Adelaide, 2000

Brown, Robert, *Nature's Investigator: the Diary of Robert Brown to Australia, 1801–1805*, Valance, T. G., More, D. T. and Groves, E. W. (eds), Australian Biological Resources Study, Canberra, 2001

Callander, John, *Voyages to Terra Australis*, Hawkes, Clark and Collins, Edinburgh, 1776

Clark, Ralph, *The Journal and Letters of Ralph Clark, 1787–1792*, P. G. Fidlon and R. J. Ryan (eds) Australian Documents Library in association with the Library of Australia History, Sydney, 1981. Also online: www.setis.library.usyd.edu.au/ozlit/pdf/clajour.pdf

Clode, Danielle, *Voyages to the South Seas: in search of Terres Australes*, Miegunyah Press, Melbourne, 2007

Coleridge, Samuel Taylor, *The Table Talk and Omniana*, Oxford University Press, Oxford, 1917

Collins, David, *An Account of the English Colony in New South Wales*, vols 1 and 2, Stratham, London, 1802. Also online: www.gutenberg.net.au/ebooks/e00010.html

Cook, James, *Captain Cook's Journal during his First Voyage Around the World in HM Bark Endeavour 1768–71*, Elliot Stock, London, 1893. Also online: www.southseas.nla.gov.au/index_voyaging.html

Dalrymple, Alexander, *An Historical Collection of Several Voyages and Discoveries in the South Pacific Ocean*, Nourse, London, 1770

Dampier, William, *A New Voyage Round the World,* James Knapton, London, 1697. Also online: www.gutenberg.net.au/ebooks05/0500461h.html

Dampier, William, *A Voyage to New Holland in the Year 1699*, James Knapton, London, 1703. Also online: www.gutenberg.org/files/15675/15675-h/15675-h.htm

Dampier William, *A Supplement to the Voyage Round the World. Voyages and Descriptions*, James Knapton, London, 1700. Also online: www.books. google.com.au/books?id=iZNCAAAAcAAJ&printsec =frontcover&source=gbs_ge_summary_r&cad=0# v=onepage&q&f=false

Dunmore, John, *French Explorers in the Pacific*, Clarendon Press, Oxford, 1965

Duyker, E. and Duyker, M. (eds and trans.), *Bruny D'Entrecasteaux, Voyage to Australia and the Pacific, 1791–1793*, Melbourne University Press, Melbourne, 2001

Dyer, Colin, *The French Explorers and the Australian Aboriginals, 1772–1839*, University of Queensland Press, Brisbane, 2007

Estensen, Miriam, *Discovery: the Quest for the Great South Land*, Allen & Unwin, Sydney, 1998

Estensen, Miriam, *The Life of Matthew Flinders*, Allen & Unwin, Sydney, 2002

Evelyn, John, *Diary*, Oxford University Press, Oxford, 1959

Flinders, Matthew, *A Biographical Tribute to the Memory of Trim*, Angus & Robertson, Sydney, 1997. Also online: www.flinders.rmg.co.uk/ DisplayDocument.cfm?ID=92

Flinders, Matthew, *A Voyage to Terra Australis: Undertaken for the Purpose of Completing the Discovery of that Vast Country, and Prosecuted in the Years 1801, 1802 and 1803, in His Majesty's Ship the Investigator, and Subsequently in the Armed Vessel Porpoise and Cumberland Schooner: With an Account of the Shipwreck of the Porpoise, Arrival of the Cumberland at Mauritius, and Imprisonment of the*

Commander during Six Years and a Half in that Island,
vols 1 and 2, G. and W. Nicol, London, 1814. Also
online: www.gutenberg.net.au/ebooks/e00049.html

Flinders, Matthew, 'Observations on the Coast of Van
Diemen's Land, etc.', Historical Records of New South
Wales, vol. 3, appendix B, Charles Potter, Sydney,
1893

Flinders, Matthew and others, *Matthew Flinders' Private
Journal from 17 December 1803 at Isle De France to
10 July 1814 at London,* Friends of the State Library
of South Australia, Adelaide, 2005

Flinders's papers and letters are also online at:
State Library of Victoria www.slv.vic.gov.au
National Library of Australia www.nla.gov.au
National Museum of Australia www.nma.gov.au
State Library of South Australia www.slsa.sa.gov.au
State Library of New South Wales (including the
Mitchell Library) www.sl.nsw.gov.au.
National Maritime Museum, London www.nmm.ac.uk
Australian National Maritime Museum www.anmm.
gov.au
Australian Dictionary of Biography www.adb.anu.
edu.au

Fornesiero, J., Montheath, P., West-Sooby, J.,
Encountering Terra Australis, Wakefield Press, South
Australia, 2004

Freycinet, Louis de, *Reflections on New South Wales,
1788–1839*, T. Cullity (trans.), Horden House Rare
Books, Sydney, 2001

George, A. S., *William Dampier in New Holland*,
Bloomings Books, Melbourne, 1999

Good, Peter, *The Journal of Peter Good: Gardener
on Matthew Flinders' Voyage to Terra Australis
1801–3*, Phyllis Edwards (ed.), British Museum,
London, 1981

Harris, Hendon, *Asiatic Fathers of America*, Warwick House Publishing, Virginia, 2006

Heeres, J. E. (ed.), *Abel Janszoon Tasman's Journal: His Life and Labours*, Frederick Muller, Amsterdam, 1898

Hélouis transcripts, *Transcripts of documents relating to Australasia and the Pacific in French archives*, transcribed by Mme R. Hélouis, State Library of New South Wales

Historical Records of Australia (HRA), series I, vols. I, II, III, IV

Historical Records of New South Wales (HRNSW), vols. I, II, III, IV, V, VI, VII, VIII

Hitchcock, Witgar, *Flinders in Mauritius, 1803–10*, special collections, Flinders University Library, Adelaide

Hooker, Joseph Dalton, *The Botany of the Antarctic Voyage of H.M. Discovery Ships Erebus and Terror*, Reeve Brothers, London, 1860

Horner, Frank, *The French Reconnaissance: Baudin in Australia 1801–1803*, Melbourne University Press, Melbourne, 1987

Horner, Frank, *Looking for La Pérouse: D'Entrecasteaux in Australia and the South Pacific, 1792–1793*, Melbourne University Press, Melbourne, 1995

Hough, R., *Captain James Cook*, Hodder & Stoughton, London, 1995

Hughes, Robert, *The Fatal Shore*, Random House, London, 1987

Hunt, S. and Carter, P., *Terra Napoleon: Australia through French Eyes, 1800–1804*, Pot Still Press, Sydney, 1999

Hunter, John, *Historic Journal of the Transactions at Port Jackson and Norfolk Island*, John Stockdale, London, 1793

Idsøe, O. and Guthe, T., *Frequency of Venereal Disease among Seafarers*, www.whqlibdoc.who.int/bulletin/1963/ Vol29/Vol29-No6/bulletin_1963_29(6)_773-780.pdf

Ingleton, Geoffrey C., *Matthew Flinders, Navigator and Chartmaker*, Genesis Publications, Guildford, 1986

King, Philip Gidley, *The Journal of Philip Gidley King: Lieutenant, RN 1797–1790*, Australian Documents Library, Sydney, 1980

Labillardière, Jacques-Julien Houtou, *Voyage in Search of La Pérouse*, John Stockdale, London, 1800

La Pérouse, Jean François de Galaup, *The Journal of Jean Francois de Galaup de la Pérouse 1785–1788*, J. Dunmore (trans. and ed.), Hakluyt Society, London, 1994–95

Lee, Ida, *The Coming of the British to Australia 1788–1829*, Longmans, Green and Co., London, 1906

Lee, Ida, 'The First Sighting of Australia by the English', *The Geographical Journal*, Royal Geographical Society, London, April 1934

Mack, James Decker, *Matthew Flinders, 1774–1814*, Nelson, Melbourne, 1966

McClymont, James R., *The Theory of an Antipodal Southern Continent during the Sixteenth Century*, Government Printer, Hobart, 1892

McHugh, Evan, *1606: An Epic Adventure*, UNSW Press, Sydney, 2006

McIntyre, Kenneth Gordon, *Governor Phillip's Portuguese Prelude*, Sovereign Press, London, 1984

Moore, George Fletcher, *Diary of an Early Settler in Western Australia 1830–1841*, Selwyn & Co., Sydney, 1884

Mountford, Charles, *Records of the American Australian Scientific Expedition to Arnhem Land*, vol. 1, Melbourne University Press, Melbourne, 1956

Mutch, T. D., 'The First Discovery of Australia, with an Account of the Voyage of the *Duyfken*', *Journal of the Royal Australian Historical Society*, vol. XXVII, Sydney, 1942

Naval Chronicle. 'Biographical Memoir of Captain Matthew Flinders R.N', vol. 32, London, 1814. Also online: www.nla.gov.au/nla.aus-vn5019873

Paine, Daniel, *The Journal of Daniel Paine*, Library of Australian History, Sydney, 1983

Pelsaert, Francisco, *The Batavia Journal of Francisco Pelsaert*, Marit van Huystee (ed. and trans), Algemeen Rijksarchief, The Hague, Netherlands, 1998; report of the Western Australian Maritime Museum, Department of Maritime Archaeology, no. 136, 1994

Péron, François, *A Voyage of Discovery to the Southern Hemisphere, performed by the order of the Emperor Napoleon, during the years 1801, 1802, 1803 and 1804*, Marsh Walsh Publishing, Melbourne, 1975

Phillip, Arthur, *The Voyage of Arthur Phillip to Botany Bay*, Hutchison, Melbourne, 1982

Preston, Diana and Michael, *A Pirate of Exquisite Mind: The Life of William Dampier, Explorer, Naturalist and Buccaneer*, Random House, London, 2004

Rawson, Geoffrey, *Bligh of the Bounty*, Philip Allan, London, 1932

Report from the Select Committee on Transportation, House of Commons, London, 1812. Online: www.catalogue.nla.gov.au/Record/1887951

Retter, Catherine and Sinclair, Shirley, *Letters to Ann*, Angus & Robertson, Sydney, 1999

Richardson, William, A.R., *Was Australia Charted before 1606?: The Jave la Grande Inscriptions*, National Library of Australia, Canberra, 2006

Scott, Ernest, *The Life of Captain Matthew Flinders, R.N.*, Angus & Robertson, Sydney, 1914. Also online: www.gutenberg.org/files/7304/7304-h/7304-h.htm

Scott, Ernest, *Terre Napoleon: a History of French Explorations and Projects in Australia*, Methuen and Co., London, 1910

Smith, Samuel, *Sailing with Flinders: the Journal of Seaman Samuel Smith*, Peter Monteath (ed. and introduction), Corkwood Press, Adelaide, 2002

Smyth, William Henry, 'Memoir of the Official Services of Captain Matthew Flinders', 1789–1814, compiled by Admiral William Henry Smyth, State Library of New South Wales, Sydney, May 1843

Stevens, Henri (ed.), *New Light on the Discovery of Australia as Revealed by the Journal of Captain Diego de Prado y Tovar*, George F. Barwick (trans.), Hakluyt Society, Liechtenstein, 1930

Tasman, Abel, *The Journal of Abel Jansz Tasman, 1642: with documents relating to his exploration of Australia in 1644*, G. H. Kenihan (ed.), Australian Heritage Press, Adelaide, 1964. Also online: www.gutenberg.net.au/ebooks06/0600571h.html

Tench, Watkin, *A Complete Account of the Settlement at Port Jackson, in New South Wales*, G. Nicol and J. Sewell, London, 1793

Tench, Watkin, *A Narrative of an Expedition to Botany Bay*, Debrett, London, 1789

Vancouver, George, *A Voyage of Discovery to the North Pacific Ocean and Round the World*, G. G. & J. Robinson and J. Edwards, London, 1798

Waterhouse, Henry, 'Account of the Battle of June 1, 1794', Bass/Waterhouse letters CY 3970, Mitchell Library, State Library of New South Wales, Sydney

Whitington, Louis Arnold, *Matthew Flinders and Terra Australis*, Pioneers' Association of South Australia, Adelaide, 1951

Williamson, J. A. (ed.), *William Dampier: A Voyage to New Holland*, The Argonaut Press, London, 1939

MAPS

Arrowsmith, A., *A Chart of Bass Strait between New South Wales and Van Diemen's Land*, A. Arrowsmith A., *Chart of Torres Strait from the surveys of Capt. Cook in 1769*, Arrowsmith, London, 1798

Arrowsmith A., *Port Dalrymple on the north coast of Van Diemen's Land as surveyed in the Norfolk sloop by M. Flinders*, Arrowsmith, London, 1801

Arrowsmith, A., *A Topographical Plan of the Settlement of New South Wales. Including Port Jackson, Botany Bay and Broken Bay*, Arrowsmith, London, 1815

Arrowsmith A., *Twofold Bay on the east coast of New South Wales examined by M. Flinders and Mr. R. Simpson*, Arrowsmith, London, 1801

Arrowsmith A., *Western Port on the south coast of New South Wales from Mr. Bass's eyesketch*, Arrowsmith, London, 1801

Perry, T. M., *The Discovery of Australia: The Charts and Maps of the Navigators and Explorers*, Hamish Hamilton, London, 1982

Other maps online:

Dixson Map Collection, State Library of New South Wales: www.sl.nsw.gov.au/discover_collection/history_nation/dixson/index.html

Early Australian Maps, State Library of Queensland: www.slq.qld.gov.au/coll/maps/aust

Maps of Australia, National Library of Australia: www.mapsearch.nla.gov.au

Australia, Matthew Flinders, electronic archive, maps and charts, National Library of Australia: www.pandora.nla.gov.au/pan/77226/20071011-0000/www.sl.nsw.gov.au/flinders/maps/index.html

South Land to New Holland: Dutch Charting of Australia, 1606–1756: www.pandora.nla.gov.au/pan/60542/20060914_0000/www.nla.gov.au/exhibitions/southland/intro.html

LIST OF ILLUSTRATIONS

First map of Australia from Nicholas Vallard's atlas, 1547
National Library of Australia

Dieppe map by Nicolas Desliens, 1566
Bibliothèque Nationale de France

The discovery of Australia by the yacht *Duyfien*
published in *Monumenta cartographica* by Martinus
Nijhoff, The Hague, 1925
National Library of Australia

Hollandia Nova by Melchisédech Thévenot, 1663
State Library of South Australia

Captain Dampier's new voyage to New Holland by
William Dampier, 1699, published by James and John
Knapton, 1729
National Library of Australia

Atlas du voyage de Bruny D'Entrecasteaux, commander
of *La Récherche* et *L'Esperance* by Charles-François
Beautemps-Beaupré, 1807
National Library of Australia

Louis-Claude Freycinet, Carte Générale de la Terra
Napoleon, 1811
State Library of South Australia

Chart of Terra Australis by Matthew Flinders, commander
of HM *Sloop*, 1814
State Library of South Australia

Carte Générale de la Nouvelle Hollande by Louis-Claude
Freycinet, 1811
National Library of Australia

General chart of Terra Australis or Australia by Matthew
Flinders, 1814
State Library of South Australia

*

Willem Janszoon Blaeu by Jeremias Falck
Digital Library for Dutch Literature

Luis Váez de Torres, 1606, by Geoffrey Chapman
Ingleton, 1938
National Library of Australia

Abel Tasman, his wife and daughter by Jacob Gerritsz
Cuyp, 1637
National Library of Australia

William Dampier by William Dobson, 1850
National Library of Australia

Captain James Cook by Nathanial Dance-Holland, *c.* 1775
National Maritime Museum, Greenwich, London

Sir Joseph Banks by Thomas Phillips, engraved by
Nicholas Schiavonetti, 1813
National Library of Australia

La Pérouse by Maurin, lithograph by Delpech, undated
State Library of New South Wales

Bruni D'Entrecasteaux, painter unknown, 1806
National Library of Australia

Cigne noir du cap de Diemen, engraving of a black
swan from Tasmania by Jean Piron from the atlas of
Labillardiére
Collection of the Australian National Maritime Museum

William Bligh
Tasmanian Archive and Heritage Office, PH30-673-14

John Hunter by William Mineard Bennett, *c.* 1812
Mitchell Library, State Library of New South Wales

Matthew Flinders and George Bass survey the Australian
coast in the tiny *Tom Thumb* with a crew of one boy
Mary Evans Picture Library / Alamy

Captain Matthew Flinders, RN, 1774–1814
Toussaint Antoine de Chazal de Chamerel, 1806–7,
Mauritius
Oil on canvas, 64.5 x 50 cm
Gift of David Roche in memory of his father, J.D.K.
Roche, and the South Australian Government, 2000
Art Gallery of South Australia, Adelaide

George Bass
Tasmanian Archive and Heritage Office, PH30-673-5

Government House, Sydney by William Westall, 1802
National Library of Australia

Nicolas Baudin by André Joseph Mécou, c. 1804
State Library of New South Wales

François Péron by Charles-Alexandre Lesueur
Allport Library and Museum of Fine Arts, Tasmanian
Archive and Heritage Office

Henri de Saules de Freycinet, painter unknown, c. 1794
State Library of New South Wales

General Charles Mathieu Isidore Decaen, painter and
date unknown

ACKNOWLEDGEMENTS

$\mathcal{R}$esearch into the exploration of Australia has benefited from the rapidly increasing amount of material made available online by our major libraries and universities. The original historical material – including journals, books, diaries, letters and other official documents – that in the past few years has become freely available on the internet is quite staggering. It is now possible to read online the complete journals of Matthew Flinders, a translation of Abel Tasman's first great voyage and a copy of the original published account of the English pirate William Dampier's first visit to Australia in the late 1600s.

I would like to make special mention of Frank Horner, whose *French Reconnaissance* (1987) and *Looking for La Pérouse* (1995) have added considerably to our understanding of the importance of French exploration of Australia. In recent decades there has been an increased interest and focus on the French role in the exploration of our continent during the past two centuries, including the establishment of the Baudin Legacy Project in 2005: www.setis.library.usyd.edu.au/baudin/

Also, my thanks again to everyone at Random House for all their guidance and advice, and particularly to my editor Catherine Hill, whose persistence and professionalism has made this a far better book than it otherwise would have been. Thanks, too, to Ian Smiley Bayliff for help with the research.

INDEX